Londonderry Revisited

A Loyalist Analysis of the Civil Rights Controversy

Paul Kingsley

Belfast Publications,
152 Albertbridge Road,
Belfast BT5 4GS

Published in 1989 by
Belfast Publications,
152 Albertbridge Road,
Belfast BT5 4GS

ISBN 0 9515549 0 5

Contents

Introduction

Bernadette Devlin described Londonderry as "the Capital City of Injustice". In his foreword to Frank Curran's book, John Hume said the city "was the living symbol of what was perceived to be wrong in the Northern Ireland created in the 1920s, the place where the injustices of the unionist state were at their most blatant....". Londonderry was judged to be the most wicked place of all during the "civil rights" era in the 1960s. This was where the Protestants were doing the most terrible things to the Catholics.

The literature about "civil rights" is monumentally one-sided. Ulster Loyalists have a poor record of writing books. Their booklets have been lost in the mists of history. Their opponents books remain on the library shelves to influence posterity. The army of academics and journalists who are supposed to fearlessly seek out the truth have not done a very good job.

Although I am an Englishman, I declare in advance that I am a committed supporter of the Ulster Loyalist cause. Practically everthing that can be said in favour of the anti-Unionist interpretation of the "civil rights" movement has been said. Here I present the other side of the story in the interests of historical balance. Read the other books, read my own and make up your own mind.

I have not been able to cover everything. What I have done is to select what my opponents would regard as the worst example of gerrymandering and discrimination, and to examine it in some detail. If we have cause to doubt the accusations in what is allegedly the most blatant example, we will have cause to doubt the rest.

Why is it relevant? Because English attitudes about Ulster were formed during the "civil rights" era and led to the formulation of government policies in the early 1970s which have changed little since. To study the "civil rights" era and its immediate aftermath is to study the Ulster Problem itself.

In Part I I examine the accusations of the "civil rights" movement about gerrymandering and discrimination in housing and employment. In Part II I look at the "civil rights" movement and come to some conclusions as to what it was all about. Part III attempts to show how attitudes acquired during the "civil rights" era have influenced British policy ever since, particularly in relation to fighting the IRA. Part IV is addressed to Ulster Loyalists and their sympathisers outside Northern Ireland. It is a call to action.

To help you find your way around this book: The Londonderry County Borough Council is more often referred to as the Londonderry Corporation. "Cameron" is Lord Cameron, a Scottish Judge and author of the Cameron Report, an infamous document which pronounced Ulster Protestants guilty on the flimsiest of evidence.

Throughout I often refer to "the English" rather than "the British". As I am usually being extremely critical of my fellow countrymen, my Scottish friends should not feel insulted at being left out. I am, in effect, absolving the Scots (with the exception of Lord Cameron) of responsibility for getting us into the current mess. Scots at least usually have some understanding of the problem.

Part I

Londonderry: Capital City of Injustice?

A.   Gerrymandering

Cameron identified a number of councils whose electoral boundaries were the subject of "civil rights" complaints.[1]

134. The basic complaint in these areas is that the present electoral arrangements are weighted against non-Unionists. In the table on page 57 we show that the complaint is abundantly justified. In each of the areas with Unionist majorities on their council the majority was far greater than the adult population balance would justify. In Londonderry County Borough, Armagh Urban District, Omagh Urban District and County Fermanagh a Catholic majority in the population was converted into a large Unionist majority on the Councils. In the two Dungannon councils a very small Protestant majority held two-thirds or over of the seats on the councils. The most glaring case was Londonderry County Borough, where sixty per cent of the adult population was Catholic but where sixty per cent of the seats on the Corporation were held by Unionists. These results were achieved by the use, for example, of ward areas in which Unionist representatives were returned by small majorities, whereas non-Unionist representatives were returned by small majorities. In Londonderry County Borough there was the following extraordinary situation in 1967:

	Catholic Voters	Other Voters	Seats	
North Ward:	2,530	3,946	8	Unionists
Waterside Ward:	1,852	3,697	4	Unionists
South Ward:	10,047	1,138	8	Non-Unionists
Total:	14,429	8,781	20	
		23,210		

The figures have become quite famous. They have been reproduced over and over again and have mesmerised a generation of academics, journalists and political commentators. Just to clarify a couple of points, by "Other Voters" Cameron actually means Protestant voters, and when he talks of "Non-

Unionists" holding 8 seats he refers to 8 members of the Nationalist Party, a purely Catholic party which sought a united Ireland.

Anyone seeing the figures for the first time will inevitably draw the conclusion that the "Non-Unionist" (Nationalist Party) candidates had won about 90% of the vote in the South Ward with a majority of nearly 9,000 and that they had polled nearly 6,000 more votes than the Unionist Party in the Londonderry County Borough. Indeed, in the subsequent literature we are often told that 14,000 electors returned 8 Nationalists while 8,000 electors returned 12 Unionists. Such conclusions would seem entirely reasonable if readers were given the additional information that 1967 was the year of the Londonderry Corporation elections, and as Cameron was outlining the "extraordinary situation in 1967" he must clearly have been basing his statements on the very latest electoral statistics available to him at the time of his investigation.

In fact Cameron's figures are not a set of election results at all. They are an analysis of the electoral register. They simply show what proportion of electors were Catholics and Protestants. Their ability to impress the reader rests on the assumption that Catholics in Londonderry supported the Nationalist Party and Protestants the Unionist Party and that any analysis of election results would yield very similar conclusions to those achieved by analysing the electoral register. Cameron himself led a generation of intellectuals to this conclusion by talking of "ward areas in which Unionist representatives were returned by small majorities, whereas Non-Unionist representatives were returned by very large majorities."[2] In other words the actual election results were said to be very much as would be expected by a glance at Cameron's analysis of the electoral register in Londonderry.

As I carried out research for this book I experienced a growing sense of unease at reading again and again the same breakdown of the Londonderry Corporation electoral register, without ever coming across any sets of local election results showing the outcome of actual confrontations between the Nationalist Party and the Unionist Party in Londonderry. If the electoral arrangements were so unjust why not print the evidence that elections yielded unfair outcomes?

Eventually I had to refer to contemporary sources to track down the 1967 local election results for the Corporation. Electors were voting for multi-member wards and hence had several votes each. This accounts for the number of votes cast being greater than the number of electors. The total votes for each party were as follows.[3]

Londonderry Corporation Election Results 1967	
Nationalist Party	26,880
Unionist Party	25,535
Labour Party	25,296
Independents	1,461

To give an idea of what would have happened if each party had fielded just one candidate in the wards they contested, I have added together the votes cast for each party's most successful candidate in each ward.

Nationalist Party	4,692
Unionist Party	5,742
Labour Party	5,251
Independents	1,461

I think it is fair to say that there is some difference between the proportion of votes actually cast for each party and the figures which Cameron's statistics led a generation of political observers to expect.

One complicating factor of course was the intervention of the Northern Ireland Labour Party. Those mesmerised by Cameron's figures have become accustomed to thinking of the contest in Londonderry as simply Protestants v. Catholics, Unionists v. Irish Republicans (euphemistically described as"Non-Unionists"). But the Labour Party, which was in favour of Ulster remaining part of the United Kingdom, drew votes from both communities.

Another important consideration was the refusal of some parties to put up candidates in all wards. The Nationalist Party only contested the South Ward and the Unionist Party fought only in the North and Waterside Wards. This meant that there was no direct Nationalist Party-Unionist Party confrontation at all. Each of them only faced contests with the Labour Party.

It might be thought that this was an unusual occurrence and that there must be plenty of other electoral evidence to support the kind of assumptions most readers make - that Irish Republican candidates beat Unionists in the South Ward by large majorities while Unionists triumphed over Republicans in the North and the Waterside Wards with small majorities.

I therefore went back to 1936 when the Londonderry Corporation ward boundaries were last revised and noted every occasion over the next 33 years (until the dissolution of the Corporation) when Catholic/Irish Republican candidates came up against Protestant/Unionist candidates in local elections.

Londonderry Corporation Elections 1936-1969 Republican v. Unionist Contests		
South Ward	North Ward	Waterside Ward

No, this is not a misprint. Not once during the period in question did a Catholic party put up even a single candidate in the North or Waterside Wards, and the Unionist Party declined to field candidates in the South Ward.

Cameron had complained that on certain councils, including Londonderry Corporation, the Unionist majority "was far greater than the adult population balance would justify". His specific objection to the Londonderry arrangements was that "sixty per cent of the adult population was Catholic but....sixty per cent of the seats on the Corporation were held by Unionists". Setting aside the assumptions this makes about Catholics voting for Catholic parties (which I shall return to shortly), Cameron's remarks have clearly misled successive eminent readers of his report into thinking that generations of Catholic candiates had heroically striven to get elected in the North and Waterside Wards only to be defeated by cruel and unjust electoral arrangements. It didn't happen. It seems likely that Cameron and his team didn't even bother to enquire whether it did.

It is not simply that there is inadequate evidence from Londonderry County Borough election results to blame the electoral arrangements for Catholic candidates' lack of success. The truth is that over the 30 years prior to the Londonderry Corporation's dissolution there is no such evidence whatsoever. This leads me to make a suggestion which, as far as I am aware, appears nowhere else in the vast literature on Northern Ireland. It may be formulated as follows:

Q: Why could Catholic parties get no more than 8 representatives elected to the Londonderry Corporation under the 1936 ward boundaries?

A: Because never at any time did they put up more than 8 candidates.

In a particularly Irish way, Catholic/Republican parties in Londonderry seemed to assume they should be able to win elections without fielding candidates.

Projections

Given that there is no record of Catholic parties standing in 2 out of Londonderry Corporation's 3 wards over the last 33 years of its existence, can we glean any clues about how they might have performed? Looking at the 1967 results we can of course compare voting figures in the South Ward with the kind of outcome the Cameron Report figures lead us to expect. Overall there is no correspondence between the actual results and the analysis of the electoral register, but perhaps there is in the South Ward.

In fact Cameron's infamous figures are again wide of the mark. In 1967 the 6 Nationalist Party candidates in the South Ward won a total of 26,880 votes to the Labour Party's 14,174. The best Nationalist candidate was supported by 4,692 electors compared with 2,701 who backed the top Labour man.[4] Even without any Unionist oppostition, the Nationalist Party could win no more than

65.5% of the votes cast in the ward. On a candidate for candidate basis, the Nationalists beat Labour by just 2,000 votes. This is some way short of the 90% share of the poll and 9,000 majority suggested by Cameron's figures.

What is interesting is to see how successful the Nationalist and Unionist Parties were in maximising their potential support. Given that the Nationalists were appealing exclusively to Catholics and the Unionists largely to Protestants, it is possible to work out how successful each was in getting the support of its target group. It will then be possible to make some projections as to how the parties would have performed if they had contested all the Corporation's wards. Although this is a rough and ready approach it is an improvement on analysing electoral registers, which is about as scientific as examining chicken entrails. It is at least based on electoral fact rather than wishful thinking.

Maximising Religious Potential - Londonderry Corporation Elections, 1967				
	Vote of Top Candidate	Religious Potential*	% of Religious Potential	% Turnout
North Ward (Un.)	2,908	3,946	73.7	71.7
Waterside Ward (Un.)	2,834	3,697	76.7	74.3
South Ward (Nat.)	4,692	10,047	46.7	66.3

* *Religious Potential figures taken from the Cameron Report's estimate of the number of Catholics and Protestants in the relevant wards.*

If we compare the last two columns it can be seen that the Unionists were very good at maximising their potential vote. On a 71.7% turnout in the North Ward we could expect 71.7% of Protestant electors to vote Unionist. In fact here and in the Waterside Ward the Unionist Party did slightly better than the turnout figure would have suggested they would do.

The Nationalist Party on the other hand did very badly. On a 66.3% turnout in the South Ward it could only get 46.7% of the Catholic electorate to support it.

Clearly its potential vote was more likely to be reduced by defections to the Labour Party, while the Unionist vote was rock solid.

The average percentage of Protestant voters who supported the Unionists in the North and Waterside Wards was 75.2% compared with the 46.7% of Catholics who voted Nationalist in the South Ward. If these percentages are projected into the respective wards not contested by the parties and are combined with actual votes cast where they did stand, we get the following figures.

Projected Performance Of Londonderry Nationalists and Unionists			
	Nat.	Un.	
North Ward	*1,182*	**2,908**	Actual vote of top candidate in
Waterside Ward	*865*	**2,834**	**BOLD**
South Ward	**4,692**	*856*	Projection in *ITALICS*
	6,739	6,598	

This also presents quite a different picture from that painted by a stream of writers on Northern Ireland who could not be bothered to ask how people actually voted in Londonderry.

Of course the results of the projections I have made about Catholic voting patterns should come as no surprise. Between March and August 1968, Professor Richard Rose of Strathclyde University carried out his Loyalty Survey of opinion in Northern Ireland.[5] Only 51% of Catholics said they supported "Nationalist" candidates such as those from the Nationalist Party and the Republican Labour Party; 27% backed the N.I. Labour Party and there were even 5% who were Unionist Party supporters.

Almost all those who voted for Catholic parties were Catholics but not all Catholics voted for Catholic parties. This fact is often obscured by our experience of polarised politics after The Troubles began.

Governor Gerry

One of the most frequent charges against the Londonderry Corporation is that it was gerrymandered. Although the word is not in common use it is assumed by most writers that everyone knows what it means. For those too shy to ask, here are a couple of definitions. First from the Oxford English Dictionary:

A method of arranging election districts so that the political party making the arrangement will be enabled to elect a greater number of representatives than they could on a fair system, and more than they should have in proportion to their numerical strength.

And secondly from Webster's Third New International Dictionary:

To divide (a territorial unit) into election districts in an unnatural and unfair way with the purpose of giving one political party an electoral majority in a large number of districts while concentrating the voting strength of the opposition in as few districts as possible.

Gerrymandering owes its name to Governor Elbridge Gerry of Massachusetts in the United States. In 1812 he is said to have pushed through boundary changes in the state legislature to give the Democratic Party more representatives in the State Senate. The story goes that one man, noting the rather peculiar shape of one of the electoral districts, said that it looked like a salamander (a kind of lizard). His friend replied that it looked more like a Gerrymander, and that's how we got the term.

It is clear that in 1967 the voting strength of the Nationalist and Unionist Parties was not evenly distributed. The projections based on actual results show that the Nationalist Party's support was concentrated in the South Ward, where most Catholics lived, although the situation was not as dramatic as the electoral register figures would suggest.

In an election where both parties contested all 3 wards it is reasonable to believe that the Nationalist Party would overall have had a marginal advantage over the Unionist Party, although with Labour Party intervention it is highly unlikely to have won an overall majority of votes. But because the Unionists had more supporters in the other 2 wards they would win more seats.

We now know that the reason the Nationalist Party did not actually win more seats is that it refused to put up more candidates. It did in fact win every seat where it fielded a candidate from 1936-1969, and it really couldn't complain about that. We also know that the Cameron Report's figures have no basis in electoral fact and hence that the sense of injustice they try to convey is not well-founded.

However, it still makes sense to ask if the electoral arrangements were arrived at in an unnatural and unfair way to benefit the Unionist Party. Some ill-informed or mischievous writers have created the impression that the Londonderry Corporation ward boundaries were constantly adjusted or gerrymandered to maintain a Unionist advantage. This is not so. As we have seen the ward boundaries in 1967 were those which were drawn up in 1936 and they had not been revised since then. The complaint therefore must be that something unnatural and unfair happened in 1936 and/or that the failure to revise the ward boundaries was unfair. The latter charge, of course, is not one of gerrymandering; not changing boundaries is in fact the only way of avoiding the accusation.

1936 And All That

Contests of any sort for seats on Londonderry Corporation had always been few and far between. The idea that places on the council were the subject of intense party political rivalry is just one of the many myths which surround the city's affairs.

In May 1966 there had been a by-election in the North Ward when the Unionist Party candidate, Jackie Allen, held off the challenge of a Protestant solicitor, Claude Wilton, who stook as an independent, by 2,464 votes to 2,021. The contest was held against the background of both Protestant and Catholic disillusionment about what they considered to be the neglect of Londonderry by the Northern Ireland government. More of this later.

But prior to that there had been no contests of any sort since 1949. In that year Irish Labour Party candidates (pro-united Ireland) unsuccessfully challenged the Unionists in the Waterside Ward and Anti-Partition candidates in the South Ward. Labour candidates of various hues also stood in the 1946 elections and some pre-war contests.

The keen eyed reader may have noted my statement that 6 Nationalist Party candidates stood in the South Ward in 1967, whereas Cameron says that there were 8 Nationalist representatives. The explanation is that the South and North

Wards each returned 6 councillors and 2 aldermen while the Waterside Ward had 3 councillors and 1 alderman. Before the 1973 reorganisation of local government in Northern Ireland, aldermen in the county boroughs were directly elected by the public in seperate elections. This was not so in England, where aldermen were appointed by existing councillors. This system was widely abused with non-elected persons from outside the council being drafted in to bolster a party's majority. As English aldermen served longer terms than councillors, it was possible for a party to be defeated at the polls only to hang on to power for some time by relying on its aldermen to outvote elected representatives. This system was phased out in the 1970s. It is, however, interestng to note how democratic the Ulster system was in comparison.

In Londonderry the aldermen's seats were in practice not contested. There was an unwritten agreement that the Nationalist Party, and before them the Anti-Partition groups, had nomination rights in the South Ward. Similarly the Unionist Party was given a clear run in nominating aldermen in the North and Waterside Wards. I have only come across one occasion since the 1930s on which a Labour candidate contested an aldermanic seat, and that was in the South Ward.

And so to 1936. In view of the abuse which has been poured on Londonderry Corporation's electoral arrangements it is surprising that there have been few real attempts to describe the events leading up to the redrawing of the ward boundaries in the year. One of the main Republican accounts is contained in the book, *Derry: Coundown to Disaster* by Frank Curran, who was for many years editor of the *Derry Journal*, Londonderry's Catholic newspaper.⁶ However, his account is so misleading that the story needs to be retold.

Up to 1936 Londonderry was divided into 5 wards: North, South, East and West on the west bank of the Foyle, and Waterside on the east bank. The North, East and Waterside Wards were held by Unionists and the South and West Wards by Republicans. The Unionists had a 24-16 majority on the council.

Then, according to Curran:

In 1936, a by-election in the North Ward resulted in a Unionist majority of only 352. Another gerrymander was imperative, and the Unionist Party duly applied to Stormont for ratification of a new ward change scheme. The Unionist scheme called for a reduction in the wards from five to three, with four seats for the Unionist Waterside, eight seats for the Unionist North

Ward, but also only eight seats for the Nationalist South Ward, which contained more voters than the other two wards together.[7]

Unfortunately it didn't happen like that.

Firstly Curran implies that the Unionists, having the evidence of the election result, then decided to redraw the ward boundaries. In fact the scheme to update the ward structure was approved by the March meeting of the Corporation. The poll in the old North Ward (which incidentally was not a by-election but the only contest in the scheduled elections) did not take place until 15 May 1936. Two seats were up for election but the opposition fielded just one candidate, Paddy Maxwell, standing as a Nationalist. The two Unionists, Sir Basil McFarland and R.J. Finlay polled 2,392 and 2,381 votes to Maxwell's 2,040.[8]

Curran suggests 352 was a narrow majority, but this was a small ward of just 4,810 electors and in a city which did not experience violent swings from one party to another, it was quite comfortable. In a typical English Parliamentary constituency of 65,000 voters it would be equivalent to a majority of over 4,700.

There is also a suggestion that trends indicated that the majority in the old North Ward was about to disappear. Unfortunately the electoral evidence is again non-existent. May 1936 was the first, last and only time a Catholic/Republican candidate challenged a Unionist in any ward under the 1923 boundaries. To find the previous contest we have to go back to 1920, that is before the foundation of the Northern Ireland State. Indeed, the May 1936 election in the old North Ward is famous for being the only occasion between 1920 and 1973 when a Catholic/Republican candidate stood against a Protestant/Unionist in the Londonderry Corporation area. This must be borne in mind when Republicans argue that they didn't have a fair opportunity to gain control of the council.

What we do have is the evidence of the head-counters. Prior to the 1936 election the electoral register had last been revised in November 1934. During these revisions both sides had registration agents to make sure all of their potential supporters were included on the register. Both tended to count heads, that is analyse the number of Protestants and Catholics in each area. Mr. Robert Irwin, one of the Unionist registration agents, is quoted in the *Derry Journal* of 28 November 1934 as saying that the Unionists had increased their majorities on the register in the North and Waterside Wards. He was not contradicted by this Catholic paper. As the Unionists had a reputation for getting solid support from Protestants, it was fair to assume that an increase in the proportion of Protestants on the register implied an increase in the potential Unionist majority. Therefore what evidence there is suggests the Unionist majority in the old North Ward was not being eroded at the time of the decision to revise the ward boundaries. What is clear is that the election result itself can have played no part in the Londonderry Unionists' decision as the contest did not take place until two months after the new ward scheme had been approved by the council.

By 1936 the following situation had arisen.[9]

	Voters	Valuation	Seats	Voters per Seat
North Ward	4,810	£82,844	10	481
East Ward	2,117	£41,091	6	353
South Ward	3,117	£21,797	8	390
West Ward	3,269	£23,156	8	409
Waterside Ward	3,632	£35,079	8	454

The valuation i.e. rateable value of each ward is given for information as the Local Government Act 1922 required that valuation be taken into account in drawing up electoral divisions. In other words it suggested that attempts should be made to equalize valuation as well as the number of voters, so that wards paid similar amounts of rates.

So what was the proposal of the Londonderry Corporation? Basically it was, with minor variations, to combine the North and East Wards to form a new North Ward, and to link the South and West Wards to create a new South Ward. The Waterside Ward would be unchanged. Thus the scheme that was put forward to the Northern Ireland government was as follows.[10]

	Voters	Valuation	Seats
North Ward	6,779	£115,398	8
South Ward	6,534	£53,491	8
Waterside Ward	3,632	£35,079	8

Now is a good time to recall Frank Curran's claim that the Unionist scheme provided for a South Ward "which contained more voters than the other two wards together". This will not be the last time a prominent writer will have been found to be talking nonsense about Londonderry.

The ward scheme was the subject of a public inquiry in October 1936 and the inspector, Vice-Admiral Archdale, reported to the Minister of Home Affairs. Curran implies that the scheme was rubber stamped. It was not. In fact few writers on the subject seem to have picked up the fact that the ward scheme was amended by the Stormont government.

The Londonderry Unionists' proposal that there be 8 seats in the Waterside Ward was based on an argument that this was the fastest growing area of the city and would soon catch up with the other wards. It does, however, seem to have been a bit of a try-on and the Ministry of Home affairs reduced the Waterside seats to 4.

The Corporation scheme had paid little attention to valuation, aiming to equalize numbers in the North and South Wards, which, under its plan, would have had a similar acreage. King's Counsel for the Corporation at the inquiry, Mr. W. Lowry, pointed out that there had been no attempt to penalise people in the South Ward simply because their valuations were low.[11]

The Minister, however, felt he had a legal duty under the Local Government Act 1922 to take valuation into account and to try and make the wards less unequal in that respect. Therefore the Northern Ireland government, in its letter to the Londonderry Corporation, amended the boundary between the North and South Wards so that it coincided precisely with the boundary between the Stormont constituencies of Foyle and the City of Londonderry. Thus the new arrangements were:[12]

	Voters	Valuation	Seats
North Ward	5,469	£105,824	8
South Ward	7,844	£63,065	8
Waterside Ward	3,632	£35,079	4

Before we look at the thinking behind the changes, let us look at their practical effect. Readers steeped in mythology about the "oppressed Catholics" of Londonderry will already have drawn the conclusion that the change transferred a large number of Catholic voters to the South Ward and hence consolidated the Protestant position in the North Ward. They would be wrong. The area transferred to the South Ward, which included Barrack Street, Ferguson Street and Dark Lane, had a Protestant majority and the *Londonderry Sentinel,* the local Protestant/Unionist newspaper, estimated that the Unionists' potential majority in the new North Ward would therefore be reduced by some 300 votes.[13] Catholic figures suggested that two-thirds of the transferred voters were Protestants.[14]

A letter from the Ministry of Home Affairs announcing its decision was placed on the table at the Corporation's meeting on 22 December 1936:

> *The principle factors to be considered by the Ministry are the valuations and populations of the various wards taken in conjunction with their representation, but the Corporation appear to have entirely overlooked the necessity for any such basis for their proposal. Thus, while the populations of the proposed North and South Wards would be approximately equal, the valuation of the former would be almost double that of the latter;* [15]

It therefore announced a change to the proposed ward boundary and said of the valuation differences:

> *While there would be appreciable disproportion it would be nothing like so great as under the original proposal, for the lower population in the North Ward is balanced by a higher valuation, and the higher population in the South Ward is balanced by a lower valuation.*

This is important to bear in mind because Patrick Buckland, in one of the more accessible accounts of this period, gets this the wrong way round, believing that the Corporation's scheme only took into account valuation and that it was only the Northern Ireland government which gave proper consideration to population size.[16]

The Ministry also noted that:

It would, however, appear that the line proposed in the scheme follows very closely, for the greater part of its length, the line dividing the Parliamentary constituencies on this side of the river, and where it departs from this line the figures relating to the areas affected by the diversion have been given.

Having considered these figures, the Ministry has been unable to see any justification or advantage in departing from this existing statutory boundary, while on the other hand, there are obvious advantages and conveniences to be gained by adhering to it. It would, moreover, to an appreciable extent, remedy the disproportions above referred to in the valuation and population figures for these wards.

Denis Barritt and Charles Carter discerned a logic behind the amended scheme. "It may be deduced that the formula used was roughly to equate an elector with £18 of valuation, and to provide one representative (including aldermen) for each 1,400 of the 'equivalent electors' so calculated."[17]

One of the Corporation's main motives in revising the ward structure was to streamline the operations of the Londonderry County Borough by reducing the number of councillors. Before the revision there were 23 committees, and all 40 council members were entitled to sit on the General Purposes Committee. The system was felt to be unwieldy. It was argued that a smaller council would attract better quality members. The changes also meant that it was possible to eliminate the imbalance in representation between the wards both in terms of population and valuation. Both objectives could not be achieved by simply reducing the number of councillors under the old ward scheme. A distribution of seats such as 5-3-4-4-4 would not have been a true reflection of the strength of each ward, and giving each ward 4 seats certainly would not.

The Northern Ireland government letter went on:

The Ministry is, however, convinced that so large a membership as 40 is altogether excessive for a body of the nature of Londonderry Corporation, and it has no doubt that if this number is to be reduced to the neighbourhood of 20 to 25, as would seem proper, no greater number of wards than 3 is necessary or desirable.

Certainly the trend throughout Ireland seemed to be towards such streamlining. Limerick, a town of 40,000 inhabitants (compared with Londonderry's 46,000), had reduced its council to 15 and Cork (80,000) had 21 members on its local authority.[18]

One of the Ministry's complaints needs to be clarified. Curran correctly states that the letter talked about the boundary line between the North and South Wards being at times difficult to define "and none of the witnesses examined on behalf of the scheme have ascertained or were aware how this boundary would actually run."[19] A study of the evidence given to the inquiry makes it clear exactly what is being said here. There was no great mystery about the boundary line itself. For most of its course it followed the Stormont boundary. The problem was one of presentation.

The Corporation had decided that its officers would present the technical information about the line the boundary would take. The council members would not concern themselves with such details but would present general arguments about why this sort of revision was necessary. But the officers made a number of technical errors. The City Surveyor's map had the line drawn in the wrong place and Mr. Lowry, King's Counsel for the Corporation, had to assure the inquiry "that the line runs down the centre of a street and not through a graveyard."[20] There were also some minor errors in the number of voters and the valuation of wards. The councillors and aldermen were not briefed on these details and hence couldn't correct the errors themselves.

The *Londonderry Sentinel* later gave them some stick for not pressing the scheme with the necessary "energy and resource", but the problem was sorted out when the inspector walked the boundary accompanied by council officers.[21] The Ministry's complaint therefore was essentially that no-one seemed to know what they were doing rather than that something untoward was going on. In the end, of course, the original scheme was rejected for other reasons and was only approved in an amended form.

Guilty or Not Guilty?

The question is whether the 1936 ward scheme was a fair one. Was Londonderry

divided in "an unnatural and unfair way" to give the Unionists an advantage?
Arguments about motives in this situation tend to be pointless. There is
evidence from correspondence between government figures at the time that
they would have liked to see Londonderry saved from Republican control.[22]
This is not unusual given that opposition councillors in the city did not owe
their allegiance to the Crown or Northern Ireland. They wanted to see the
overthrow of the state. The worst that could be said about government
ministers is that they might have been prepared to keep Londonderry in
Unionist hands by fair means or foul. If that was true then it is clear they would
have faced a dilemma if the choice had been between a fair ward scheme which
gave control to the Republicans, and an unfair scheme which left Unionists in
control of the Corporation. It seems to me that the key question is: where they
faced with that dilemma or did they have available to them a fair ward scheme
under which the Unionists could win a majority?

The only way that question can be answered is by examining the ward scheme
and making an objective assessment of its merits. If it was a fair scheme then
the Northern Ireland government faced no moral dilemma in approving it.
What this means is that the examination of motives is ultimately inconclusive.
Because the government, on purely pragmatic grounds, would have had a
preference for a defensible rather than an indefensible scheme for maintaining
control, even if it had the blackest of motives, the question "Was Londonderry
gerrymandered?" can only be answered by looking at the merits of the scheme
itself to see if it was unnatural and unfair. If it was fair the motives of the
government become irrelevant.

I believe there was no gerrymander in 1936. Here are some of my reasons:

1. The Corporation made an honest attempt to equalize numbers in the North
   and South Wards. Under its own proposals the North Ward would actually
   have had more electors.
2. The original line followed for the most part the Stormont Parliamentary
   boundary and only deviated from it to make the wards equal in size. The
   revised scheme approved by the Northern Ireland government used the
   Stormont boundary in its entirety. It was therefore logically based.
3. The imbalance of electors between the North and South Wards arose from
   a statutory requirement to make ward valuations more equal, and the
   formula used to balance numbers of voters and rateable values was quite
   consistent.
4. This imbalance between wards was not severe and the 1936 revision cannot

be blamed for the big differences which had emerged by 1967.

5. The Northern Ireland government's revisions to the scheme did not benefit local Unionists. Their likely majority in the new North Ward was actually reduced by taking valuation into account.

6. Unionists lost 12 council members and the Republicans only 8 through the reduction in the size of the Corporation.

7. Mr. J. C. McDermott, King's Counsel, representing business ratepayers with premises which had a total valuation of £45,000 (including all the shirt and collar firms which employed 8,000-10,000 people) stated: "My clients believe the scheme is an improvement and is more likely to make for efficient government and more likely to promote the prosperity of Derry."[23]

8. The Republicans failed to suggest an alternative scheme.

On this last point, the complaint of "civil rights" minded Republicans was often that they were not enjoying British standards. I therefore wrote to the Local Government Boundary Commission for England during the course of my research to check on the latest standards. I asked them how they would guard against gerrymandering. They confirmed they can only take note of certain objective criteria in assessing schemes submitted to them. They seek to ensure such things as equality of representation and the preserving of community ties. But the only ultimate safeguard against gerrymandering is for aggrieved parties to submit alternative schemes and convince the Commission that these are better than the original proposals.

According to the *Londonderry Sentinel* reports of the public inquiry on the ward scheme: "Mr W. F. McCoy, counsel for independent ratepayers supporting the proposals, in a powerful plea for the adoption of the scheme, asked why had the Nationalists, if they thought the division line 'absurd and grotesque', not brought in an alternative plan, and said the only answer was that the Nationalist opposition was not sincere and has as its only foundations the political, religious, and party cries."[24]

It was a conclusive argument. At the end of the day the Republicans had cried "gerrymander" and complained bitterly that they were not to control the Corporation, but they put forward no constructive alternative. They seemed more concerned to use the inquiry as a political platform.

The Passage of Time

Over the years, what had been a fair distribution of voters between the 3 wards had become unbalanced.[25]

| | **Number of Voters** | | |
	1936	1967	Seats
North Ward	5,469	6,476	8
South Ward	7,844	11,185	8
Waterside Ward	3,632	5,549	4

On a strictly pro-rata basis, the South and Waterside Wards were under-represented in 1967. Or to look at it another way, if the number of seats in these 2 wards are accepted as having been in the correct proportion, the North Ward had too many representatives. Disregarding valuation altogether, as most authorities were doing at this time, an updated scheme would probably have given the North Ward 5 seats. As the Unionists controlled areas containing 12,025 voters and the Republicans represented 11,185 voters, the Unionists would still have retained control on a strictly pro-rata basis of ward representation. Splitting the South Ward into 2 electoral divisions with 4 seats each would not, of course, have changed this. The above point has often been obscured by the way the infamous Cameron figures were presented.

One problem the Republicans had was that their supporters were concentrated in certain areas of the city, whereas the Unionists were more evenly spread. Thus, not only in 1967, but thoughout Londonderry's history, they would always have been more likely to "waste" votes by piling up big majorities in certain areas. How such concentrations of population built up is a matter of dispute, and will involve an examination of housing policy, which I shall turn to in the next chapter. Whether the phenomenon of support concentrated in certain areas which leads to wasted votes is at all unusual, I shall explore shortly. What can be said is that it is not at all clear that an updating of the 1936 basis of representation would have led to Republican control, but it is certain that Republicans would have increased their representation on the council, even if only in percentage terms.

So, was Londonderry unusual in not having its electoral divisions revised for so long? Was it alone neglected, indicating perhaps some devious plot? If we look at the 2 other most important institutions in Northern Ireland, Belfast Corporation and the Stormont Parliament, it becomes apparent that the Londonderry situation was not unusual. Belfast at this time was operating on ward boundaries drawn up in 1896 and the Stormont constituencies had not been revised since 1929. In fact since 1923 only 5 local government boundaries had been redrawn.[26] We must therefore ask who benefitted from this general failure to update electoral arrangements.

Ian Budge and Cornelius O'Leary have carried out a study of the situation in Belfast. They noted that some unusually small wards such as Falls and Smithfield had been specifically created to provide Catholic representation. They concluded: "From our account of the circumstances surrounding the initial drawing of ward boundaries in 1896 it is apparent that if anyone was favoured then it was the Catholics and Nationalists."[27] At the time the boundaries were fixed Smithfield was the smallest ward with 1,985 voters and Pottinger (in Protestant East Belfast) was the largest with 4,307 electors.[28] All wards had 4 seats. By 1967 the ward discrepancies had become more marked. Catholic Smithfield was still the smallest with 3,115 but the largest was now Protestant Clifton with 22,500.[29] It is interesting that the Catholic wards of Falls, Smithfield and Dock with 12 seats between them contained a total of 22,614 electors, about the same number as in the single Unionist ward of Clifton, which had just 4 seats on the council.[30] Such inequalities make the Londonderry situation pale into insignificance.

Budge and O'Leary found that "Unionist wards throughout the entire period were more heavily populated. This is supported by inspection of actual ward populations. The central wards of Falls, Smithfiled and Dock, with a heavy Catholic population, have always been among the smallest, while such staunchly Protestant areas as Shankill have always had a larger population."[31] By 1967 the average Republican-held ward had 7,538 voters, while the Unionist wards averaged 14,528 electors.[32] Budge and O'Leary also concluded that "the Unionists have more generally had votes pile up in useless superfluity than had them weighted in their favour."[33] In fact in 3 times as many cases. Thus the passage of time exaggerated the disadvantage suffered by the Unionist Party under the Belfast ward scheme; the wards with Protestant majorities had less seats than was justified by their number of electors.

From a reading of Tim Pat Coogan the Stormont situation certainly seems more promising for those in search of oppressed Catholics.[34] He states: "The unionists were also (in the absence of a body such as the Westminster Boundary

Commission) able to manipulate constituency sizes so that they varied from as many as 43,000 to as few as 7,000." Coogan was the editor of the Dublin-based newspaper, the *Irish Press*, from 1968 to 1987, and is the author of a very well known book on the IRA. It might be assumed that such an esteemed journalist would not mislead us. Catholics must have been corralled into huge constituencies so as to under-represent their strength at Stormont. But what Coogan omits to say is that most of the small constituencies were Republican held and all of the large ones were safe Unionist seats.

Shortly before the 1969 Stormont general election the average geographical seat (that is excluding the university seats) had about 19,000 voters. Only one of the Catholic/Republican constituencies had an above-average electorate and that was the Londonderry seat of Foyle with 19,875 voters. However, due to population movements a number of huge constituencies had grown up, notably Mid-Down (45,754), Carrick (41,669), South Antrim (37,095), Antrim (33,347) and North Down (30,286). All were ultra safe Unionist seats. At the same time there were Catholic/Republican constituencies like Belfast Central (6,384) and Belfast-Dock (7,212) which were tiny in comparison.[35]

Until the 1969 general election Stormont had 4 members who were elected by graduates of Queen's University, Belfast. This antiquated arrangement was then scrapped and 4 new geographical constituencies were created. This enabled the huge divisions mentioned above to be cut down to a more manageable size. Funnily enough this meant that the university MPs, who usually contained one or two opponents of the Northern Ireland government, were replaced by Unionist supporters elected on a more democratic basis.

Now that there were 52 geographical constituencies instead of 48 the average size of constituency came down to 17,500. The Catholic/Republican seats, which had been unaffected by this minor change, still only included 2 constituencies which were of above average size. The 3 smallest seats in Ulster were Catholic/Republican areas and in spite of the changes, 26 of the 27 biggest seats were controlled by Unionists. The average Republican area had 14,000 voters while the average Unionist division contained 18,400 voters.[36]

If the Unionist government had manipulated constituency sizes, it had manipulated them to its own disadvantage. In fact the differences in the size of electoral areas had grown up due to population changes, no amendments having been made to boundaries between 1929 and 1969. The result was that Protestant voters were packed into large constituencies which were under-represented in comparison with the smaller seats held by Republican MPs. An updating of arrangements would have led to an increase in Unionist representation.

It might also be pointed out that the passage of time had left Ulster under-represented at Westminster. By the 1970 general election, for instance, Unionists were representing giant constituencies such as South Antrim (143,544 voters) and North Down (120,788 voters). At the same time the British Labour Party held a considerable number of constituencies with tiny electorates such as Birmingham Ladywood (18,734), Glasgow Kelvingrove (18,935), Glasgow Central (20,312), Manchester Exchange (21,074), Liverpool - Scotland (29,292) and Leeds South East (29,876). These 6 constituencies between them didn't have as many voters as South Antrim.[37] It was noticeable that Harold Wilson, who had been quick to level ill-informed complaints against Ulster's electoral arrangements, had been in no hurry to update the Westminster boundaries.

The inevitable conclusion therefore is that delays in revising the electoral divisions of the most important political institutions in Northern Ireland worked, on balance, to the Unionists' disadvantage. Londonderry had not been singled out for special treatment. It was unusual in that the inequalitites in ward representation which had emerged had operated, potentially at least, in the Unionists' favour. We shall never know for certain because the Republicans refused to submit themselves to the electorate outside the South Ward for over 30 years. Overall, however, the failure to update boundaries did not work against Republicans and hence could not have been a plot against them.

Why then was there such a policy or non-policy? The Unionists' experience of boundary revisions in the 1920s and 1930s had been that they were a pain in the neck. Unless such revisions actually handed control to Republicans there were going to be screams of "gerrymander" and the reviews would become political battlegrounds. It is also clear that any general policy of revising boundaries would have led to a reduction in Republican representation on Belfast Corporation and in the Stormont Parliament (with Gerry Fitt in all probability losing his seats in both institutions).[38] In the relatively peaceful decades after the Second World War many Unionists would have regarded it as stoking up unnecessary trouble to make such changes.

Gerrymander By the Sea?

We have seen that potential supporters of Irish Republican candidates in Londonderry were concentrated in one of the three wards up to 1969. We have also seen that if the Nationalist Party had ever bothered to seriously contest elections it might, according to projections based on actual results, have polled marginally more votes than the Unionist Party overall. The question then arises whether such concentrations of support, which "waste" votes by building up large majorities in certain areas, are alien to British politics. By having supporters of a particular party unevenly distributed between the Corporation's wards, was Londonderry falling short of a British standard?

The answer has to be no. The accumulation of large majorities which are "wasteful" of votes is a common and constant feature of the British first past the post system. For most of this century it is the Labour Party which has been the main loser by deriving much of its support from closely knit working class communities, particularly in heavy industrial areas, where a large number of votes have been "wasted" returning a relatively small number of candidates.

Demographic changes and the Thatcher Revolution have broken down many of the Labour strongholds and hence I have chosen the Conservative town of Brighton for a small case study, just to show that both main parties can suffer from this phenomenon. It was of course at Brighton's Grand Hotel that an IRA bomb almost wiped out the British Cabinet in 1984, so there is an unfortunate connection between the town and the problems of Northern Ireland.

It will be useful to start our case study in the year 1987 when the Brighton Borough Council elections in May can be compared with the general election results just one month later in June. Brighton Borough is divided into 2 Parliamentary constituencies, Brighton Pavilion and Brighton Kemptown. In June 1987 they returned the following results:[29]

	Pavilion	Kemptown	Total	Total %
Conservative	22,056	24,031	46,087	52.2
Labour	12,914	14,771	27,685	31.3
Liberal/Social Democrat	8,459	6,080	14,359	16.5
Con. Majority	9,142	9,260	18,402	

You will see why I described Brighton as a Conservative town. At the 1987 General Election the party had a majority of 18,402 over its nearest rival, Labour. This represented a 21% margin. Students of politics would however have been surprised to learn that just one month earlier the Labour Party had retained control of Brighton Borough Council by winning in half the wards and then relying on the casting vote of the Labour mayor. How was the huge Conservative majority overturned?

One explanation might be that people voted very differently at the local elections, so let us compare the figures.[40]

	General Election % (June)	Borough Council % (May)
Conservative	52.2	46.8
Labour	31.3	33.8
Liberal/Social Democrat	16.5	18.2
Green	-	1.2

It can be seen that the Conservative share of the vote was down, because more of its supporters stayed at home in a low turnout at the Borough Council elections. However the Tories still had a 13% margin over Labour, outpolling their rivals by over 8,000 votes. And yet both parties won 8 seats on the council with the Liberals winning one. (Normally Brighton elects 16 councillors in each of 3 out of every 4 years, but one member had resigned in 1987: hence the need to elect a seventeenth councillor. Labour's previous results meant that there was a tied council with the Socialists holding exactly half of the seats.)

The key to understanding the apparent paradox of a Conservative electoral majority and Labour control of the council lies, of course, in examining the distribution of votes in Brighton. Tory votes are concentrated in what I shall call the "Conservative Belt" - the arc of northern and eastern suburbs which return big majorities over Labour: Westdene, Patcham, Preston, Woodingdean, Rottingdean. These districts return 5 of the 16 councillors normally up for election. The other 11 councillors represent the more marginal central and seafront wards. The Conservative strength is that they can bank on winning 5 seats quite easily; their weakness is that they usually have quite a battle in the other wards, where victory is never assured. For ease of reference I shall refer to these other wards as covering the "Central Area". So here is the breakdown of the May 1987 Brighton Borough Council elections.

1987	Votes				No. of Seats	
	Conservative Belt		Central Area		Con. Belt	Central Area
	%	No.	%	No.		
Conservative	61.5	13,418	39.2	16,520	5	3
Labour	14.2	3,108	44.0	18,521	0	8
Liberal/Social Democrat	23.2	5,056	15.6	6,561	0	1
Green	1.1	251	1.2	488	0	0

	Total Votes		Seats
	%	No.	
Conservative	46.8	29,938	8
Labour	33.8	21,629	8
Liberal/Social Democrat	18.2	11,617	1
Green	1.2	739	0

It is clear that the Tories "wasted" votes in the Conservative Belt building up a huge majority of 10,000 votes over Labour to win just 5 seats. In the Central Area, Labour converted a smaller majority of 2,000 over the Conservatives into an 8-3 advantage in councillors returned. Hence a Tory majority of 8,000 was transformed into a mere equality of seats. The way party votes are distributed throughout the wards can clearly work to the disadvantage of the Conservative Party, but before drawing any firm conclusions let us look at the very interesting figures produced by the 1988 Brighton Borough Council elections.[41]

1988	Votes				No. Of Seats	
	Conservative Belt		Central Area		Con. Belt	Central Area
	%	No.	%	No.		
Conservative	64.1	11,738	38.6	14,141	5	0
Labour	19.8	3,629	53.1	19,460	0	11
Liberal/Social Democrat	15.1	2,762	6.9	2,539	0	0
Green	1.0	188	1.4	500	0	0

	Total Votes		
	%	No.	Seats
Conservative	47.1	25,879	5
Labour	42.0	23,089	11
Liberal/Social Democrat	9.6	5,301	0
Green	1.3	688	0

One of the main features of the 1988 results was the collapse of the Liberal and Social Democrats' vote to half its 1987 level. Labour was the sole beneficiary. Whereas the Conservatives' share of the vote remained at around 47%, Labour improved by over 8%. This swing helped the Socialists to win all of the Central Area wards, gain 11 seats to the Tories' 5, and take outright control of the council.

1988 saw the Conservatives' doomsday scenario come true. They were penned back into their 5 stronghold seats and lost in all the more marginal wards. However the most interesting point is that although the Tories got hammered in terms of seats they actually managed to poll nearly 2,800 votes more than Labour throughout the Borough, a clear margin of 5%.

We can therefore say that the ward boundaries in Brighton can produce an equality of seats even when the Conservatives poll many more votes than Labour; or they can lead to Labour winning twice as many seats as the Tories even though it gets less votes. They have therefore worked in the Labour Party's favour.

But Brighton is not gerrymandered and its boundaries are not out of date. It is quite simply an example of how, even under ideal conditions, minority votes are quite often transformed into a majority of seats. Brighton's ward boundaries have been regularly updated. They are accepted by all the parties concerned. Wards are of fairly equal size and are drawn up by an independent body according to generally accepted principles. It is difficult to think of anything further that could be done to remove the disadvantage suffered by the Conservatives. When it comes down to it, those who are most likely to vote Tory have chosen to huddle together in certain areas, just as the Catholics congregated in the Bogside, and in council elections their votes are therefore often "wasted". But in the Brighton case we are at least talking about actual votes and actual electoral evidence. In the case of Londonderry in the sixties we have to speculate or examine chicken entrails to find alleged shortcomings.

Electoral imperfections are inevitable under the first past the post system, and they are not in themselves proof of malpractice. Stripping away the layers of confusion and prejudice from Londonderry's electoral arrangements in the 1960s, it can at worst be said that by 1967 the wards had become unequal in size and one ward had more seats than it should have had. But as the Brighton case study has already shown, an updating of arrangements cannot overcome the problem of one party having its supporters unevenly distributed throughout an area and such supporters are quite often so distributed for quite natural reasons because of historical or social factors. This problem is a common feature of British electoral arrangements and Londonderry was not unusual in this respect. That it was deemed to be so could justly be described as English hypocrisy brought on by an overdeveloped guilt complex about the Irish Catholic population.

Out of Date

The strange thing is that before a "civil rights" demonstrator had completed a chorus of "We Shall Overcome" (let alone thrown a brick in anger) the complaints about boundaries had been overtaken by events. There had been an announcement in the Queen's Speech at Stormont in 1965 that there was to be a reorganisation of local government. The massive task of reviewing the whole structure began in 1966. Northern Ireland had 68 local councils at this time and this was certainly too many for a population of 1.5 million. A Statement of Aims was published in 1967 and on 2 July 1969 a White Paper was produced, proposing 17 single tier authorities, the ward boundaries to be drawn up by an independent statutory commission. The plan looked for the economies of scale which motivated the reduction in the number of councils on the Mainland a few years later. One new council covering both the Corporation and the Rural District Council areas was proposed for Londonderry.[42]

At the 16 May meeting of the Londonderry Corporation immediately before the 1967 local elections the Unionists were already agreed that this would be the last set of elections to the Londonderry County Borough Council.[43] The next elections would be for a new council operating under different boundaries. A Londonderry Area Steering Committee, with representatives from the Corporation, the Londonderry Rural District Council and the Londonderry County Council, assisted by outside consultants, had been working on an Area Plan since 1965. The final report, published in March 1968, assessed the needs of the wider Londonderry area. I shall return to the Area Plan again. For our current purposes, however, it was evident by the mid-1960s that, with all the talk of fewer councils under reorganisation and the work of the Steering Committee well advanced, the new structure would provide for a Londonderry local authority stretching beyond the Corporation boundaries with a new ward scheme.

That all of this was going on is often omitted from accounts of Londonderry's electoral arrangements. Any inequalities in representation were to be dealt

with under reorganisation, and this was well known to all parties before the first
"civil rights" march took place. Those who wanted an overnight reorganisation
of local government rather than one based on careful planning only displayed
their ignorance of such matters. Even with lots of planning, local government
reorganisation on Mainland Britain in the 1970s was still able to cause
considerable chaos. Therefore not only were many of the complaints about
Londonderry's ward boundaries founded on incorrect assumptions, but by the
time of the "civil rights" era, they were also out of date. They referred to
structures which were about to be superceded.

One Man, One Vote

*The demand for 'one man, one vote' raised by the Civil Rights movement in
the late 'sixties did not only have the merit of telling simplicity. Since no one
in Britain knew to precisely what it referred, it subtly conveyed the
impression (widespread even among the relatively sophisticated on this side
of the Irish Sea) that the Catholics of Ulster were actually and statutorily
disfranchised.*

T. E. Utley[44]

*The fact that 'One man, one vote' became the banner under which the CRA
[Civil Rights Association] marches took place was, I believe, no coincidence.
It sounded, to a world attuned to such protests, a positive humanitarian cry
from an oppressed people.... Many well-meaning but ill-informed people,
even in Britain, were under the impression that the 'evil Unionist government'
had made it illegal for Catholics to vote in elections.*

Brian Faulkner[45]

What was this all about? Until 1948 Ulster's system of voting was similar to
that on the British Mainland. All adults over 21 could vote in Parliamentary
elections (in Ulster's case for Westminster and Stormont), but in local elections
there was a ratepayers franchise. In 1948 Mainland Britain abolished the
ratepayers vote and brought in a universal franchise for council elections.
Northern Ireland did not make that change and hence remained in line with
many Commonwealth countries.

What this meant was that in local government contests only ratepayers
(whether owners or tenants) plus their wives could vote. Other occupiers of
their houses, such as lodgers or relatives over 21, had no local government vote.
There was also a company vote in local elections which allowed limited

companies to nominate an elector for each £10 of rateable value, but firms could not have more than 6 votes each.

The philosophy behind such a franchise was one of "he who pays the piper calls the tune", in other words that those who pay the rates should determine how they are spent. It explains why, in pre-war years, attempts were made to equalize the valuation of wards. It was thought unfair that areas with equal representation should pay unequal amounts of rates. Strangely, the same issues which led to such a system being operated throughout the United Kingdom before the war have re-emerged during the term of Mrs. Thatcher's government. High rates in certain Labour authorities led to a controversy about business ratepayers having no vote and hence no chance to influence the level of rates. This time round the problem was met by introducing a statutory duty for councils to consult business interests before setting a rate, rather than reintroducing the business vote. Similarly the community charge or "poll tax" which was introduced to replace rates, was, amongst other things, an attempt to get round what the Conservatives saw as the problem of non-ratepayers voting for high expenditure they would not have to pay for. Instead of taking away votes, the British government has tried to make more people pay the new form of rates. Whether this is a good or bad thing I cannot go into here.

Certainly there was concern in 1930s Londonderry that with the 2 Unionist wards paying three quarters of the city's rates, a Republican council would use Protestants' rates to further Catholic interests. After the war, however, concern with the "rights of property" receded.

What was the effect of the ratepayers' franchise? In 1967, 973,724 people were eligible to vote in elections to the Stormont Parliament, while 694,483 could vote in local elections.[46] Thus about a quarter of the adult population didn't have a vote at a local level. Sarah Nelson reminds us that Independent Unionist MPs like Tommy Henderson "opposed property qualifications for local elections which disfranchised more working class Protestants than Catholics."[47] "Civil rights" campaigners did not see it like that.

T. E. Utley has summarised their position:

> *The argument that this was a measure of sectarian discrimination (an argument which it was not commonly thought necessary by the Civil Rightists to spell out) ran thus: because of the economic inferiority of the Catholic population, the proportion of Catholic ratepayers was smaller*

than that of Protestant ratepayers. Catholic households were commonly also larger than those of Protestants. Accordingly a ratepayers franchise discriminated against the Catholics and, taken in conjunction with the gerrymandering of constituency boundaries, ensured that Catholics were grossly under-represented in local government.[48]

The findings of Richard Rose must, however be borne in mind: "Catholics are proportionately more numerous in the bottom income group, and less numerous in the upper income group. Given their larger numbers in the population, however, there are *more poor Protestants than poor Catholics* in Northern Ireland, just as there are more well to do Protestants."[49] Thus even if being disenfranchised were related to poverty then, numerically, more Protestants than Catholics would have lost votes under the ratepayers franchise. In fact Christopher Hewitt estimated that just under 60% of those disenfranchised throughout Ulster were Protestants.[50] Budge and O'Leary, in a Belfast study of the ratepayers franchise, concluded "that the bias is so unsystematic as not to be the result of any concerted plan."[51]

Maybe so, says Paul Arthur of the University of Ulster, but "The bias was systematic in areas like Londonderry County Borough."[52] As usual this is not supported by statistical evidence. Christopher Hewitt found that in Londonderry 22.3% of Catholics and 18.6% of Protestants had a Parliamentary vote but couldn't vote in local elections.[53] The difference is so small as to make no difference to election results.

Why did the argument summarised by Utley fail? Firstly, I think, because the link between economic disadvantage and disenfranchisement was a tenuous one. Budge and O'Leary, in a Belfast survey which used a very small sample, discovered that manual workers made up 70% of electors and 64% of non-electors and those in semi-professional jobs were more likely to be without a local government vote, thus lending no support to the claim.[54] Wealthy owner occupiers and poor tenants all had the same right to vote in local elections. Secondly, the economic disadvantage of Catholics was overstated (as we shall see in the next chapter). Thirdly, the bigger Catholic households were largely made up of offspring under voting age rather than disenfranchised adults. Hence it was that a Catholic was only slightly more likely to have no local government vote than a Protestant, and throughout Ulster many more Protestants than Catholics had no opportunity to elect their local councils.

In Londonderry there were about 990 company votes (3.9%), wielded by both

Protestants and Catholics and companies with headquarters outside Ulster who were probably difficult to classify. Throughout Northern Ireland company votes made up 0.48% of the local government electorate.[55] When the Stormont government announced that this form of franchise was to be scrapped, Eamonn McCann, one of the leading "civil rights" activists in Londonderry, said that "company votes accounted for a miniscule proportion of the local government electorate" and the announcement was therefore a "derisory gesture".[56] It is difficult, therefore, to know what all the fuss was about.

The end of the restricted local government franchise was announced at Stormont in April 1969. Both communities thus gained thousands of voters but it made little difference to the balance of power. The controversy had never tackled the real issue - whether Protestants and Catholics who didn't pay rates should be deprived of local government votes - which should have been easily resolved. Because the issue was wrongly defined as a question of Protestants oppressing Catholics, it all became very difficult, and the concession of a universal adult franchise for local government in such circumstances had unforseen consequences.

After The Revolution

In November 1968 the suspension of the Londonderry County Borough Council and the Londonderry Rural District Council was announced. They were to be replaced by an unelected Development Commission, which took over in April 1969. Later it was decided to take away many key functions from all local councils and place them in the hands of different organisations. This move overturned the 1969 White Paper proposals for local government reorganisation, caused a complete rethink and delayed the whole process. It was therefore not until 1973 that the first elections were held for the reorganised councils, now 26 in number. A new Londonderry City Council, covering the old Corporation and Rural District areas, had been created.

Those who had complained about Londonderry's electoral arrangements had been given everything they could possibly want.

a. The ratepayers franchise had gone, to be replaced by universal adult suffrage.

b. The company vote had been abolished.

c. The boundaries of the 5 new wards had been drawn up by an independent boundary commission and representation was strictly in proportion to the number of voters.

d. The voting age had been reduced to 18, benefitting the younger Catholic population.

e. The Corporation boundary had been extended. This had been a key demand, which I shall return to in my discussion of the housing situation. This had the effect of bringing in Unionists from the smaller Londonderry Rural District population, but the new Londonderry City Council area still had 64.3% of its population made up of Catholics and they must therefore have constituted at least 59% of the electorate.[57]

Once again each ward returned several members. With a fair system in place all the pundits knew there would be a big victory for the Catholic parties. The coming of the Troubles and the resulting polarisation meant the Northern Ireland Labour Party's support had collapsed. People had long ago stopped talking about "civil rights". The issue was what it always had been - whether Ulster should remain part of the United Kingdom. Parties lined up for or against the Union, and a big anti-Unionist majority was inevitable. Those for the Union in the election were the United Loyalist Group (ULG) and the new Alliance Party which had the support of some liberal ex-Unionist Party members like former minister, Sir Robert Porter, and former Stormont MP, Richard Ferguson. Although the Alliance Party appealed then, as now, to both communities it has over the years got its main electoral support from middle class Protestants.

When the votes of each organisation's candidates were added up there was one clear winner, both in terms of its combined vote and its leading candidate's vote, in 3 out of the 5 wards. That winner was the United Loyalist Group. The 2 pro-Union contestants, the ULG and the Alliance Party, between them polled an absolute majority of votes cast in the Londonderry City Council area.[58]

One thing and one thing only saved the Republicans from a humiliating defeat, and that was the application of electoral standards which were not acceptable on the British Mainland. The "civil rights" demand for British rights and British standards was forgotten as Northern Ireland became the only place in the United Kingdom to have imposed upon it a proportional representation system which no British government this century would have found acceptable in England, Scotland or Wales. Ironically, it was in October 1968, the month of the first "civil rights" march in Londonderry, that Jack Lynch, the Irish prime minister and leader of the strongly Republican Fianna Fail party, had unsuccessfully sought to abolish P.R. in the Irish Republic by means of a referendum. Eamon de Valera had tried to do the same thing in 1959. But what wasn't good enough for Fianna Fail or Mainland Britain was deemed good enough for Ulster.

The United Loyalist Group had won the 1973 contest on first preference votes, indicating that it would have won control of the council in a traditional British first past the post election. However, when the subsequent preferences were taken into account and votes transferred under the P.R. system, the breakdown of seats looked like this:

Anti-Union		Pro-Union	
Social Democratic & Labour Party	10	United Loyalist Group	9
Nationalist Party	3	Alliance Party	4
Republican Clubs	1		13
	14		

The crucial distortion made by the P.R. system was that the SDLP with just 11,008 first preference votes won 10 seats, but the ULG with 12,483 first preference votes secured only 9 seats. If we look at the accumulated votes (first preference plus votes transferred from other candidates) which it took to get the successful candidates elected, the disparity is even greater. The 10 SDLP men required just 9,165 votes to get elected and the 9 ULG councillors 12,319 votes.

The drawing of ward boundaries under a P.R. system is less crucial as long as the proportion of voters to seats is fairly uniform in all the wards. I said earlier that representation under the 1973 ward scheme was strictly in proportion to the number of voters. This was not quite true. The wards, which were known rather unimaginatively by letters of the alphabet, had the following number of seats.

Ward	Voters	Seats	Voters per Seat
A	10,295	6	1,716
B	10,115	5	2,023
C	9,024	5	1,804
D	6,836	5	1,367
E	12,450	6	2.075

Wards A, B, C and E had representation in the range 1,716 to 2,075 voters per seat on the council. The odd man out was Ward D, which covered the Bogside and the Fountain, a small Protestant enclave. It had a large Catholic majority. It can be seen that if this ward had had 4 seats instead of 5 there would still have been only 1,709 voters per seat, the lowest ratio in Londonderry. It would therefore seem that Ward D had too many seats according to any fair criteria aimed at equalizing representation.

What was the effect of this? Under the P.R. system candidates can be elected on first preferences alone if they reach the relevant quota of votes. The sole ULG candidate, Marlene Jefferson, and one SDLP man, Dr. R. McClean, were elected in this way. The rest had to undergo the complicated process of transferring second preferences between candidates until they reached the quota necessary to be elected. Under this procedure the remaining 3 councillors were elected one after each other on Counts 9, 11 and 12. If there had been only 4 seats in Ward D, the fifth and last person to be elected in 1973 would not have been able to sit on the council. That person was James Hegarty of the Nationalist Party, who had been the leader of its group on the old Corporation.

Therefore under a strictly fair system of representation, the anti-Union forces on Londonderry City Council would have had only 13 councillors, the same as the pro-Union ULG and Alliance Party. The Republican Clubs member in fact boycotted the council and didn't take his seat. The much-maligned Londonderry Protestants might therefore be forgiven for thinking that Londonderry was, at the end of the day, only delivered into Republican hands because of unfair and easily remedied electoral arrangements. It was, perhaps, the final irony.

1973 Londonderry City Council Election Results			
Anti Union		%	Seats
SDLP	11,008	32.4	10
Nationalist Party	2,850	8.4	3
Republican Clubs	2,091	6.2	1
Ind. Republican	71	0.2	0
	16,020	47.2	14
Pro-Union			
ULG	12,483	36.8	9
Alliance Party	4,930	14.5	4
	17,413	51.3	13

Other candidates of indeterminate loyalties made up of the remaining 1.5%.

The Roaring Twenties

A general reader may be surprised at the extent to which opponents of Unionism sought to dig deep into history to find evidence of wrongdoing. But this did not stop in the 1930s. Many have looked at electoral arrangements in the 1920s to try and bolster the "civil rights" case. It might be thought that a discussion of such issues cannot be relevant to the 1960s and that they can safely be ignored. I feel that this is not the case.

The anti-Unionist delving into history is an attempt to locate some dreadful electoral fiddle from which stem all subsequent wrongs. It is also an attempt to locate the source of Protestant guilt; to uncover some ancient electoral misdeed so dreadful that a massive act of atonement is required. The power of such arguments can be seen from the Cameron Report, which itself drank from the same well. Therefore to give this whole subject adequate treatment it will be necessary to briefly dispose of any residual guilt feelings.

Cameron said: "We note too that there have been times when other electoral systems and boundaries permitted non-Unionists majorities in Omagh Urban District, Armagh Urban District and Londonderry County Borough. Accordingly it is our view that the arguments used to justify the existing arrangements when they were introduced, mainly rationalised a determination to achieve and maintain Unionist electoral control."[59] In the case of Londonderry he is referring to a brief period between 1920 and 1923 when the city was under Republican control. The elections in January 1920 took place before the formation of the Northern Ireland State.

The implication is that the boundaries at that time were fair and the subsequent ward boundaries were not. If the 1920 boundaries led to Republican control, why did later schemes wrest control from Catholic parties? Some terrible fiddle must have taken place. The key to understanding this lies in Cameron's use of the phrase "other electoral systems and boundaries". The 1920 election was held under a system of proportional representation which was abolished in time for the 1923 contest. It is therefore necessary to determine what part the 1920 ward boundaries (as distinct from the P.R. voting system) played in the Republican victory.

The answer is: none at all. For the P.R. election Londonderry was divided into 4 wards. The West Ward had 8 seats, the North Ward 11, the South East Ward 12 and the Waterside Ward 9. There was no contest in the West Ward and 8 "Nationalists" (a coalition which included Sinn Fein supporters, Redmondites and Labour candidates) were elected. In the other 3 wards the Unionists won clear majorities in straight fights with the Nationalists. It was the first such confrontation since 1897.[60] (Hence in the 76 years between 1897 and 1973 there were only 2 occasions when the Republicans took on Unionists in Londonderry council elections.) The number of first preference votes cast was as follows:[61]

	Uns.	Nats.
North Ward	1,923	1,297
South East Ward	2,035	1,809
Waterside Ward	1,613	960

Under a traditional British first past the post system Unionists would have won all the seats in these 3 wards. They would therefore have had a 32-8 majoirity on the Corporation, compared with a 24-16 result under the 1923 boundaries and a 12-8 split under the 1936 arrangements. There is therefore no truth in the rumour that the 1920 boundaries handed control to the Republicans or even contributed to such a handover.

It should be noted that in 1923 Londonderry simply went back to the 5 wards that had been in operation from 1896 to 1920. This change also made no contribution to the transfer of power back to the Unionists. They would actually have had a bigger majority under the 1920 boundaries. Patrick Buckland hints at dark deeds by suggesting that the Republican wards after 1923 were "significantly larger" than the Unionist wards.[62] This statement is completely untrue. The authority Buckland cites for this, Sydney Elliott's PhD thesis, says nothing about the ward figures.

The population figures contained in the 1911 and 1926 Census returns are set out below:[63]

	1911	1926
North Ward	10,788	11,791
South Ward	7,683	8,666
East Ward	4,409	5,133
West Ward	8,730	9,347
Waterside Ward	9,170	10,222

Even though population figures tend to overstate the position in the Catholic wards (because the younger Catholic population had a smaller percentage of voters than of the population as a whole) it can be seen that throughout this period the Unionist North and Waterside Wards were always the biggest. The East Ward had less representatives than the rest to make up for its small size.

Proportional Representation

The temporary transfer of power to Republicans was in fact solely due to the introduction of a proportional representation system for the 1920 local government elections throughout Ireland, which was then all still under British rule. In the South East Ward the Unionists beat the Nationalists by 200 votes but secured only 6 of the 12 seats. They came within about 40 votes of winning the extra seat they needed to deny the Republicans control but they ended up losing the election by 21 seats to 19. The abolition of P.R. returned the city to the Unionists.

The question that is usually raised is whether or not the abolition of P.R. in Northern Ireland was a cynical political manoeuvre. I think the more interesting question is whether it was the introduction or the abolition of P.R. which fell into that category.

In the December 1918 Westminster elections, Sinn Fein with its commitment to physical force won a landslide victory in the Catholic constituencies of Ireland by triumphing over the more moderate Nationalists of the United Irish League, formerly led by John Redmond, who died in March 1918.⁴⁴ But there was a tremendous difference between the 6 counties which were to make up Northern Ireland and the 26 counties which were to become the Irish Free State. In Ulster the Nationalists won 4 seats to Sinn Fein's 3 (the Unionists taking the other 23 constituencies). However in Southern Ireland Sinn Fein won 70 seats, the Nationalists 2 and the Unionists 3. This alarmed the British government, who would have preferred a victory for Nationalists committed to Home Rule, a limited form of self-government. Local elections were to be held throughout Ireland in 1920 and there was a prospect of Sinn Fein winning total control of councils throughout the South, which would have made administration of the country very difficult.

While this was going on the Sligo Corporation was getting ready to burst into the news.⁶⁵ This council was in financial difficulties and had only limited rating powers. It wanted to extend these powers and this required an act of Parliament. The Ratepayers Association objected, saying it wanted guaranteed representation on the council before it would support such a move. The Local Government Board arranged a deal under which proportional representation would be introduced to ensure that ratepayers candidates could win some seats on the council. A private act, the Sligo Corporation Act 1918, was passed at Westminster and in January 1919 Sligo became the first place in the British

Isles to hold an election under P.R. The result was of great interest to the British government. There was no Sinn Fein landslide and the other candidates, including those from the Ratepayers Association, won seats on the council. The issue was probably decided when in January 1919 the Sinn Fein MPs declared themselves to be the Parliament of an Irish Republic.[66] On 25 February 1919 the Local Government (Ireland) Bill was announced. It provided for P.R. in council elections throughout Ireland. It is difficult to view this sudden conversion to proportional representation (especially as it was deemed inappropriate on the British Mainland) without a certain amount of cynicism. It was simply designed to nobble Sinn Fein. The Ulster Unionists, themselves no lovers of Sinn Fein, from the very beginning took a principled stand against the change. Sinn Fein boycotted Westminster and took no part in the Parliamentary debate. The Nationalists opposed the way the change was to be introduced with the Local Government Board being given wide-ranging powers to draw boundaries without reference to local authorities or ratepayers.

Sir Edward Carson supported the criticism, saying: "They will frame the constituencies to cut out the Sinn Feiners or to make the Sinn Feiners as harmless as possible."[67] There was a feeling that this was far too important an issue to be playing politics with. Carson went on to say: "I regard the whole of this bill with the greatest contempt. It is the most wretched, miserable bill and nobody wants it."[68]

When the bill had its third reading not a single Ulster MP of any persuasion would vote for it. Only 2 of the 105 Irish MPs gave it their support. Carson justifiably objected to what he saw as discriminatory legislation passed against the wishes of Irish MPs. In case anyone was unclear about the Ulster Unionists' position, Captain C. C. Craig, the future Lord Craigavon's brother, spelled it out at Westminster a year later: "We hate the system in the North and so far as I know everybody is of the opinion that we will reverse it and go back to the present system of election."[69]

There are a number of things, therefore, we can say about the introduction of proportional representation:

1. It was simply a way of halting the advance of Sinn Fein and there was little thought as to its objective merits.
2. It was introduced to deal with a Southern Irish problem - the annihilation of the United Irish League. This was not a problem in Ulster.
3. Not a single Ulster MP supported this legislation.

4. The Ulster Unionists made clear their opposition from the very beginning
and left no-one in doubt that they would get rid of P.R. as soon as possible.

The legislation setting up the Northern Ireland government in 1920 gave it the
power to change back to the British system of voting, and it can have come as
no surprise that Ulster voted to realign itself with the rest of the United
Kingdom. It was therefore the temporary introduction of P.R. which was the
political fiddle, and by repealing the measure the Unionists were simply
showing they would not be discriminated against by legislation which was not
acceptable on Mainland Britain.

Stormont

Accusations of gerrymandering have not been confined to the local government
boundaries in Londonderry. Some have levelled the same complaint against
constituency boundaries for elections to the Northern Ireland Parliament at
Stormont. Tim Pat Coogan says the Londonderry City seat was won by
Nationalists in 1920 and was held by them until 1929. "Then the predominantly
Catholic South City Ward was joined to the Foyle constituency, which had a
Catholic majority, but the City's electoral division was extended into the
county of Derry. The net effect of this gerrymander was that the Derry City
constituency ceased to return a nationalist and the seat went to the unionists."
He sees this as an example of "blatant unfairness".[70]

Liam de Paor, in a widely circulated Penguin paperback account of the Ulster
situation, states that "in a rearrangement of boundaries the city was divided in
two, the bulk of the urban population, crowded into the Catholic ghetto on the
west side of Derry, being taken into the 'Foyle' constituency, and the 'City'
constituency having its boundaries extended eight miles to the east into the
countryside of Co. Derry to create a Protestant majority."[71]

I think it would not be an overstatement to say that both writers have made
complete fools of themselves. The first elections to the Stormont Parliament
were held in 1921 under a system of proportional representation. County
Londonderry, which of course included the city, was assigned just one
constituency. It elected 5 Stormont MPs. Between 1921 and 1929 there was
no seperate Londonderry City constituency, nor was there a Foyle constituency,
and hence no Republican represented either of them.

The Northern Ireland government had been unable to complete the administrative arrangements necessary to rid Stormont of the P.R. system in time for the 1925 election. However by 1929 it had drawn up 5 single member constituencies to cover the County of Londonderry.

Coogan's account makes it sound as though a Catholic area of Londonderry was joined to an existing Foyle constituency, which already had a Catholic majority. This would have led to an accumulation of "wasted" Catholic votes. At the same time it seems that an existing City constituency not only rid itself of a major part of its Catholic electorate but also bolstered its Protestant majority by extending its boundaries to bring in more friendly voters. The net effect of this would have been to leave the Foyle constituency under Republican control and to transfer the City constituency to the Unionists by a form of electoral confidence trick.

This story has no basis in fact. As neither the Foyle nor City of Londonderry constituencies existed until 1929 there was no transfer of voters between them and as non-existent constituencies have non-existent boundaries, no boundaries were extended. There was no such fiddle.

What had happened was that those drawing up the new boundaries realised that Londonderry City was too big to have just one Stormont constituency. Their aims were not to let constituencies cross county boundaries and to disturb the 1921 distribution of seats as little as possible. Thus the County of Londonderry would have 5 MPs as before. At this point it should be noted that for much of this century census returns have made it easy to identify the population of quite small electoral areas. Identifying the number of voters or adults is not so easy in Northern Ireland. Thus many writers quote population figures, often with misleading results, rather than electorate figures. Some of the relevant government papers refer only to population and I have had to use this where the electorate is unavailable.

The government draftsmen saw that if the city, with its population of 45,000, had one seat, the other 4 county constituencies would each have populations of about 23,600.[72] The city seat would also be far larger than any other seat in Northern Ireland. In order to get 5 seats of roughly equal size they had to ignore the city boundary. This was the practice adopted at the 1983 UK revision of Westminster boundaries where a city was too big for one seat and too small for two eg. Oxford.

In Londonderry this was achieved by including part of the surrounding Rural

District areas in both Stormont constituencies. The Foyle division consisted (with minor variations) of the old South and West Wards (which became the new South Ward in 1936) plus the Upper, Middle and Lower Liberties from the Rural District area on the west bank of the River Foyle. The City of Londonderry constituency was basically made up of the North and East Wards, the walled city, the Waterside Ward and the 4 east bank country areas which adjoined the River Foyle: Glendermott, Waterside, Lough Enagh and Eglinton.

The estimated population figures were as follows[73]

Constituency	From the City	From the Rural District
City of Londonderry	22,383	4,940
Foyle	22,595	3,816

It is therefore quite false to state, as de Paor does, that the bulk of the urban population went to the Foyle constituency. It is also clear that the City of Londonderry seat would have had a comfortable Protestant majority even without the addition of the Rural District voters. The latter made up less than 20% of the constituency's population and in no sense did the so-called "extension of the boundary" create a Protestant majority. There was one there already. The only significant consequence of including Rural District voters in the City and Foyle seats was the creation of a safe Republican majority in the adjacent Mid Londonderry constituency.

Before 1929 Unionists held 3 out of 5 County Londonderry seats. After the changes in 1929 they elected exactly the same number of MPs. Barritt and Carter noted that "in Londonderry City and County together the Unionists get three out of the five seats, and since they claim a bare majority of the population this result might be achieved under any fair system."[74] In fact the electoral majority was not so bare. In the County Londonderry constituency the Unionists achieved a 56.2% share of the vote in 1921 and 57.9% in 1925.[75]

It will be recalled that the Stormont boundary was used as the dividing line between the North and South Wards in the 1936 ward scheme. Dr. Sydney Elliott found that although there were other objections to the Stormont boundaries at the time by George Leeke (a Londonderry Nationalist MP) in the

Northern Ireland Parliament, there was no opposition to this dividing line, and Elliott concluded that this part of the boundary was acceptable in 1929.[76] It therefore presumably formed a satisfactory basis for the 1936 ward scheme. The only minor objection Leeke had about the west bank dividing line was that it included all of the walled city in one constituency by detaching that small portion of the West Ward which fell within the walls. The contemporary government papers say that only 250 people (and therefore less than 200 voters) lived in this area and hence the dispute was of no electoral significance.[77] It was more a dispute about symbolic control of a site of historical significance to Protestants because of their heroic defence of the walled city during the Siege of Londonderry in 1688-89.

The objections of Patrick Buckland of Liverpool University's Institute of Irish Studies are more atmospheric than specific.[78] His comments create the feeling that something nasty was going on, but you don't know what. In some areas "the ideosyncratic distribution of the Catholic population provided at least a plausible justification of the government's scheme of redistribution. It was otherwise in the city of Londonderry. There the government's actions were determined solely by the interests of the Unionist Party." This recalls the comments of Paul Arthur about the effects of the restricted local government franchise. Londonderry was for many people the wickedest place of all.

The Northern Ireland government apparently "now had the power to neutralise, if they wished, the nationalist majority in the city" and was looking for a way of "preventing the city from falling into nationalist hands". But Buckland doesn't explain how the 1929 boundaries can be said to have achieved this. After all the Catholic population was not "neutralised". The constituency boundaries assured that a Republican would always be elected to represent Londonderry in the Foyle division.

The idea that Londonderry City should form one constituency was a non-starter because of its size. It would have been under-represented, and Catholics could well have complained that this was a sign of gerrymandering. Buckland may have had in mind his criticism of Belfast where "the government readily tolerated inequalities" and "Unionist constituencies of 18-20,000 contrasted with a nationalist constituency of over 30,000". He seems to be referring to the Central division which had a population of 33,694.[79] What is certain is that 45,000 is a very much bigger population than 33,000 and it cannot therefore be argued that the size of the Belfast Central constituency would justify having one seat in Londonderry City.

In fact the main reason for the Belfast inequalities was the government's decision to divide each of the city's Westminster seats (which were not equal in size) into 4 Stormont divisions. To compare like with like, in the West Belfast Westminster area Belfast Central was only the second biggest Stormont constituency. The biggest was the Unionist-held Woodvale (population 34,464). Unionist St. Anne's was only slightly smaller than Central and the smallest division was the Republican Falls.[80] Central therefore did not stand head and shoulders above the Unionist areas as implied by Buckland. Nor is there evidence that Catholics were disadvantaged by being allocated large constituencies. The smallest seat in Belfast was Dock, which had a Catholic majority. Buckland's comment therefore seems to be just a cheap crack made without due regard to the government records he has examined.

A Decent Burial

It only remains to give the Cameron Report's conclusions about electoral arrangements in Londonderry a decent burial. So let us deal with his other complaints. Writing about the Corporation elections he says:

> ....the electoral outturn in these areas was unrepresentative, and was felt to be so by a significant number of people. In such circumstances it is idle to argue that artificial majorities are not unique to Northern Ireland.[81]

Cameron claims that the electoral outturn was unrepresentative in Londonderry. In fact it was perfectly representative. Which other political group in the world could complain about the fact that in all elections between 1920 and 1973 only one of its candidates was ever defeated? The Republicans won those elections they contested. The outturn was perfectly representative of the number of candidates nominated.

There is clearly here a reference once again to the analysis of electoral registers in terms of Catholics and Protestants. As long as there were English politicians and Scottish judges prepared to take them seriously, Republicans were laughing. They must have regarded politics as an easy business, because whereas everyone else had to go out and persuade people to vote for them, all the Republicans had to do was count names on a register to show the gullible how many supporters they had. The Northern Friends Peace Board thought that voters associations in Londonderry could "tell the voting strength very accurately at any time, taking for granted that no-one will vote out of line".[82] It was wrong.

The actual performance of the Nationalist Party in Londonderry's South Ward elections showed there was no evidence to support the view that all Catholics were Nationalist Party voters. The quoting of electoral register figures led to inflated claims of Republican support, hence suggesting that there was some terrible wrong which needed righting by an English knight in shining armour. There is a sense in which this claim only remained credible in the absence of actual electoral evidence. A whole series of contests would have shown the Nationalist Party was unable to mobilise the Catholic population in sufficient numbers. The absence of any contest at all between 1949 and 1966 certainly helped the myth-makers. The 1967 results, however, gave the game away.

This does rather assume that, if there had been a whole heap of electoral evidence, a few of the authors of the vast number of books criticising Londonderry would have bothered to do the necessary research. I must admit that I have no reason to believe that this is the case. They have, after all, acted as though the 1967 results didn't exist.

In another sense the absence of electoral contests was the Republicans' achilles heel. If they had come to the English public and said: 'Our electoral system is so unjust but we actually have no evidence of this because we have only fought the Unionists once in the last 50 years', it is likely they would have got a different reaction.

As it was, the army of academics, journalists and political commentators, who came to Ulster flaunting their integrity and sense of social justice, didn't ask and didn't want to know about electoral evidence. They preferred to wallow in the myth of the "oppressed Catholics". Republicans would have been entitled to believe that there is one born every minute.

To turn to another of Cameron's points, is it "idle to argue that artificial majorities are not unique to Northern Ireland"? Well no, it is not. The whole thrust of the "civil rights" argument was that Ulster Catholics were not having British standards applied to them, and this was said to be the basis of their grievances. Jim Callagan, the Home Secretary in the British Labour government during the "civil rights" era, believed that "the Unionist Government failed to put right civil grievances that would not have been tolerated in the rest of the United Kingdom."[83] It was hypocritical nonsense.

But then it rather depends on what is meant by "artificial majorities". There are some things boundary revisions can solve and some they cannot. They could, for instance, have done away with the tiny Parliamentary constituencies held by Jim Callaghan's party and eliminated its artificial majority in the House of Commons in 1964 and 1974. What boundary revisions cannot do is to overcome the awkward habits of electors who insist on voting for third parties; fail to vote for the parties they are supposed to vote for; refuse to keep switching allegiance from one party to another; split the vote of movements which the pundits would like to see win; take up patterns of residence which are inconvenient for the parties who are chasing their votes; and do not vote for parties who fail to put up candidates.

Adjusting the ward boundaries could not save the Brighton Conservative Party. The 1973 boundary revisions could not save Londonderry Republicans from being beaten in 3 of the 5 wards and securing only 47% of first preference votes. Even under a P.R, system which distorted voters' first choices, they could only scrape a council majority of one, and then only because of malapportionment of seats. Indeed, in not one of the other areas said by Cameron to be gerrymandered - Dungannon, Armagh, Omagh and Fermanagh - could Republicans win a majority of seats in 1973. The myth of the Londonderry gerrymander had been laid to rest, but no-one noticed.

B.   Housing

Under the ratepayers franchise the local government vote was essentially restricted to the householder and his wife. His house might be full of other adults, but they could not go to the polls. In order to get a vote they needed a house so that they too could become ratepayers. Hence no house, no vote. Therefore by refusing to allocate houses to people, a local authority could deny them votes.

It was argued by "civil rights" activists that the Londonderry Corporation built and allocated houses unfairly so as to minimise the electoral threat from the opponents of Unionism. By not giving Catholics their fair share of houses the number of Catholic voters was kept down. There were also complaints about the location of houses and the areas in which Catholics were allocated homes by the Corporation. The housing needs of Roman Catholics were allegedly not being met.

Conor Cruise O'Brien, writing in 1968, stated that the Protestant Unionist majority held a "near-monopoly" of housing in Londonderry.[1] The Northern Friends Peace Board felt that "The allocation of houses appears to be badly biased and the main purpose appears to be to maintain the established voting balance, and thus prevent any challenge to the party controlling the Council."[2] A much younger Max Hastings (who is now editor of the *Daily Telegraph*) wrote that "Until 1969, housing in Ulster was largely in the hands of local councils, and there was the clearest evidence that in many areas Protestant-dominated councils had used their powers to discriminate against Catholics in the distribution of accommodation." He went on: "With political power of such an invincible kind, the Unionists could leave the Catholic minority to beg in vain for crumbs from the Protestant table."[3] Gerry Adams, current President of Sinn Fein, says: "I began to realise that Catholics were being denied houses because that meant they could be denied votes."[4]

The Northern Ireland Housing Trust

Londonderry County Borough Council was the local housing authority, but it was not the only public body providing accommodation in the city. The Northern Ireland Housing Trust (NIHT) had been set up in 1944 to supplement the efforts of local authorities. It was a kind of QUANGO funded by the

Stormont government. The NIHT outlined its relationship with councils as follows:

> *The Trust recognises that the Local Authority with which it is working is a colleague in a partnership. The Local Authority has full knowledge of conditions in its district and its advice and guidance to the Trust is invaluable. In the choice of sites, the Trust must co-ordinate its plans with those of the Local Authorities, which, it must be remembered, are charged with providing the majority of the houses in their respective areas. The Local Authority provides sewerage and other services for the Trust and no scheme can be successfully carried out without the most complete co-operation. The trust warmly appreciates the helpful and friendly attitude of representatives of the Local Authorities with whom it has had dealings. In many cases, Members and Officers, including County Officers, have gone to much personal trouble to resolve difficulties and expedite decisions.[5]*

It should be noted that the Trust was not able to breeze into town and start erecting houses against the wishes of councils. It needed their consent and positive co-operation. Thus local authorities had to positively agree that they wanted NIHT houses in a particular place. It followed that, in assessing their housing needs and how they might be met, councils took into account the part the Trust could play in assisting them. Therefore it is reasonable to count both council and Trust-built houses in looking at how good an area was in tackling its housing problems. All public house building would have been endorsed by the local authority and should thus be viewed as part of the housing programme it wished to see implemented.

The position in Londonderry was very clear cut. All the Trust's projects were carried out at the suggestion of the Corporation, which took the initiative in each case. This is how the NIHT described the initial approach:

> *Before the Trust was formed, Londonderry Corporation had acquired 257 acres at Creggan. This is an elevated site, pleasantly situated on the outskirts of the City at the Rosemount Bus Terminus. It would ultimately accommodate some 1,500 houses, with churches, schools, shops and community centres and other amenities.*

> *The Corporation invited the Trust to share the site, and it was arranged that the Trust would act as its agents in a joint scheme, laying out the whole Estate, and building the first 500 houses and the necessary roads; half of the*

houses should then become the property of the Corporation and be paid for by it. The other half would remain the property of the Trust which would pay the Corporation for the land on which these houses were situated.

This scheme has proved a happy example of co-operation, involving as it does the joint consideration of many problems and the Trust warmly appreciated the energy and enthusiasm with which the Londonderry Corporation Housing Committee and its staff have contributed to the combined effort.[6]

The NIHT went on to build further parts of the Creggan estate and also undertook the Lecky Road/Rossville Street redevelopment in the Bogside, all in the South Ward. This incidently saved Londonderry ratepayers a lot of money. The City Accountant, Mr. D. C. White, told the Bogside public inquiry in 1961 that the scheme would cost the council £22,000 per year in loan charges compared with £41,000 per year if the Corporation had carried out the whole redevelopment itself. A *Londonderry Sentinel* editorial in 1968 estimated that the whole NIHT housing programme had saved the Corporation between £32 and £38 per house per year in loan charges.[7]

Barritt and Carter said of the Trust: "It has a world-wide reputation for the provision of well planned and competently administered housing estates. It selects its tenants from both direct applications and from the local authority waiting lists, using a strict points system to determine priority." They also said: "We have heard many tributes to the fairness and just dealing of the Housing Trust with members of both communities, and virtually no complaints;[8] The Northern Friends Peace Board said: "It is spoken of on all sides as being fair and just".[9]

Who Got the Houses?

Let us start our calculations on the basis of figures provided by the Catholic organisation, the Campaign for Social Justice. At the beginning of 1965 it published an analysis which can be presented as follows:[10]

Corporation Houses	Catholic Tenants		Protestant Tenants		Total
North Ward	39	(9%)	395	(91%)	434
Waterside Ward	119	(20%)	480	(80%)	599
South Ward	995	(99%)	6	(1%)	1001
	1153	(57%)	881	(43%)	2034
NIHT Houses					
South Ward	1059	(96%)	43	(4%)	1102
	2212	(71%)	924	(29%)	3136

If we accept these figures as accurate, it is possible to estimate what happened over the next few years to assess the state of play at April 1969, when the Corporation was dissolved.

NIHT annual reports indicate that in the 4 years up to that date 507 further dwellings had been completed as part of the redevelopment of the Bogside as well as 137 houses at Southway in the Creggan.[11] The first lot of houses were for those who had had their homes in the Bogside demolished. Hardly any Protestants lived here and therefore almost all the houses would have gone to Catholics. There is no reason to believe that less than 96% of the Southway houses would have been allocated to Catholics, just as they had in other parts of the Creggan.

The Corporation's housing programme produced about 300 homes between 1965 and 1969, and most of these seem to have been at Gobnascale on the east bank.[12] Today this is an almost 100% Roman Catholic estate, but in the early days some Protestants lived there. It would be safe to estimate that between a half and three-quarters of these new Corporation lettings were to Catholics.

Thus it seems likely that of approximately 944 houses built between April 1965 and April 1969, about 782 to 857 (500+132+150 to 225) would have been given to Catholic tenants. This would mean that Roman Catholics received somewhere between 2,994 and 3,069 out of 4,080 public sector houses in

Londonderry; in other words 73-75%. Although Roman Catholic adults never at any time outnumbered Protestant adults by more than 2:1 during this period, they received about 3 times as many houses according to calculations based on Catholic figures. The overall percentage is also in line with Protestant estimates.[13]

The South Ward Corral

Eamonn McCann thought Catholics were "corralled" in the South Ward.[14] It implies they were forced to live there against their wishes. It also raises the question of how Catholics came to be concentrated in certain areas. A common complaint was that this was the result of the Corporation's housing allocation policy.

In fact the patterns of residence in Londonderry had more ancient origins. The social geographer, Alan Robinson, found that by 1835 a number of clearly defined areas outside the Walls had appeared. Edenballymore to the north was largely Presbyterian. This was where the merchants and better off people lived. It was the basis of the North Ward. To the east was a Protestant working class area called "the Wapping", later known as the Fountain (through which runs Wapping Lane). The "Bogside and Wells" district to the south was where the Irish Catholics lived. Robinson says it was a "reception area" for newcomers, largely from Donegal. Communities were separated and segregated as they had been 200 years earlier.[15]

By 1926 Catholics made up 70% of the population in the South Ward and 97% in the West Ward.[16] These were natural concentrations of population which had grown up over the centuries. They were not engineered by drawing boundary lines in odd places. Nor were they the result of public housing policy. Northern Ireland did not have the benefit of English housing legislation between the wars and it was not until 1944 that proper financial assistance became available to councils to build on any scale.[17] Help with slum clearance did not arrive until 1956. Thus Londonderry did not have a public housing programme until after the Second World War.

The pattern of settlement in estates built by the Corporation and the NIHT did no more than mirror the patterns which had been established for over a hundred years. Strange, therefore, that no-one bothered to consider that if people had chosen to live in certain areas over such a long period they might have continued to choose to do so in the post-war era. Almost all writers seem to have assumed that if Catholics took houses in the South Ward it was because they were forced to do so. No-one asked the simple question: "Where did Catholics want to live?"

We might begin to doubt the orthodox view if we look at the way the Trust allocated its houses in the Creggan. We have seen that the NIHT used a points system for allocating houses and was praised for its fairness. Why then did it give 96% of the dwellings it built to Catholics? The Corporation was, we are told, controlled by wicked Unionists and they could be expected to corral Roman Catholics in the South Ward, but the Trust had no such motive. Yet its pattern of allocations in the Creggan was very similar to that of the Corporation. The answer is very straightforward. Then, as now, housing applicants were asked where they would like to live. The Creggan was very popular with Catholics and very unpopular with Protestants. Therefore the houses went to Catholics. Most of the new tenants came from the overcrowded Bogside. The Creggan, which is adjacent to the Bogside, had a convenient location which meant that applicants had to move only a fairly short distance. Family, friends and churches would still be accessible.

This attachment to the area and what English liberals might call "ghetto living" was underlined during the redevelopment of the Bogside. Public inquiries were held into this scheme and one in Belfast. The Trust, in one of its annual reports felt that the lesson that had been learnt from these inquiries was that "People are afraid of being moved to other areas away from their work, churches, schools, relations, friends and neighbours." The attitude of older people could be summed up when they said: "I was born in this house in this street and I want to die in it."[18]

A significant section of the Bogside's population was told in the early 1960s that its slum houses were to be demolished. It was their big chance to say that they wanted to break out of the corral within which they had been allegedly penned by the Unionists. Instead they exerted intense pressure to rehouse as many of their number as possible in exactly the same area.

The Corporation and the Trust came up with a clever scheme which was to be implemented by the latter. The key to the plan was the initial building of houses on some playing fields, and hence arose the myth of Meenan Park. Russell Stetler, articulating the received wisdom on the subject, says: "Building new houses so as to confirm patterns of segregation not only aggrevated the effects of the gerrymander; it also took away the playing fields and open spaces which had kept Bogside youth off the streets. The former Meenan Park playing fields in Bogside, which had once included four or five football pitches, had given way to flats, without appropriate steps to replace the recreational facilities."[19] The wicked Unionists had even concreted over the park in their efforts to keep people within the corral!

The reality was rather different. Before you knock down someone's house you have to put them somewhere else. If they do not want to leave the area, you have the problem that you have nowhere to build their new home until their old home is demolished. Catch 22. The Bogside was very densely populated and the only way of starting the cycle of building and demolition was to "borrow" the 9 acres of open space at Meenan Park. The first building would take place there, new tenants would be moved in from elsewhere in the Bogside and their houses could then be demolished. The new space created could be used for building more houses and so on. Recreational space would be provided at other sites in the Bogside.

The position was neatly summed up by Mr. C. A. Nicholson, QC for the Corporation at the public inquiry: "Without this park on which to build houses to start with, it would be like starting a game of draughts with all the places filled. The people will not be dispossessed of their homes in the place where they have their roots, and, in addition, they will have 13 acres of open space which is more than the recommended modern standards. There is ample compensation elsewhere in the vicinity for the loss of playing pitches at Meenan Park."[20]

Not surprisingly the redevelopment scheme was approved unanimously by both sides of Londonderry Corporation in February 1961.[21] It was by no means perfect. The flats were unpopular with many, but it was inevitable that a small number of blocks would be built if as many locals as possible were to be rehoused in the area. Most got houses with gardens. The central idea of the scheme was very advanced. In England there was a preference for destroying communities and sticking people in tower blocks in the middle of nowhere.

We must also not overlook the role of the Roman Catholic Church in supporting the existence of concentrations of its adherents in particular areas. Mary Holland talks of Unionist plans to "herd" Catholics together in the Creggan. "But the Church, seeing the advantage of keeping its flock together, around its chapels and its schools, accepted the plans. In return it got control of the area. No Unionist would dare to interfere with what the [Catholic]

Church thought fit for the people of Creggan."[22]

The ordinary Roman Catholic wanted to live in the South Ward. His very influential Church also wanted him to live there. There was no compulsion, no corralling and no herding by Unionists. But by the beginning of the 1960s some Republican politicians were beginning to realise that such concentrations of population were electorally very inconvenient. There was absolutely no possibility of persuading ordinary Catholics to break up their ghettos or accept large numbers of Protestants into their midst. City of Londonderry Stormont MP (and a recent Lord Mayor), Albert Anderson, said of the Creggan: "It is fair to say that when this estate was established, Londonderry Corporation tried to mix religions here but, unfortunately, this only led to strife and almost all the Protestants have now been removed and put elsewhere ."[23] The Catholic politicians' complaints therefore amounted to a claim on houses in other areas without giving up anything their supporters already held.

The housing needs of Catholics had been substantially met in the Bogside and Creggan, where they wanted to be housed. It therefore followed that the Corporation was left to meet at least part of Protestant housing need in the other small estates, although the share of homes they received throughout Londonderry was less than might be expected in view of the make up of the adult population. If the Republican demands had been met to the extent of giving a simple majority of houses in other wards to Catholics, it would have meant that by early 1965 at least 82% of all public sector dwellings would have gone to their religious group. Giving two-thirds of these houses to Catholics would have pushed their overall share to 87%, a ratio of nearly 7:1.

Integration

Perhaps over-influenced by foreign examples, few writers have been able to come to terms with the fact that the main impetus for segregated living came from the Roman Catholic Church with the overwhelming support of its community. Over the centuries the practice of occupying separate areas became a way of living peacefully together because of the feeling of security it gave, particularly in troubled times. To suggest it was imposed on Catholics by Protestants is a long way wide of the mark. After the "civil rights" movement had unleashed violence onto the streets, the Housing Executive, which took over responsibilities from the councils and the NIHT, soon came to see the naivity of 1960s liberal views on integration. In its first annual report it said: "We believe that people should have the maximum freedom of choice in where they wish to live. The Executive does not believe that forced integration is any more desirable than a policy of deliberate segregation."[24]

It is also interesting to note the comments of Charles Brett, who had been a Board member of the Housing Executive since 1971 and its Chairman from 1979 to 1984. He is a past Chairman of the Northern Ireland Labour Party and a prominent critic of "discrimination" in the 1960s. Writing in 1986 he said:

> Visiting politicians of all parties find the sectarian divisions in the housing estates of Northern Ireland incomprehensible. A surprising number of them (again of all parties) appear to believe that, by tolerating segregation of the two communities, the Housing Executive is itself guilty of perpetuating such divisions. Indeed, some of them are so naive as to believe that, if all Catholics and all Protestants were compelled to live in mixed estates, the fears and antagonisms of the past three centuries would immediately disappear. Would that it were so simple![25]

He then tells the story of an employee of his firm of solicitors. Brett was able to offer this man's son and daughter-in-law a privately rented house in the Ardoyne.

> I was greatly taken aback by his response: 'Oh, no, sir, that would never do, there were bad troubles in that street before the war, it wouldn't be a safe place for them to live at all.' I thought him unreasonable, ungrateful, and characteristically pusillanimous. I assured him that those bad old days were dead and gone forever; I urged him to think again; but he refused to change his mind. He was proved dead right, and I was proved dead wrong: that street was one of the first to burst into open conflict in the renewed troubles of 1969: within a few weeks every family of his denomination had been burned, intimidated or frightened out, and the whole street had become once again the exclusive territory of the other denomination.[26]

Brett notes the collapse of attempts by the NIHT to create an integrated estate at Twinbrook outside Belfast. It is now completely Catholic. Incoming Board members of the Housing Executive were reluctant to give up such ideas but had to come to terms with reality. A question had to be included on the housing application form asking whether the applicant would prefer to live in a mixed, Protestant or Catholic estate.[27] Brett concluded: "Practically nowhere, and practically never, does the possibility exist of encouraging, still less imposing, integrated housing in the public rented sector."[28]

It is noteworthy that the naive and ill-founded "civil rights" complaints about segregated housing, blaming as they did only the Protestants, succeeded only in increasing tensions and making the situation worse. Londonderry became more segregated than ever.

Points Systems and the Allocation of Houses

A points system is one where housing applicants are awarded points for such things as overcrowding, disrepair and lack of amenities in their existing accommodation. Those with the most points are deemed to be in the greatest housing need and hence are given priority in the allocation of public rented housing.

However in Londonderry, says Eamonn McCann, "The mayor, on his own, allocated the houses. He was not required to report to the sub-committee or to the Corporation. The operation was completely secret. There were no set criteria to guide him. The only way to get a Corporation house, therefore, was to convince the mayor that you *ought* to get one, and members of his local Orange Lodge were obviously better placed than Bogsiders."[29] If this was so it would seem strange that most houses were given to Catholics, but we shall pass on for the moment.

This situation seems to have come to an end in November 1968. Richard Deutsch and Vivien Magowan wrote the standard chronology of events for 1968-73, and their work contains the following entry for Friday 8 November 1968: "Derry Corporation voted in favour of a Nationalist proposal to adopt a points system for the allocation of houses."[30] Max Hastings agreed: "the Corporation of Londonderry announced the switching of housing allocation from the personal discretion of the mayor to a points system based on need."[31] Frank Curran tells us that at its November meeting the Corporation set up a 3 man Housing Allocation Sub-Committee "pending the adoption of a points system by the Council."[32] Almost immediately, however, the dissolution of the Corporation was announced. It was to be replaced by a Londonderry Development Commission in April 1969. Therefore, says Curran, the Nationalist Party and the Derry Citizens Action Committee "demanded that the commission be allied with a points system for allocating houses."[33]

Of all the political beliefs about Northern Ireland that are most certain and unchallengable, the most certain of them all must be the belief that the

Londonderry Corporation did not use a points system for the allocation of houses. Take an opinion poll of academics interested in Ulster politics and they will all tell you the same thing. They are all wrong. Readers unfamiliar with the controversy will be able to accept this with equanimity but there are, at this moment, others who are trying to work out whether I am insane for suggesting that one of the political crimes of the century did not, in fact, take place. I shall therefore tell the story as clearly as I can.

The meeting of the Londonderry Corporation on 8 November 1968 passed the following opposition motion: "That the Housing Sub-Committee be requested to base allocation of houses on a points system approved by this Council."[34] It was wonderfully ambiguous. The Republicans were able to present it, for propaganda purposes, as a great victory. The Corporation was to adopt a points system, which was still to be drawn up. The Unionists, by this time rather tired of the opposition's constant complaints, probably saw no harm in voting for a motion that did no more than reflect existing practice. The Corporation had been using a points scheme for a long time. It was probably an eloquent comment on the standards of journalism at the time that the truth did not come over.

The Corporation did in fact also agree to set up a 3 man Housing Allocation Sub-Committee. A meeting of what must have been a slightly puzzled Housing Sub-Committee took place on 14 November 1968 and considered the Council's resolutions. It passed a resolution of its own:

(1) That the points system for the allocation of houses, approved by the Housing Sub-Committee on 5 July 1946, he employed in the meantime, pending receipt of such recommendations, if any, as the Committee [the Housing Allocation Sub-Committee] referred to in (3) below may consider appropriate.[35]

Far from being slow to adopt a points system, Londonderry had been one of the first authorities in Northern Ireland to do so. The Stormont Ministry of Health and Local Government had issued the Housing (Management of Accommodation) Regulations (N.I.) 1945 on 10 December 1945 under powers contained in the Housing Act of that year. These applied to both local authorities and the Northern Ireland Housing Trust. They stipulated the maximum number of persons who should live in houses of particular sizes and set out some general guidelines about who should be given preference in public sector housing e.g. those in premises unfit for human habitation or so overcrowded as to be prejudicial to the health of their occupants. Preference would also be given to members of the armed forces returning from the war.

One way of complying with these regulations was to draw up a points scheme. The Corporation had obviously been quick to consider this approach because there is a letter in the files at the Londonderry Guildhall dated 7 March 1945 from the Ministry of Health and Local Government to the Town Clerk, J. C. Donnell, enclosing examples of English and Scottish points schemes "as promised".[36]

After a points scheme was adopted by the Housing Sub-Committee in July 1946 it received a delegation from the Londonderry and District Housing Action Council led by Stephen McGonagle a few days later and told them that a points system was to be used.[37] This was reported in the local papers.

A report by the Londonderry Housing Manager on the selection of Council tenants dated 25 February 1953 was presented to the Housing Sub-Committee the following day. This was reconsidered by the same committee on 5 June 1958. The methods of selection were again judged satisfactory and they thus continued until 1968. As the report is, in the context of this subject, a major historical document, I reproduce it in full.

Copy/

To/

The Members of the Housing Sub-Committee

Gentlemen,

Report on Selection of Council Tenants

   As instructed at last Meeting I submit this general report on method of selection of Council tenants.

   Every salient feature of each case is recorded on application form, which gives details of applicant's family - sex, age, accommodation and other essential information. From the housing register, and information supplied by interview or correspondence, files are continually revised, and following investigation a "priority pool" is compiled of those cases which are considered to warrant priority. I should point out here that I endeavour to prevent undue weight being given to cases who constantly call at this Office, or contact members of the Council.

When houses become available for letting, from the "priority pool" I prepare a list of those applicants to whom, in my opinion , allocations can be justified. In drawing up such list regard has to be given to number of bedrooms contained in the dwellings available. Whilst "points" awarded in accordance with scheme approved by Corporation are the guiding factor, (a most necessary piece of administrative machinery), consideration is given to other aspects, VIZ., number of children in family, sex, age - length of time on waiting list - period of residence in City, and most important factor - housing need. The prepared list is then discussed at length by Mayor and Housing Manager and selections agreed.

Since my appointment I have enquired from Officers in other Local Authorities as to their methods of allocating houses. I remain convinced that no scheme, however devised, will give satisfaction to those who still await rehousing. I feel that the success of any method must be judged by the extent to which it ensures that the applicants selected are those in the greatest need of a house.

I am, Gentlemen,
Your obedient Servant,

Signed D. A. S. Murphy

HOUSING MANAGER

Dated this 25th Day of February, 1953

Before unearthing this report I had earlier had personal interviews with those who served on the Corporation in the 1960s and their description of the procedures tallies with the account of the Housing Manager. The main point is that it was the Housing Manager who drew up the shortlist of those most in need of housing at any one time - the "priority pool". This list was compiled according to objective criteria. The points scheme tended to throw up many people who had an equal number of points and therefore more detailed information about individuals' circumstances had to be taken into account in deciding who got houses. The discussions between the Housing Manager and the Mayor were therefore something of a tie-breaking operation. It was totally untrue to say that the Mayor alone allocated houses without reference to any set criteria. His role was a minor one. The Housing Manager determined who was in most need of Council property.

Early points schemes (including that of the NIHT) were fairly rudimentary and did not cover every category of housing need.³⁸ In fact neither do the very modern ones. Most of the latter use a "group plus points" scheme which allocates houses without any reference to points to certain categories of people eg. those in houses which are the subject of closing orders or affected by redevelopment, and applicants in some kind of "emergency situation". The Housing Manager therefore had to consider all categories of need in drawing up his "priority pool".

From September 1965 a list of persons allocated houses and the accommodation allocated was tabled on a monthly basis at meetings of the Housing Sub-Committee. There is no record of any great objections to the selections made. When the Housing Allocation Sub-Committee of 3 Council members took over the role previously carried out by the Mayor, the Nationalist Party nominated Alderman Hegarty as its representative. No great scandal was uncovered and no objections to existing procedures were raised. Hegarty confined himself to making a constructive suggestion. The minutes of the Housing Sub-Committee meeting of 20 January 1969 read:

> *18. ALLOCATION OF HOUSES -POINTS SCHEME:*
> *Alderman Hegarty drew attention to the Council's existing Points Scheme for the allocation of houses, and suggested that the present scheme should be amended (pending receipt of a new model scheme from the Ministry of Development) so as to award points for (a) length of time on the waiting list and (b) chronic illness."*

The Ministy's model scheme was to be recommended to all housing authorities. At this stage it was inviting comments from councils on its draft scheme. The Housing Sub-Committee took on board Hegarty's suggestions and as the days of the Corporation were numbered, dealt with them as follows at its February meeting:

> *8. The Committee noted that the House Allocation Sub-Committee would continue to exercise discretion in the allocation of dwellings, using the present points scheme as a guide and also taking into consideration factors*

affecting housing need not covered by the scheme.[39]

Meanwhile the fledgling Londonderry Development Commission was making great play of the fact that it would be using a points system when it took over. This wrankled with members of the Housing Allocation Sub-Committee and its minutes of 12 February 1969 state:

> 5. *The Committee felt that it should be made known, once again, to the press that houses were being allocated by the Council at the present time by means of a points system, and directed the Town Clerk to issue a suitable statement to the press.*

History records that the world outside Londonderry wasn't listening.

According to press reports of the Commission's first meeting in February 1969 "preliminary arrangements were made for a study of suitable points schemes."[40] It was therefore with great interest that the city waited for this new body to take over. It was apparently to sweep away the wicked allocation policies of the Corporation and bring justice and fairness into the world.

The Development Commission met on 21 April 1969 to discuss housing matters in the Mayor's Parlour at Londonderry's Guildhall, now in full control of the city. The official Memorandum of the meeting records the following:

> *14. POINTS SCHEME FOR THE ALLOCATION OF DWELLINGS:*
> *Having heard the views of the Clerk, it was agreed that the Points Scheme presently in use in Londonderry County Borough be employed in the allocation of dwellings situated in the area of Londonderry Urban District until further notice.*[41]

The political commentators said how wonderful the Commission was. The Loyalist population was left speechless.

Houses and Votes

Let us return to the accusation that by denying Catholics houses Unionists could deny them votes. In Londonderry there was something of a paradox. Republicans would argue in support of their claim for more Council seats that the percentage of Catholics on the electoral register was increasing. At the same time they would say that they were being denied a fair share of houses.

But if no house meant no vote under the ratepayers franchise, it was difficult to see how both arguments could be sustained at once. The only way a community could increase its percentage of voters was by getting a larger share of the available houses than the other community.

Public sector houses made up only a minority of homes in the city, and to get a full picture of how dwellings were shared out we need to show the position in both the public and private sectors. According to Liam de Paor: "A Catholic, even with money in his pocket, could only with the greatest difficulty, and only by subterfuge, buy a house in a Unionist ward."[42] As the majority of private landlords were Protestants it would seem that there would have been enormous opportunities for a combination of the Unionist Corporation, home-owners and landlords to deny Catholics houses, and hence votes.

So let us see what happened. In 1936 the *Derry Journal* published a religious breakdown of the local government electorate after the revision of the ward boundaries.[43] The Cameron Report published a similar breakdown, obtained from Catholic sources, relating to the position in 1967 (as shown earlier in this book). By comparing the two we can see to what extent the number of Protestant and Catholic voters increased or decreased.

		1936	1967	Change	% of Net Increase
North Ward	Caths.	1928	2530	+ 602	65
	Prots.	3615	3946	+ 331	35
South Ward	Caths.	6230	10047	+ 3817	100
	Prots.	1618	1138	- 480	0
Waterside Ward	Caths.	1334	1852	+ 518	27
	Prots.	2298	3694	+ 1396	73
Total	Caths.	9492	14429	+ 4937	80
	Prots.	7531	8778	+ 1247	20

Hence, of the 6,184 voters who were added to the electoral register between 1936 and 1967, 80% (4,937) were Catholics. But as votes could only increase with the number of houses occupied under the ratepayers franchise, it is therefore reasonable to conclude that 80% of the net increase in the number of all houses went to Roman Catholics. The 1937 and 1966 Census returns indicate that the numbers of houses in the Londonderry County Borough in these years were 8,563 and 12,254. Thus about 2,953 (80%) of the 3,691 extra houses which appeared in the borough would have been occupied by Catholics.

The wicked Protestants of Londonderry, who held a "near monopoly" of housing according to Conor Cruise O'Brien, had presided over a policy which had allocated public sector housing to Roman Catholics in the ratio of 3:1. They had also allowed the additional housing which had appeared since 1936 (both public and private sector) to go to Catholics in a ratio of 4:1.

Far from denying Catholics votes, the Protestants had handed them out in bucketfuls. Even in the "sensitive" North Ward, 65% of the extra houses and votes had gone to Catholics, even though 65% of the electorate had been Protestant in 1936.

But what if the Unionists had gone further and handed control of the Corporation to their opponents? And what if those opponents had adopted an anti-Protestant housing allocation policy to the extent of letting 87% of public rented houses go to Catholics as mentioned earlier? (With them keeping what they held in the Bogside and Creggan and receiving two-thirds of the Council houses in the two other wards.) Using the 1965 Campaign for Social Justice figures, and assuming the creation of 2 votes for every house, Protestants would have lost (and Catholics acquired) 500 votes in the North Ward. The transfer of votes in the Waterside Ward would have been 560. This would not have created a Catholic majority in either ward. The accusations about using allocations to maintain political control therefore seem rather lame.

Where They Built the Houses

The next ploy by the opponents of Unionism is to say that the location of local authority housing was designed to safeguard the Protestant position. Some people have thought that all houses were built in the South Ward. Others, like Eamonn McCann, believed that "While the Bogside bulged with people, iron law decreed that insufficient houses be built".[44] "When building land in the South Ward began to run short the Corporation was faced with the problem of either housing Catholics in other wards or not housing them at all. It opted for the latter."[45] Paul Arthur follows McCann a little too closely when he says that "a problem arose when the Corporation ran out of land in the Catholic South Ward. Electorally, it could not afford to house Catholics in the remaining wards, nor could it contemplate extending the city boundaries since that might require an examination of the ward boundaries. Its solution was to do nothing; it stopped building houses."[46] I shall deal with the question of boundary extension shortly.

The central thrust of the above arguments is that building land was available in other wards, but was not built on for political reasons. To begin to understand the problem you have to understand the geography of the area. The Londonderry County Borough had a population of 55,681 crowded into 2,200 acres. The surrounding Londonderry Rural District Council area had 25,189 people living in 83,322 acres. Thus nearly 70% of the population of what was to be the Londonderry City Council area was packed into 2.5% of the acreage.[47] To appreciate how tightly this borough boundary was drawn is to be half way to enlightenment.

When the Londonderry Corporation began work on its housing plans in 1944, the only large expanse of building land within the borough was at the Creggan. There was nowhere else to build a couple of thousand houses. Over the next two decades the smaller areas available within the city were built up and by the mid-1960s there was little building land left. The NIHT said in its annual report: "there is virtually no land left for housing within the City boundary".[48] The Corporation could not pick and chose where to build - it filled in all available spaces. The North Ward, which was traditionally considered "marginal" (for no good reason), really had no vast expanses of building land to house anyone, Catholic or Protestant. New building, which never stopped completely, did slow down when land began to run out.

When the consultants to the Londonderry Area Steering Committee, the James Munce Partnership, presented their report in 1968 they actually recommended reducing the population within the Corporation boundaries by 10,000. This area was badly overcrowded and the Londonderry Area Plan, which was to be implemented by the new Development Commission, identified all future sites for new building as being outside the County Borough.[49]

But many people were keen to perpetuate the distortions. It is interesting that Frank Curran has printed a map of the city at the front of his book, showing areas developed since 1968. He has put in the boundary between the

Corporation's North and South Wards, but not the boundary between the County Borough and the Rural District. Therefore it seems as though a lot of new building took place in the North Ward. Not so. The only significant building in the ward was in redevelopment areas such as Rosemount and the Fountain, which did not result in a net increase in housing. The rest was outside the Corporation boundary.

Boundary Extension

The Cameron Report said of the Londonderry County Borough Council: "In recent years housing programmes declined because the Corporation refused to face the political effects of boundary extension, even though this was recommended by all its senior officials."[50] The Campaign for Social Justice thought that "Even the Housing Trust, which has built large numbers of flats and dwellings, has been seriously hampered in its house-building efforts by the continued refusal of the Corporation to extend the City boundary."[51]

What would a boundary extension have involved? It basically implied taking land from one local authority and transferring it to another. In this case it would have meant pinching part of the Rural District Council's area adjacent to the city and handing control of it to the Londonderry Corporation. The Stormont government would only approve such things with the agreement of the parties concerned. Would it therefore have been a straightforward matter to apply for such a boundary extension?

In was in fact common knowledge that the Rural District Council and the powerful Londonderry County Council would have raised strong objections. The problem was that by the time people started discussing the issue in the 1960s the areas immediately surrounding the city had become built up to a significant extent. This did not imply there was a shortage of space, it simply meant that it would be difficult to transfer a decent tract of land without including part of the Rural District's housing stock, and with it an amount of rate income. There was also a general incentive for suburban authorities to have a city's housing needs met by others within their boundaries to generate additional income from rates without any capital expenditure.

Belfast had exactly the same problem. It had nowhere near enough land to meet its housing needs. "The [Belfast] Corporation had asked for the county line to be extended, the last such extension had been in 1896, but this had been refused because of the pressure from surrounding authorities." "Eventually the

Housing Trust stepped into the breech and took over responsibility for house-building in land between the city boundary and the Mathew stop-line. In fact in the period 1954-59 the Housing Trust housed nearly twice as many people in the Belfast area as did the Corporation. The need to solve the more fundamental dispute, about the area over which the Belfast Corporation should have jurisdiction, and in particular over which land should be allocated for housing Belfast's overspill population was one reason why Mathew was brought in, in 1960 to provide his regional plan for Belfast."[52]

So what would have been the "political effects of boundary extension" mentioned by the Cameron Report? Usually it is said extension would have meant a re-examination of the ward scheme and this would have been inconvenient to Unionists. The logic is difficult to follow. The Rural District Council population had a clear Protestant majority, and boundary extension would undoubtedly have improved the Unionist position in the city. As we have seen, the only real problem with the ward scheme by 1967 was that the North Ward had become slightly underpopulated in relation to the number of Council seats it possessed. It would not have been too difficult to bring in all or part of the adjacent Middle Liberties area sometime during the preceding decades if political control was the only consideration. Such a move would have required no major upheaval in the ward boundaries. Neither would it have affected the Unionist majority on the Rural District Council. The Unionists could then have built houses for Protestants in the Middle Liberties if they had wanted to.

We have seen that Belfast managed to extend its boundaries in 1896 when the climate was more favourable. In the same year it was proposed that the Londonderry County Borough should take in 25 square miles of the surrounding countryside. There was strong opposition to this from local Irish Republican politicians and the plan had to be dropped.[53] If they had not been so obstructive perhaps the housing crisis in Londonderry would not have become so acute.

These early objections did point the way to later Republican divisions on the issue. The Nationalist Party was pressing hard for boundary extension, and yet Gerry Fitt, then of the Republican Labour Party, had a different view on the matter. Speaking at an outdoor meeting in the Foyle Street car park in July 1968 he said the Unionists would not give up the city. "They are going to extend the city boundary - they are going out into the country and bringing in pockets of Unionist voting strength."[54] Londonderry Protestants must have been well and truly confused. They simply could not win.

No account of the boundary extension issue would be complete without a reference to Frank Curran's version of events. The Nationalist Party put a motion calling for a boundary extension to the July 1966 meeting of the Corporation which was, as he says, rejected by the Unionist majority. The officers of the Council had been asked to submit reports on the city's housing needs and "To the intense embarrassment of the Unionists, the Chief Officers then tabled their reports, unanimously favouring boundary extension. But embarrassed or not, they still managed to reject a proposal that the Reports to be sent to the Ministry of Development for comment; instead they ordered them to be pigeon-holed and forbade their publication."[55]

Curran says of the officers: "As they set about their task, London consultants Messrs. Lovell, Mathews and Partners issued an outline plan for the Waterside area, to conform with a design for the improvement of Duke Street. Their report concluded: 'Any new plan for the Waterside must take into account the growth requirements of the hinterland. In order to achieve logical growth patterns it will probably be necessary to extend the city limits.'"[56]

The Unionists were actually not opposed to an extension of the city limits. All they were opposed to was the idea of achieving this by an application for a boundary extension (taking land away from the Rural District) which was bound to fail. So defined a boundary extension was not the only way of extending a boundary, although the Nationalist Party seems to have bamboozled Lord Cameron's team on this point. Some form of local government reorganisation would do the job just as well.

This is what the Unionist Deputy Mayor was reported in the press as saying at the July 1966 Corporation meeting:

Councillor Beattie, referring to the report of Lovell, Mathews and Partners, planning consultants for the Waterside development scheme, saying that there were different ways of meeting the problem of extending the city's limits, said: 'My contention is that it would be pure foolishness for us to say we will accept in principle the extension of the city boundary, until we have considered what the further possibilities are.'

He said the consultants had stated that there were many methods of overcoming the problem of extension , ranging from an extension of the city boundary to a federation of all the authorities concerned and added: 'It might well be argued that we have already embarked on one of them which has taken place in the setting up of the Steering Committee.'[57]

The reports of the Housing Manager, Executive Sanitary Officer and City Surveyor outlining housing requirements from 1966-81 of course indicated that these could not be met within the existing Corporation boundaries. Everyone knew and accepted that. The only subsequent difference with the opposition councillors was over the best means to gain access to more building land.

It is quite wrong of Curran to say that the reports of the officers were "pigeon-holed". The minutes of the Housing Sub-Committee meeting of 7 July 1966 confirm that the reports were submitted to the Londonderry Area Steering Committee and they were to play a vital role in shaping the Londonderry Area Plan. It would have been pointless sending the reports to the Ministry of Development, because it was this very ministry which, with the Steering Committee, had jointly instructed the James Munce Partnership to prepare a plan for the area. It wanted to be told the solution, not the problem.

Further officers reports were called for over the coming months and the General Manager of the Housing Trust was invited to attend the November meeting of the Housing Sub-Committee to discuss them.[58] He declined on the grounds that "the Trust saw little prospect of making any physical progress with its schemes until the report of the Steering Committee was made known.'[59]

Strategic planning as had been known in England for some time did not really arrive in Northern Ireland until the 1960s. We have seen that the problems of Belfast were not resolved until Sir Robert Mathew drew up the *Belfast Regional Survey and Plan* and the difficulty over boundaries was tackled through local government reorganisation. The same was true of Londonderry. Until the Steering Committee presented its interim suggestions on housing on 7 July 1967 there was uncertainty about where houses could be built and where "green belts" would be preserved. This created an unfortunate lull in housebuilding and planning approvals for a year or two, which was misrepresented by anti-Unionist agitators, but it was necessary to set out zones for different activities if an unplanned urban sprawl was to be avoided.

First the Development Commission and then local government reorganisation gave Londonderry the extended boundary it wanted (although the new council was never to exercise powers over housing). Once the review of local government had begun in 1965 there was never going to be a chance of an orthodox boundary extension being considered by the Northern Ireland government. An application for such a boundary extension agreed between the councils in Coleraine and Portrush was suspended by the Minister of Development on the grounds that it would be superseded by local government reorganisation.[60]

Finally, the question of boundary extension did not affect the Housing Trust at all. It was not restricted by boundaries. To help Belfast out of its difficulties the NIHT built estates outside the city limits at places such as Rathcoole, Andersonstown and Cregagh. Realising that there was a lack of building land, the Londonderry Corporation had, on 21 June 1965, resolved "That in order to alleviate the housing situation in this City, we request the Northern Ireland Housing Trust to contact the Londonderry Rural District Council with a view to undertaking a substantial programme of house-building in the vicinity of the City." An estate was subsequently built by the NIHT at Shantallow.

Goodbye to the Londonderry Corporation

In April 1969 the unelected Londonderry Development Commission took over the functions of the Londonderry Corporation. A centralised Housing Executive started work in May 1971 with the job of managing all public sector housing in Northern Ireland. It immediately acquired the NIHT's housing stock in the Londonderry area but the Development Commission did not hand over the once council-owned properties until January 1973.[61]

Both the "civil rights" activists and the liberal Unionists clustered around Terence O'Neill liked to stress that an enormous change in housing policy had taken place when the Development Commission took over from the Corporation. The former group did so to emphasise their victory over the wicked Protestants of Londonderry and the latter group wanted to stress that the allegedly bad old days were gone forever.

The reality was different. The Londonderry Area Steering Committee was set up by the Corporation, the Rural District Council and the County Council in 1965. The splendid Londonderry Area Plan, which appeared under the name of the Steering Committee and the James Munce Partnership (consultants) was presented to the Minister of Development and the 3 councils in March 1968. They all unanimously endorsed the plan, which covered the period up to 1981. The document was a comprehensive survey of the area's economic needs and dealt with everything from shopping facilities, roads and schools to the need for a second bridge across the Foyle. But its main recommendation was that 10,000 new houses be built in the Rural District Council's area at Ballyarnett/ Shantallow, Eglinton, Strathfoyle, Waterside/Drumahoe, Lettershendony, Prehen and New Buildings.

This plan was the achievment of the old councils, not the Development Commission. When it appeared they enthusiastically pushed for its implementation. The consultants were retained to list priorities for the councils and to do some basic cost accounting.[62] A conference of the 3 councils concerned urged the consultants to press on as quickly as possible with a District Plan for the Ballyarnett/Shantallow area.

A report on the Conference to the Corporation Planning Committee on Monday stated that those present recognised the necessity for planning the district as a whole in order to provide for all necessary services and its development in an orderly fashion.

A case for special financial assistance from the Government was urged and it was agreed in principle that the three Councils - the Corporation, the Rural Council and County Council - should approach the Minister of Development as soon as possible after the James Munce Partnership had produced the requested list of priorities and the cost of implementing the proposals in the Area Plan.[63]

The cost of implementing the Area Plan was later announced as being £108,000,000, £84,000,000 of it public expenditure. Housing alone would cost £35,500,000.[64] The annual budget for the Corporation in 1968-69 to cover all the services of this unitary authority (except the Electricity Department) was just £734,805.[65] It underlined the fact that the problems of the area were quite beyond the financial resources of the local authorities. However with assistance from the Northern Ireland and British governments they could have implemented the Area Plan.

The Unionist local authorities in the Londonderry area had made enormous progress before the first "civil rights" march in the city took place in October 1968. A massive housing programme had been approved and was in effect only waiting for Harold Wilson's government to agree to finance the project. This was because the Stormont government had negligible powers of taxation and relied on the British government transferring to it a share of tax income collected centrally.

When the Northern Ireland cabinet finally announced it was giving a "very high priority" to the implementation of the Londonderry Area Plan on 19 November 1968 (no doubt after consulting Wilson) it surprised everyone by almost immediately announcing the dissolution of the Corporation and the Rural District Council.[66] Terence O'Neill's excuse that the ordinary machinery of local government was not designed to cope with a project on this scale did not hold water.[67] The Development Commission was simply a bunch of part-timers presiding over the former staff of the local councils.

Those who have recorded the recent political history of Ulster tell us that the Commission made up for the deficiencies of the Unionist Corporation. In fact it did no more than implement the Area Plan drawn up and endorsed by the Corporation, starting by allocating houses using the same points system as the Corporation. The only difference was that money was now no object as far as Wilson's government was concerned. But the Commission got all the credit.

Miscellaneous Myths

A keen reader of books about Northern Ireland will find quite a number of stories about housing in Londonderry during the "civil rights" era. Before concluding this chapter with an examination of Protestant housing need, I thought it would be useful to deal with a number of the miscellaneous myths that have grown up about the city.

The first is the story of the Belmont policemen. Frank Curran says that at the meeting of the Corporation in July 1959 "tempers flared" because some houses on the Belmont estate had been given to policemen only a few weeks in the city.[68] Presumably the Londonderry Corporation was to blame for giving preference to policemen over needy local people. One problem is that Belmont was outside the city boundary and therefore if any local authority was to blame it was the Rural District Council. But then again it didn't own the houses. They belonged to the Housing Trust. And even it had no say in the matter. The 1958-59 Trust Annual Report points out that agreement had been reached in advance of building them that 40 houses would be leased to the Ministry of Home Affairs, who wanted them for housing policemen. These homes were not built for the general public.[69]

It is also noteworthy that Republicans such as Curran complained that nearly all of the 200 houses at Belmont were given to Protestants. Of the other NIHT properties built in and around Londonderry up to April 1969 (approximately 2,062), only about 76 went to Protestants. That Republicans complained in such circumstances said a lot about their concern for fairness.[70]

There are also two stories told, but not originated, by Charles Brett of the Housing Executive. "One of the last actions of the Londonderry Rural Council was to pre-allocate almost entirely to Protestants the not-quite-completed Ballynagard housing development at Culmore Road in order to pre-empt the possibility that the Commission might use it to relieve Catholic overcrowding."[71] 43 houses were involved. What Brett omits to say is that all the cases were reviewed by the incoming Commission in April 1969. 37 of them were confirmed for immediate occupation and the other 6 applicants were told they would get a house by the end of the year.[72]

"The Commission set about its task energetically, and was seen to act fairly; it resumed building at Shantallow where the old Corporation had refused to allow the Housing Trust to build on specious grounds of bad drainage; it built Gobnascale, implemented the area plan, and opened up new sites in every part of the city irrespective of electoral considerations."[73] Dealing with the last point first, Gobnascale and the Area Plan were, of course, the Londonderry Corporation's ideas. The Corporation had 1,040 houses in the pipeline at October 1968 (that is over and above those in the Area Plan to be built outside the boundary).[74] Many of these were in redevelopment (slum clearance) areas but the others filled up the last remaining building spaces. The Commission simply took over this programme and took credit for it. It did not open up new sites left vacant for political reasons. That was just another myth.

But what about Shantallow's sewage? Firstly the Commission did not carry out any building here. It was all done by the NIHT and the Housing Executive. Then Brett's geography is rather shaky. Shantallow lay outside the city boundary and hence the Corporation had no say over what was built there. He must mean the Rural District Council, and it did not oppose building at Shantallow. An estate containing 316 houses was completed by the NIHT in 1968 and an adjacent site with planning permission had been acquired in 1967. An application to acquire (by means of a vesting order) another 250 acres went to the Minister of Development in November 1968.[75] So many houses were due to be built at Shantallow that massive works were needed to ensure a water supply and adequate drainage. The report of the James Munce Partnership and the Steering Committee pointed out that untreated sewage from Shantallow was being discharged into the River Foyle and that "although the design of schemes for new or extended disposal works and sewers is at an advanced stage in most instances, the availability of sewerage services will impose some restrictions in the short term."[76]

It was no more than a short delay. A £2,500,000 water and sewerage scheme was discussed by the Rural District Council in October 1968[77] and there were already facilities for 1,000 houses.[78] When the Commission took over it simply received reports on progress to date from the Londonderry Corporation Surveyor and the Rural District Council Engineer and resolved to continue with the plans being worked on by consultants engaged by the two councils.[79] It implemented other people's ideas.

What it all tends to show is that even chairmen of the Housing Executive frequently don't know what they are talking about when it comes to the subject of Londonderry.

Then there is the story of the Derry Housing Association, run by a Catholic priest, Father Tony Mulvey, with the help of John Hume as Chairman. It is told by their old pal Frank Curran:

The Housing Association bought 50 acres of land at Pennyburn from Dr. McDonald, owner of Monarch Electric, with the intention of building several hundred houses. That could have been a considerable contribution towards easing the housing pressure. But then they came up against the sort of snag that was insurmountable in gerrymandered Derry. The land was in the Unionist north ward, and the erection of a large housing development which would obviously have been occupied entirely by Catholics would have created a real threat to the artificially created Unionist majority in the ward. The Unionists reacted as they had throughout the past hundred years, turning the planning application down on the grounds that the land had been originally zoned for industrial purposes.[80]

In fact the site had been used by Monarch Electric until earlier that same year, 1967. Its tragic closure put nearly 2,000 people out of work. The priority was to get new jobs and industrial sites had to be made available. It made no sense to build on a site so recently vacated by a major industry. The Londonderry Area Plan zoned Pennyburn for industrial purposes. In seeking to impose some kind of order on the city's unplanned and overcrowded streets, the consultants noted that many industries were occupying "unsatisfactory premises in unsuitable sites" without adequate road access and parking facilities. They identified

Pennyburn as an area where "industrial uses at present incompatible with the Central Area pattern could be relocated."[81] When the Derry Housing Association appealed to the Ministry of Development, Mr. G.R. McSheffrey of the James Munce Partnership testified that the project would be contrary to the Area Plan.[82]

Barry White noted that "Even the Nationalist members of the Corporation were hostile, seeing a better alternative in a long-term area plan and a 'new town' development at Shantallow, north of the city."[83] It would have been planning madness to pack more people into the city and obliterate what few sites were available for industrial and recreational purposes. The 1960s were seeing a determined drive against urban congestion and sprawl. All the planners agreed that housing development would now have to take place in the Rural District. For this reason a planning application from Messrs. A.L. and J.E. Rosborough to build 100 houses at Strabane Old Road on the east bank was turned down even though they were represented by Desmond Boal QC, a hard-line Unionist MP who was originally from Londonderry. The City Solicitor said: "This straggled urban growth must stop somewhere."[84]

But Curran gives the game away when he says the houses "would obviously have been occupied entirely by Catholics". Why? Because everyone in Londonderry knew that Catholic housing associations, unlike Protestant councils and Protestant landlords, did not give houses to people of a different religion. The political idea of settling an area where Protestants need not apply was probably so attractive that it overruled all other considerations. In spite of these antics the Corporation was very helpful to the Association in other projects it undertook.

Protestants Don't Need Houses

Perhaps one of the most offensive things that has been implied by a whole range of writers about the "civil rights" era is that Protestants had very little need of public sector housing. On many occasions it has been said that in Londonderry they were significantly better off and those in need could acquire council housing more easily than Catholics. So easily that almost all those in need of housing by the late 1960s were Catholics.

The Bogside and the Fountain faced each other across an open street. For the best part of the decade the Protestants had watched the slum houses of their Catholic neighbours being demolished and replaced by new homes with all the amenities the Bogsiders had previously lacked. But the occupants of the Fountain were part of the Protestant ascendancy. They didn't need houses.

But then the Corporation's Executive Sanitary Officer carried out a survey of 217 houses in the Fountain Street area which might also be considered for redevelopment. Figures he gave to the Redevelopment Sub-Committee showed that 76% of them had no inside toilet, 70% had no hot water supply and 83% had no bathroom.[15] Many families lived in a "storey-and-a-half house", one room and a kitchen in a single storey building, where the occupants slept in the roof space. What need had these people of new council houses?

By looking at the Census returns we can get a wider view of the housing conditions enjoyed by the Protestant ascendancy.[16]

	1961		1971		
	% No Hot Water Tap	% No Fixed Bath	% No hot Water Supply	% No Fixed Bath/ Shower	% Outside Flush Toilet Only
Londonderry County Borough	43.9	45.9	21.2	25.8	21.0
North Ward	38.4	40.2	20.6	26.0	19.5
South Ward	46.7	49.3	23.3	27.4	23.1
Waterside Ward	43.9	45.4	18.0	22.7	18.7

Apart from the general improvement in standards, the most noticeable thing is how marginal the differences were between the various wards. The Protestants in their wards were living under very similar conditions to the Catholics in the South Ward.

Even though the Corporation ceased to function in April 1969, the only housing schemes completed in the city up to 1971 were those it had initiated. It was therefore responsible for the housing position in the Census year. So let us compare the situation in Londonderry with that in Belfast, which was three-quarters Protestant. In particular let us compare Londonderry's South Ward with the 12 Unionist-held wards in Belfast.[17]

Belfast's 12 Unionist Wards - Better Off Than the South Ward? (1971)					
Hot Water Supply		Bath/Shower		Inside Toilet	
Wards Better Off	Wards Worse Off	Wards Better Off	Wards Worse Off	Wards Better Off	Wards Worse Off
5	7	3	9	0	12

There was great resentment in the Protestant areas of West Belfast about the "civil rights" agitation and it was here that there was a backlash at the start of the Troubles. Let us see if we can find any reason why there might have been such resentment by taking a closer look at the 4 Unionist wards in this area. (1971 figures).[18]

	% No Hot Water Supply	% No Fixed Bath/Shower	% Outside Flush Toilet Only
Londonderry's South Ward	23.3	27.4	23.1
Belfast County Borough	23.6	37.1	38.7
Shankill Ward	28.6	48.0	47.8
Woodvale Ward	29.5	46.2	44.3
Court Ward	46.6	65.6	62.7
St. George's Ward	58.2	88.6	87.5

The Court Ward (Lower Shankill) and St. George's Ward (Sandy Row), which had large Protestant majorities, were the worst areas in Belfast. When rioting broke out in the Bogside, it was these Protestants living in their slums who were expected to believe that it was because of how badly the Londonderry Catholics had been treated. Protestants in both cities, who were living in conditions which were just as bad or much worse than those in the South Ward, tended to make an assessment of the Catholic complaints in the light of direct experience rather than the myths readily swallowed by gullible journalists and academics. They formed their own view about the validity of those complaints and the likelihood of their being the real reason behind the agitation.

What we can say, reviewing the situation 20 years later, is

1. That those in Londonderry's North and Waterside Wards were suffering from similar housing conditions to those in the South Ward. Protestants were not noticeably better off.
2. "Protestant" Belfast had worse housing conditions than "Catholic" Londonderry.
3. The "oppressed Catholics" of the South Ward were living in significantly better conditions than working class members of Belfast's "Protestant ascendancy".

The Brave New World

When the Londonderry Corporation was wound up it should, according to the myths, have signalled an increase in the share of housing going to Catholics. In fact the exact opposite was the case. A glance at the annual report of the Londonderry Development Commission for 1969-70 shows that of the major schemes in progress, those at Kilfennan, Newbuildings, Nelson Drive and Eglinton were to benefit the Protestant community.[89] Likewise with the redevelopment scheme at Fountain Street. The Housing Trust was building homes at Shantallow which would be occupied by the Catholic community, but there can be no doubt that in the Brave New World of the Development Commission, covering the few short years after the demise of the Corporation, Protestants would, if anything, have received a greater share of public housing than they enjoyed up to 1969. (This was not to last, however. Londonderry Councillor, Gregory Campbell, estimates that between 1970 and 1985, 85% of new houses were allocated to Roman Catholics.)

I believe there are two main reasons for this temporary phenomenon. Firstly, in the Corporation era all the slum clearance work had been in Catholic areas.

The Bogside was given priority over the Fountain. Therefore hardly any Protestants benefitted from houses built in redevelopment areas. By the end of the 1960s it really was about time the Protestant slums were tackled, and schemes were finally got under way. Secondly, there was the effect the post-war housing programme had had on reducing the number of large families on the housing list.

It was well known that Catholics tended to have much bigger families than Protestants, one reason being their Church's opposition to all forms of "unnatural" contraception. Other things being equal, housing authorities gave preference to those living in the more overcrowded conditions. More controversially those with big families often got preference over smaller families living in houses which were in a worse state of disrepair and had fewer basic amenities. Certainly under the selection scheme currently operated by the Housing Executive it is quite easy for a big family in a perfectly good house to obtain more points than a family with two children in a home where the damp and state of disrepair is so bad "as to be a threat to the health or physical safety of the occupants."[90]

The consequence of this practice was that Catholics were able to gain some preference over Protestants in the allocation of housing. Largely as a consequence of this however, by the mid-1960s the proportion of large families on the waiting list had fallen. When the Corporation updated its list in 1967, it found that the percentage of applicants with 4 children or more had fallen to 5% from 13% in 1961.[91] Thus the Catholics' ability to gain preference was somewhat diminished. Protestants and Catholics, living in similarly bad housing, were in a greater position of equality in competing for new houses.

If the Development Commission did help the less privileged religious group to catch up, it did so by giving some long overdue assistance to the Protestant community.

C. Employment and Regional Development

There were basically two complaints which "civil rights" campaigners made about employment practices in Northern Ireland. The first of these alleged that at least some Unionist local authorities discriminated against Catholics in the making of appointments. The second complaint was that the Unionist Northern Ireland government had discriminated against the "Catholic" West of the Province by deliberately diverting industry and public investment to the "Protestant" East. The River Bann, which runs through the middle of Ulster from north to south, was often referred to as the boundary line. Areas West of the Bann were said to be those which were neglected.

Employment at Londonderry Corporation

One of the more obscure publications of the Campaign for Social Justice gave a breakdown of the religious composition of the Corporation's salaried staff as at 1 April 1964. All 15 heads of departments were Protestants and the rest of the workforce was made up of 145 Protestants earning a total of £94,004 a year and 32 Catholics earning £20,400.[1] The figures are probably correct.

The first thing to note is that the figures are for salaried (white collar) employees only. These and a whole range of selective statistics published elsewhere by others tend to give the impression that the Corporation's workforce was overwhelmingly Protestant. It was not. Albert Anderson, who had been Lord Mayor of the city before becoming a Stormont MP, put the record straight as follows:

> *The Corporation itself employs far more Roman Catholics than Protestants. I admit not many of the top jobs have gone to Roman Catholics but, when one examines the records, one finds that very few Roman Catholics have applied for them.*[2]

We can therefore settle one point of controversy straight away. The Corporation did not deprive the Catholic population of employment, contrary to what most people believe. Most of its workforce was Roman Catholic. Therefore the Catholic community as a whole in Londonderry did not suffer from high unemployment as a result of a decision to share out the available council jobs

in the Protestants' favour. The worst we might find is that Catholics were given
lower paid rather than higher paid jobs.

It was the gradual realisation in the late 1960s that, statistically, the Corporation's
employment policies had no effect on Catholic unemployment which pushed
this particular "discrimination" argument into the background and made it far
less important than the "gerrymandering" and housing issues in raising
temperatures. The matter has, however, burned deep into the English consciousness
and is worth exploring further.

The Unionist councillors I have spoken to could not recall any Catholic
applying for a head of department's job in the Londonderry Corporation.
Indeed it seems that the only Roman Catholic to apply for a senior post in the
period after the War was John Hume, who unsuccessfully sought the job of
Deputy Director of Education. Hume had no experience of either local
government administration or the state education system. The Catholics'
approach therefore paralleled their approach to elections. They expected to be
given jobs without applying for them. But why did so few Catholics apply for
white collar posts?

There were two main reasons: antipathy towards the Northern Ireland state and
lack of educational achievement. When the South seceded from the United
Kingdom in the 1920s most Catholics wanted to see the majority in Ulster
forced against its wishes into joining Eire in a united Ireland. They opposed the
very existence of the Northern Ireland state and councils controlled by
Republicans often refused to recognise the government and pledged their
allegiance to the Irish Free State. A view emerged among the Catholic
population that it was disreputable to work in a public sector job which helped
administer the Northern Ireland state. This was most clearly seen in appointments
to the Stormont civil service, where few non-Protestants applied. Patrick Shea,
a Catholic who did join this branch of the civil service and went on to a very
senior post, summed up his community's view of people like himself by saying:
"we had joined the enemy; we were lost souls".[3]

Former Northern Ireland prime minister, Brian Faulkner, said:

*Nationalists had traditionally shunned any part in the administration of
Northern Ireland affairs. They boycotted all official functions and turned
down appointments to public boards, or even as Resident Magistrates.
Those who accepted such appointments were ostracized by the politically*

committed among their community.[4]

Loyalists were therefore particularly annoyed when, in the 1960s, "civil rights" propagandists drew up lists of public boards which had an under-representation of Catholics and claimed this was evidence of discrimination. What was happening was that some Catholics' views on participation in the affairs of the state were changing.

In the meantime the ways in which a good Catholic showed he was withholding support from the state were rather difficult for an outsider to comprehend. Working for the Northern Ireland civil service was out, but a job controlled by Whitehall, in what was then known as the Imperial civil service, was alright. Thus Barritt and Carter estimated that 50-55% of staff working for the Post Office throughout Ulster were Catholics.[5] An under-representation in one service was made up for by an over-representation in another. The Post Office in Londonderry was overwhelmingly Catholic, and a former member of the Ulster Special Constabulary remarked to me how strange it was when his colleagues were assigned to guard the building knowing that there were several IRA supporters inside.

Attitudes towards local authority employment were also not always easy to follow. Working for a Republican controlled council was permissable. A manual job with a Unionist council did not attract criticism, but a white collar job administering the same council's policies under an oath of allegiance to the Crown was definitely dubious. This residual suspicion of being seen to support the state was one reason for the low number of applications from Catholics for salaried posts in the Corporation.

The other was the question of education. The Catholic Church has consistently opposed the idea of sending its flock to secular state schools. It has insisted on private Catholic schools to educate its adherents within a "Catholic ethos". It is therefore the Catholic Church which has segregated education in Northern Ireland. In the Sixties less than 2% of Catholic children were sent to state primary schools although a few more went to non-Catholic secondary schools.[6] Liberal Unionist policies at the time tended to perpetuate the segregation by giving far more generous financial asistance to Catholic schools than was available in England and Wales. The Minister for Education, Captain W.J. Long, estimated that 95% of the cost of providing and running these private schools was being met from public funds.[7]

Although Catholic pupils of grammar school age would have made up over 40% of their age group, only 27% were in fact pupils at grammar schools in 1961. Barritt and Carter noted the difficulty of providing enough places by voluntary (Catholic) effort.⁸ Although capital grants of 65% (80% from 1968) were available the Catholic Church was unable to keep up with the demand and their community thus suffered by opting out of state education. Examination results in Catholic schools were consistently poorer than in the state sector. Large Catholic families also meant that many of their children had to leave school early to help bring in extra income. Barritt and Carter remarked that "few seem to realize that even if there were no discrimination at all, fewer Catholics than Protestants would get good jobs because (in this generation) relatively fewer are qualified to fill them."⁹ Also "the principle of 'the best man for the job', will often give a large proportion of Protestants at the higher levels, simply because the advancement of Catholics is hampered by low social status."¹⁰

Professor Richard Rose, writing in 1971, noted that "There is moreover, no tendency for public authorities to favour unqualified Protestants; 56 per cent in public jobs have at some time obtained a qualification by examination; among Catholics the proportion is 46 per cent."¹¹ In his survey 8% of Protestants and 7% of Catholics had someone in the family currently publicly employed.¹²

Thus the general pattern was that similar proportions of Protestants and Catholics were employed in the public sector but not necessarily in the same proportion in all parts of the public sector, and not necessarily in the same kind of jobs. In the case of Londonderry, Catholics would have been less qualified for a white collar post with the Corporation. Those who did have the qualifications would have been happier applying for jobs in the Imperial civil service (such as in the Inland Revenue, Customs and Excise and the Post Office), as did Eddie McAteer before he became the Nationalist Party MP for Foyle, or as a teacher, as did John Hume.

Having said that, there was some element of preference likely to be given to Protestants in border areas like Londonderry. Because so many Catholics withheld support from the state they were not unnaturally regarded as security risks in a Province periodically assailed by IRA campaigns. It was known that at least one Unionist Councillor did not want Catholics working in the Londonderry Guildhall (where about 35 people were employed) for this reason, although other areas were not regarded as being so sensitive. As long as Catholics overwhelmingly identified themselves as being anti-British such attitudes could not be dismissed as unreasonable. The Conservative MP, John Biggs-Davison, who was himself a Roman Catholic, wrote: "If the Border was the only election issue, and many Catholics felt themselves 'second class citizens' much of the blame must fall on those who behaved as if they were not citizens at all and conspired against institutions cherished by the vast majority."[13]

The question then arises as to how influential such Unionist preferences were in Londonderry. In the 1960s, with Catholics becoming more ready to participate in the running of the state without being considered traitors, and with rising educational standards (particularly since the 1947 Education Act) we could expect a growing number of Catholics to be employed in white collar posts at the Corporation. Also those who had bothered to apply for posts at an early stage and been accepted on merit would, without religious discrimination, be receiving similar salaries to Protestant employees. An absence of both phenomenon would indicate that discrimination played a significant role.

In fact the 1964 Campaign for Social Justice figures show that in the posts below that of departmental head (ie. those which Catholics actually applied for) 145 Protestants earned £94,004 a year and 32 Catholics earned £20,400. Thus Catholics making up 18.08% of staff earned 17.83% of the salaries, indicating an absence of internal discrimination.

The Cameron Report found that in October 1968 30% of white collar staff at the Londonderry Corporation were Catholics. In April 1964 16.66% of all such employees (ie. including departmental heads) were Catholics.[14] Bearing in mind the low turnover of staff, an increase such as this over a relatively short period could only have taken place if discrimination at the point of entry was insignificant. It was therefore not true to imply, as the Cameron Report did, that Catholics did not apply because they had no real prospect of getting jobs. In Londonderry, when Catholics began to apply for jobs they got more of them and those who were employed enjoyed equality of opportunity with Protestant workers.

Catholic Discrimination

The Cameron Report could not seriously claim to be even-handed in its investigation of claims of discrimination. It spent just 8 lines talking about the Republican-controlled Newry Urban District Council (it looked at no other non-Unionist council), and swept the whole problem under the carpet by saying that Protestants "do not have a serious unemployment problem, and in Newry there are relatively few Protestants". In any case, says Cameron, "two wrongs do not make a right".[15]

Writers are often reluctant to discuss Catholic discrimination and when they do they seem not to appreciate its significance in the context of the "civil rights" controversy. A typical view 20 years ago would have been that of the young Max Hastings. He noted that the Catholic Church insisted on exclusively Catholic schools. "But excluding education it is only the Protestants who practise real discrimination."[16]

As we shall see later, the whole thrust of the "civil rights" campaign was to portray Catholics as innocent victims. They had been badly treated by Protestants and had finally reacted against injustice. The British role was to intervene on their behalf and force the Protestants to make changes. The strategy involved instilling feelings of guilt in the British public by painting a picture of Catholics as downtrodden and oppressed. But above all it was necessary to present the minority community as themselves free from guilt and hence able to occupy a position of moral superiority in the eyes of British opinion.

Protestants were not tremendously efficient at gathering statistics about Catholic discrimination, but some did make an effort. Senator Joseph Fisher pointed out that at the Newry Urban District Council all of the 70 outdoor staff and 20 clerical workers were Catholics. Protestants made up about 19% of the adult population at the time. The Newry Gas Works, owned by the Council, employed 30 Catholics and 1 Protestant. At the Newry Technical School there were 18 Catholic and 2 Protestant full time teachers. The Newry Port and Harbour Trust had 18 employees, all of them Catholics. The Daisy Hill Hospital was managed by a Board of Governors appointed by the Republican Newry Urban District and Rural District Councils. It employed 93 Catholics and 8 Protestants. Of the 765 houses owned by Newry Urban District Council, only 22 were let to Protestants.[17]

Robert Ferris, then Chairman of the North West Young Unionist Association, told the 1964 Unionist Party Conference that during the years that Nationalists had control of Enniskillen Council not one house was allocated to a Unionist (ie. a Protestant), and of the 220 houses built in Strabane, Unionists received only a 10% share.[18] Later Major G. S. Glover (a Corporation member) told the Waterside Ward Unionist Association that there was only "one of our people" (ie. one Protestant) employed on the staff of Limavady Rural District Council.[19]

Unionist politicians also found that few Protestants were employed in Strabane and Ballycastle.

The pattern was repeated in private employment in Londonderry. In criticising a report by the Society of Labour Lawyers, the *Londonderry Sentinel* stated that "it is beyond question that the Unionist, or Protestant, section of the Ulster community does not confine employment to its 'own side of the house' - a practice that is not, unfortunately reciprocated by members and followers of the Nationalist Party".[20] It had earlier pointed out that "Here in Londonderry it would be practically impossible to find an instance of a non-Catholic worker being employed by a Catholic business concern".[21]

Certainly Unionist councillors can recall James Doherty, who was to become Nationalist Party Chairman, standing up in the Council Chamber during the 1960s and announcing that he only employed Roman Catholics. Rev. Robert Dickinson drew the attention of James Thompson to the fact that neither of the Catholic businessmen, Messrs. R. Toland and T. Gallagher, appointed to the Londonderry Development Commission, employed any Protestants.[22] So extreme was the discrimination practised by Catholic employers that Councillor Jackie Allen was able to taunt Alderman Hegarty by asking at a Corporation meeting: "We employ Roman Catholics, why don't you employ Protestants to show you are not discriminating?"[23] The opposition was unable to reply. Back in the 1930s the Unionist MP, Rowley Elliott, had challenged Republican members in a Stormont debate to name Roman Catholics in their areas who employed Protestants.[24] There were no takers.

The situation was that in the 1960s complaints were made about discrimination in a small number of Unionist councils which constituted just over 10% of the total under Unionist control. The case against the Londonderry Corporation is not proven and it is likely that some of the other accusations were exaggerated or ill-founded. On the other hand Unionists had complaints against about half of the smaller number of Republican-controlled councils. It should also be noted that the nature of each side's charges was different. Republicans complained that inadequate numbers of Catholics were employed (and taking all kinds of council staff into consideration this was not established in the case of Londonderry) or that Catholics were not in the best jobs. Unionists were objecting that no Protestants or hardly any Protestants were employed by some Republican councils. The charge therefore was that a typical Catholic council was not only more likely to practise discrimination but where it did it would be in a more extreme form than its Protestant counterpart.

Private employers in Londonderry certainly followed this pattern. It was difficult to find a Catholic employer who didn't practise discrimination and the norm was for Protestants to be completely excluded from the workplace. On the other hand most Protestant firms employed Catholics and often in very large numbers, such as in the shirtmaking factories.

This was never publicised by Mainland journalists, academics or political commentators. To have done so might have been to undermine the moral basis of the Catholic case. Catholic propagandists fed this friendly audience a whole string of selective statistics. Where Catholics were under-represented in a workforce this was due to Protestant discrimination. Where they were over-represented they kept quiet and could rely on tame journalists not to ask too many questions.

Frank Curran talks about the dockers of Londonderry: "Sons followed fathers, who had inherited jobs from grandfathers."[25] Traditionally this group of workers contained few Protestants. A *Londonderry Sentinel* investigation in the 1930s found that entry to the closed shop was governed by one rule - whether the applicant's father had been a docker and a union member in good standing.[26] Thus Catholic fathers handed relatively well paid jobs on to Catholic sons in the succeeding decades.

In 1969, the Unionist Stormont MP, Joseph Burns, took up in the case of some Protestants who had been intimidated at the new Molins Machinery Co. factory on the Maydown Industrial Estate. It emerged that only about 25 of the 600 employees were Protestants.[27]

The Conspiracy Against the West

The argument that the West of Ulster had been neglected by the Northern Ireland government as a way of discriminating against Catholics was one which was most closely identified with John Hume. In July 1965 he made an influential speech outlining his views at the Fulham Town Hall in London at a meeting organised by the Campaign for Democracy in Ulster, a group led by a number of British Labour MPs. Hume said:

> *And so the plan stands clear. The minority in Northern Ireland resides mainly in the western counties of Derry, Tyrone and Fermanagh. To develop these areas is to develop areas opposed to the Government and to lose the few Unionist seats held there. The plan is, therefore, to develop the*

strongly Unionist Belfast-Coleraine-Portadown triangle and to cause a migration from West to East Ulster, redistributing and scattering the minority so that the Unionist Party will not only maintain but strengthen its position.[28]

A glance at the population breakdown of Northern Ireland in the 1961 Census would reveal that there was something strange about the argument. Catholics made up only 52% of the population in the counties of Londonderry, Tyrone and Fermanagh and actually constituted a minority of the adult population. It was certainly not true that the minority community mainly resided in these counties. They were relatively thinly populated rural areas where only 25% of Ulster's citizens lived. This meant that 63% of Catholics lived in the eastern counties of Antrim, Down and Armagh. There were actually more Catholics in Belfast than there were in the combined population of Counties Londonderry and Fermanagh.[29]

Any policy of regional discrimination on the lines suggested by John Hume would therefore have affected as many Protestants as Catholics in the West and would have benefitted a large majority of Ulster's Catholic population. Nevertheless, let us look at three of John Hume's specific complaints: regarding the development of a new town at Craigavon, the closure of railway lines and the siting of a university at Coleraine.

Craigavon Versus Londonderry

In 1963 the Mathew Report recommended the establishment of a new town in North Armagh, which was later to be given the name Craigavon. The idea was to attract industry as well as build houses on the site. The cry went up that Craigavon was being established as an alternative to developing Londonderry. The new town, which would be near Protestant Portadown on the River Bann would take jobs which should properly have gone to Londonderry. Frank Curran wrote: "It was obvious that such a conception could only be undertaken at the expense of Derry" and "the conviction that Derry was to be by-passed in Stormont's plans for future expansion became inescapable."[30] The decision was therefore an act of anti-Catholic discrimination.

The accusations vary very little and they are repeated ad nauseam in the literature on Northern Ireland. It is clear that hardly any of the writers have actually read the Mathew Report. Its actual purpose is indicated by its title: *The Belfast Regional Survey and Plan.* Sir Robert Mathew, from the University of Edinburgh, had been asked to look at the problems of the Belfast Region and his investigation was limited to the commuter area around the city bounded by the towns of Larne, Ballymena, Portadown and Downpatrick:

> *The origin of this Regional Report lies in the increasing pressures on land round the fringes of the built-up area - an area now extended far beyond the administrative boundary of the City of Belfast.*[31]

He observed that there was "an unregulated sprawl spreading over the surrounding countryside, congestion at the centre, a vague coalescence of hitherto identifiable communities."[32]

Mathew calculated that there was room for 600,000 people in the Belfast Urban Area but trends indicated that without planning the population would be 700,000 in 20 years time. There would be more people than Belfast could adequately house. There had in the past been an absence of planning and there were no clearly defined green belts around the city. There were no effective limits to unregulated development. The Report therefore established what became known as the Mathew Stop-Line, a "line of demarcation between town and country" which was to be "held sacrosanct" for 20 years to achieve effective planning.[33]

The limits on the population which Belfast could sustain meant that there would be an overspill population which would have to be housed elsewhere, and those who might otherwise have migrated to Belfast would have to be dissuaded from doing so. Sir Robert Mathew felt that government had to "demagnetize the centre, and invigorate the many attractive small towns in the Region."[34]

The Report calculated that, taking account of the natural increase in population as well as the overspill, 128,000 extra people would have to be accommodated in the Belfast Region outside the Belfast Urban Area. The proposal was that 64,000 of them should be absorbed at a "new Regional Centre" between Lurgan (half of whose population is Catholic) and Portadown which would present "a unique opportunity, not simply to bring Northern Ireland into step with town planning elsewhere, but to take a step forward in the development of a modern, multi-purpose community, fully meeting the complex needs of modern life and work."[35] A largely unplanned Ulster was to get a new town created by planners. Its population would need 22,000 houses and 15,000 jobs. The attraction of Lurgan and Portadown was that "Their Location beyond the head of the Lagan Valley is in the natural direction of development into the hinterland and close enough to Belfast to attract industrial enterprise."[36]

This was important. The plan was to move people from Belfast to locations elsewhere in the Region. Therefore the jobs that they would have held in Belfast also had to be diverted. The locations which employers were to be expected to operate in would have to have similar attractions to Belfast, which normally meant nearness to the ports in the city and in Larne for Ulster's largely export-orientated industries.

It was proposed that the other 64,000 people could be accommodated in 7 other "centres for development" at Antrim, Ballymena, Bangor, Carrickfergus, Downpatrick, Larne and Newtownards. The Report also had this to say:

In the remainder of the Province industry should be concentrated in the following key centres:
Londonderry, Coleraine, Omagh, Dungannon, Enniskillen, Newry,
in an effort to arrest the drift from the rural areas to Belfast and further afield.[37]

Mathew pointed out that:

As this Report is confined to the Belfast Region, proposals for urban development are restricted to towns within approximately 30 miles of the City, but the same principles and criteria could be applied for future development in the Province as a whole.[38]

The Belfast Regional Survey and Plan laid the groundwork for a planning structure for the whole Province. It recommended that planning surveys be carried out throughout Ulster and development plans prepared for all areas. Among other things this meant that the job requirements of all parts of the Province should be ascertained.

Many writers have seen Sir Robert Mathew as a Father Christmas figure with a number of jobs to give away. These were thought to have been dispensed to Craigavon instead of areas like Londonderry. Even a cursory reading of his report would reveal that this was not the case. He was concerned with making provision for Belfast's overspill population. The Wilson Report (finished in 1964 and published in 1965) estimated that of the 100,000 people to be diverted from Belfast, 60,000 would be living in the city and would actually have to leave, and 40,000 would be those who would normally be expected to move to Belfast who would have to be persuaded to go to the growth areas instead.[39] A large number of these 40,000 would be living in other areas in the East of the Province.

John Hume, even with the benefit of reading the Wilson Report, was complaining that "One would have thought that the most logical and indeed essential way of solving overcrowding in the Belfast area would have been to develop the other end of the province which has an already large centre in Derry."[40]

Firstly, it was patently ridiculous to suggest that any significant proportion of the 60,000 surplus Belfast residents could have been persuaded to move the 70 miles to Londonderry, let alone their Belfast employers. History shows that the Craigavon concept failed because, even though it was only 20 miles from Belfast, it was considered too far away and people preferred to move to growth areas nearer to the city. Hundreds of houses have had to be demolished at Craigavon because people couldn't be found to fill them. The same considerations applied to many of the migrants and their potential employers, who were looking for an area not far removed from the geographical advantages and amenities which Belfast could offer. It is also likely that Hume's co-religionists might have had something to say about a massive influx of largely Protestant migrants into Londonderry. What is clear is that the jobs supposedly up for grabs at Craigavon would only have gone to Londonderry with potential workers attached to them and that is not what John Hume had in mind at all.

He also seemed determined to miss the point that the Mathew Report specifically stated that Londonderry should become a growth centre "in an effort to arrest the drift from the rural areas to Belfast and further afield." Craigavon was to be developed as well as, not instead of, Londonderry. The Government Statement on Economic Development, which formed Part I of what was to be known as the Wilson Report, endorsed Sir Robert Mathew's recommendations about growth centres.[41] Professor Tom Wilson of Glasgow University wrote Part II as The Report of the Economic Consultant, and stated: "Growth areas need to be developed and this involves a highly complicated exercise in planning in order to co-ordinate the expansion of industry, housing and the public services."[42] He said of Londonderry: "What is badly needed is a phased plan for public investment and the proposed working party would be expected to make detailed recommendations ."[43] In the Summary of Main Conclusions and Recommendations we find: "Londonderry. A development plan is needed and should be put in hand."[44] This follows logically from the Mathew Report's recommendations about planning surveys and development plans.

The establishment of the Londonderry Area Steering Committee was announced in the same year as the publication of the Wilson Report, and it was to go on to recommend in 1968 a target of 12,000 new jobs. The *Derry Journal* reported the news that the Committee was to be set up under the front page headline "CRAIG WANTS 'MASTER PLAN' FOR NORTH-WEST" after the Minister of Development had addressed members of the Corporation.

> *Mr. Craig told the Finance Committee that any future development plan would involve a general urban renewal programme of the city itself. It was obvious in planning it one had to look at a much wider area than the city and both Derry City Council and Derry Rural Council would be involved. He had, therefore, proposed the formation of a steering committee on a similar basis as those set up for Craigavon, Antrim, Ballymena and Coleraine.*[45]

The introduction to the Londonderry Area Plan states:

> *One of the recommendations of the Belfast Regional Survey and Plan, prepared under the direction of Sir Robert H. Mathew and published in 1963, was that in the remainder of the Province outside the Belfast region industry should be concentrated in a number of key centres one of which should be Londonderry. Following this in 1964, the Report of Professor Thomas Wilson on 'Economic Development in Northern Ireland' proposed that Londonderry should be one of the Provinces' growth centres.*[46]

In assessing the Londonderry area's land requirements the Steering Committee's consultants, the James Munce Partnership, took into account "The Wilson concept of Londonderry as a growth centre attracting immigrants."[47] These would typically be people from the West of the Province.

In the Brave New World when the Londonderry Development Commission set out to implement the Londonderry Area Plan it was, as with housing policy, assumed that some radical change of policy had taken place. In the bad old days Londonderry had been passed over in favour of Craigavon but now the policy of neglect had been reversed. This was nonsense. The development of Londonderry was provided for in the Mathew Report back in 1963. There was a consistent thread running though the Wilson Report to the Londonderry Area Plan. They were stages in the same strategy.

While this was going on in Londonderry similar things were happening in other growth centres. For instance the Antrim Steering Committee and the Coleraine, Portrush and Portstewart Steering Committee produced Area Development Plans in 1968, the same year as Londonderry. Ballymena had reported in 1966 and the 3 areas of North Down, West Tyrone and Downpatrick in 1972.

Benson and the Railways

John Hume's second reason for believing that there was a plan to do down the West of Ulster was that the Benson Report had, in 1963, recommended the closure of both Londonderry's railway lines. Sir Henry Benson's examination of the Northern Ireland railway system was published just a few months after the Beeching Report. It reflected the same philosophy, viewing the railway as a commercial concern which had to pay its way.

The Northern Ireland railway system had been nationalised in 1948 to prevent its closure but, said Benson, "it is clear from the wording of the 1948 Act that there was no intention either that railway losses were to be accepted as inevitable or that, once nationalised, the railways should be directly subsidised by the Government."[48] The 1958 Transport Act (Northern Ireland) set a final time limit of 30 September 1964 (extended by 2 years in 1962) to eliminate losses. There had already been a drastic programme of line closures, particularly since the War, which had reduced the system from 1,200 miles of railway in 1914 to 297 miles at the time of the Benson Report.[49] These closures had affected all areas and towns like Newtownards, Enniskillen, Saintfield, Cookstown, Newcastle, Magherafelt, Ballynahinch, Dungiven, Banbridge, Armagh, Ballyclare, Ballycastle and Downpatrick had all lost their railway links.

This left just 3 "commuter lines" from Belfast running east to Bangor, west to Portadown and north to Larne, which accounted for 74% of all passenger journeys, and 3 other lines. These were the Dublin route running south from Portadown via Newry, the line from Belfast to Londondery via Ballymena with its branch line from Coleraine to Portrush, and a western route from Londonderry to Portadown via Strabane, Omagh and Dungannon.

Benson noted that half of Ulster's population lived in the Belfast Urban Area and its surrounding towns, and that the outlying sections of the railway system were little used. An increase in car ownership, road improvements and the cheapness of road transport had led to a fall in the number of railway passengers. The rolling stock and station buildings were very old and a lot of capital investment was required. A £5,000,000 investment scheme would not prevent losses increasing by £50,000 a year.[50]

The 3 commuter lines were said to be paying their way and closure would lead to increased traffic congestion in Belfast, so Benson recommended that they be kept open. The western line was making huge losses and was doomed. The other 2 lines were also lossmakers and an examination of the passenger journey figures indicates that they were used to about the same extent. However Benson only recommended that the Dublin line be kept open "because it is a link between the North and South of Ireland and it is desirable that there should be a fast rail link between the two capital cities. If this line was to be shut a difficult situation would arise because travellers to and from the South would have to disembark at the Border and transfer from road to rail or vice versa, which would be both delaying and inconvenient."[51]

The recommendation was that the whole of the Belfast-Londonderry line be closed. This would have cut off Londonderry from the railway system and hence was seen as anti-the West and hence anti-Catholic, but it should be pointed out that most of this line serviced staunchly Protestant towns such as Antrim, Ballymena, Coleraine and Portrush, and all of these places would similarly have lost their rail links. The Dublin line, which was always to remain open, benefitted a disproportionate number of Catholics.

In the event the Northern Ireland government overruled Benson and, acting on the advice of the Wilson Report, decided to keep the Belfast-Londonderry line open. The western line from Londonderry to Portadown via Omagh was however closed. It was the victim not of anti-Catholic discrimination, but of a commercial philosophy which was applied to all railways in the United Kingdom at that time. Between 1961 and 1971 British Rail's passenger network was cut from 13,653 miles to 8,980 miles. With improving and relatively uncrowded roads outside Belfast, the case against substituting buses for trains was not so strong as on the Mainland. Londonderry got an express bus route to Dublin via the western counties of Ulster.

The University Issue

Sir John Lockwood, Master of Birkbeck College, London, and a former Vice Chancellor of London University, had been asked to chair a committee to look at the future of higher education in Northern Ireland. Its report, presented to the Stormont Parliament in February 1965, dealt with a number of matters but the only real political hot potato was the proposed location of a second university in Ulster.

Both the communities in Londonderry were keen that the university should come to their city. In January 1963 the Corporation produced a glossy booklet presenting the case for Londonderry to the Northern Ireland government. Subsequently there was a long campaign and a big demonstration outside Stormont attended by Albert Anderson as Mayor of Londonderry and John Hume, showing that both Protestants and Catholics in the city wanted the university decision to go their way.

Lockwood recommended that Coleraine be the site of the second university. The recommendation was ratified after a heated Stormont debate during which some Unionist MPs opposed the decision. Desmond Boal, who was to become one of Terence O'Neill's fiercest hard-line critics, voted against the government. The issue really did cut across all the normal divisions. But "civil rights" agitators tried to turn the decision into an act of anti-Catholic discrimination because "Protestant" Coleraine had been preferred to "Catholic" Londonderry.

Eddie McAteer of the Nationalist Party said: "I honestly thought that even Stormont would have to listen to the united voice of Derry; but not even I realised the depth of the Stormont will to refuse justice to this city."[52] John Hume thought that:

> *The isolation of the west policy was to be continued under O'Neill as rigidly as under any of his predecessors. He lost all credibility in Derry as a crusading premier, and reinforced among the Catholic community all over the North the conviction that the Unionist leopard could not change its spots, and that change would have to be wrested from them.*[53]

Even in 1988 the *Independent's* Ireland correspondent, David McKittrick, was saying of the university issue that there was "a decision which seemed explicable only in sectarian terms."[54]

The new university was another one of those things which was regarded as a Christmas present which should have been given to Londonderry because it was more needy. There is in all the discussion very little consideration of whether Londonderry would have been good for the university. Lockwood was an English academic who did consider this question, but such was the irrationality generated by the decision that readers will find hardly any mention of Lockwood's reasons for choosing Coleraine in the literature on Northern Ireland. It is likely that only a handful of people actually read his report.

Lockwood considered 3 locations: Londonderry, Coleraine and Craigavon. He felt that the new university should be "well away from the pull of Belfast to ensure that the character and background of the new university will make it different from Queen's University."[55] Craigavon was therefore rejected as "Its close identification with the Belfast region involves the danger that a university located there might be unduly influenced to develop along technological lines as an attraction to new industry."[56]

Londonderry already had Magee University College in the city, and this was thought by some to be a good basis for a second university. It was a small college with 245 undergraduates who were unable to complete their degrees on the site. There was a rather odd arrangement under which most students attended courses at Magee for 2 years and then had to move to Trinity College, Dublin for all or part of their last 2 years, depending on the degree taken. A handful of undergraduates spent one year at Magee and then took the rest of their course at Queen's in Belfast.[57]

The new university was meant to take 2,000-3,000 students by 1973 and grow to accommodate 6,000.[58] In chosing a site Lockwood's committee took account of the criteria used by the University Grants Committee on the British Mainland. The chosen area should have good amenities to attract students and staff, and consideration would have to be given as to "whether there are sufficient numbers of students lodgings to supplement university residential accommodation."[59]

Any reader of the report will soon realise that this was to be the crunch issue for Londonderry. Paying attention to the UGC criteria, Lockwood said:

Allied to the question of houses for the staff is that of lodgings for students. The availability of lodgings in appreciable numbers is a short-term advantage which should be weighed against long-term considerations. Yet it is a decided advantage in the context of the future development of higher education in Northern Ireland. It will be essential in the years immediately ahead to concentrate financial and material resources, and the necessary skills and manpower available, on the provision of academic buildings rather than on student residences. Our recommendations in other fields of higher education will lead to heavy calls on these same resources.[60]

In its submission to the government the Londonderry Corporation had stated:

The housing of 1,500 or more students during term-time each year is a problem of no mean significance. For many reasons, and not least because it affords opportunity for the intermingling of students pursuing different courses of study and the consequent interchange of experiences and ideas, it is now accepted that the majority of students should be accommodated in students' hostels. Magee has followed a policy for some years of providing hostel accommodation for as many of its students as possible, and will no doubt continue to do so, as far as its finances permit, to meet the demands of expansion.

There is, however, always likely to be a demand for private lodgings for students. The council is satisfied that there will be little difficulty in meeting this demand.[61]

In the summary it was claimed: "Accommodation of students and staff presents no major problem."[62]

The document was published around January 1963 but just 5 months later we can find the following in the minutes of the Corporation's Housing Sub-Committee:

13. LODGINGS FOR STUDENTS - MAGEE UNIVERSITY COLLEGE

Letter dated 24th May, 1963, from the Hon. Secretary, Students' Representative Council, Magee University College, Londonderry, was submitted. The letter referred to the acute difficulties experienced by an increasing number of students in obtaining lodgings locally, and enquired whether the Corporation would permit Council-house tenants to take in lodgers.[63]

We know that at the time the Lockwood Committee was carrying out its investigation in 1964 there were 245 students at Magee and about 100 were resident in the College's hostels.[64] We can therefore say that about 150 students in search of lodgings were stretching Londonderry's capacity to accommodate them. This was the city which hoped to house 2,000 students by 1973 and 6,000 in due course, and where "Accommodation of students and staff presents no major problem."

Examined in the cold light of day the idea of locating such a university in

Londonderry was absurd. Students would have ended up sleeping on the pavement. Lockwood said he made his choice because "the Coleraine area satisfies our criteria better than any of the other areas we have considered" and "This area alone can provide the residential facilities which must be available in the critical years immediately ahead and it has amenities which can be greatly developed."[65] Londonderry had many of the right qualities but at the end of the day it didn't meet all the criteria and Coleraine did. The nearby seaside resorts of Portstewart and Portrush had an ample supply of lodgings.

John Hume was incensed that a lack of "boarding houses" should be considered an important factor. Hume had taken his degree at St. Patrick's College, Maynooth in the Irish Republic whilst studying to be a Roman Catholic priest. He lived a near monastic existence on the college premises where students were not permitted to speak before 8.00am and where newspapers, magazines, radio and television were banned.[66] He had no personal experience of normal student life.

My own experience as an undergraduate indicated that students were greatly concerned about having somewhere to live. Halls of residence were often considered expensive and restrictive and most students welcomed the opportunity to live in the community. But even if students had all been prepared to live in hostels, it was quite unreasonable to expect the government to divert millions of pounds from providing academic buildings and educational facilities in order to build homes for thousands of students which Londonderry couldn't accomodate. There was a perfectly good alternative 30 miles away on the River Bann in Coleraine, Co. Londonderry.

The Lockwood Commitee recommended that Magee University College be closed, but the Northern Ireland government came up with a good compromise. Magee would form one campus of the New University of Ulster, although most students would be based at Coleraine.[67] This was much more sensible and over the years the Magee campus has seen a modest expansion. Londonderry got its university after all.

But such was the hysteria generated at the time that John Hume stated: "when the university went to Coleraine, the chances of orderly change in Northern Ireland probably disappeared."[68] On such flimsy foundations was the "civil rights" movement based.

The Economics of the Periphery

In spite of everything there was always a feeling that Londonderry was being neglected by the Northern Ireland government because it contained a lot of Catholics. This feeling was probably reinforced by a look at the unemployment statistics. In February 1967 unemployment in Britain was 2.6%, Scotland 4.1%, Northern Ireland 8.1% and Londonderry 20.1%.° The city was beginning to learn again what life was like on the periphery.

Professor Tom Wilson had said: "There is no disguising the fact that Ulster seems a discouragingly remote area on the very fringe of Europe."⁷⁰ And Londonderry was on the fringe of Ulster. The social geographer, Alan Robinson, said: "the city is marginally placed with regard to the mainland of Britain, and despite its port facilities, is remote from the centres of industrial activity and growth" and "Derry cannot escape a geographical situation which neither the removal of the border nor the establishment of a free-port would appreciably change."⁷¹ The Northern Ireland Economic Council concluded that "Londonderry is located at the periphery of industrial Britain. That is basically its handicap. Industry tends to be drawn to the centre and to congregate there."⁷² Eamonn McCann, a "civil rights" campaigner who was never really convinced by the regional discrimination argument, wrote in a letter to the *Sentinel:*

> *The root cause of the disproportionately high unemployment west of the Bann, for example, is the inability of any Tory government to reverse the natural tendency of capital to attract capital, and for investment in Northern Ireland to drain into the Lagan Valley. That this is so is demonstrated by the most cursory examination of the situation in the Twenty-six counties where the plight of Leitrim, Sligo, Roscommon, Mayo, parallels precisely that of Tyrone and Fermanagh; nothing short of the most radical economic reorganisation can alter this trend.*⁷³

The harsh reality was that a neutral government policy would always mean that Londonderry in the West would be worse off than Belfast in the East. In the Irish Republic, a country of over 26,000 square miles, one third of the population is crammed into the area around Dublin on the east coast, because this is where the main sources of employment are, near the main port for trade with Britain. The Wilson Report pointed out that "the whole of Northern Ireland has 'development district' status, in the sense that the industrial inducements are available in all parts of the country"⁷⁴ and it is true that the government was glad to attract industry to any part of Ulster, but its policy was not neutral.

Terence O'Neill , the then Northern Ireland prime minister, visited Londonderry with Edward Heath in October 1965 and was asked if he would give greater incentives to firms to come to the North West:

I think that a very short answer to that is that if a firm will come out to the north-west the Ministry of Commerce will give it more favourable incentives than if the firm were to go to the greater Belfast area. But very often the dreadful moment arrives when the firm says that if it is not allowed to go to the greater Belfast area it would go to Scotland. That is the moment of truth when I feel that sometimes there are some people in the north-west who feel that if the firm cannot come to the north-west they would rather, in fact, that it went to Scotland. That is the moment when my Government has to decide that Ulster is one unit and that they would rather that the new firm came to Ulster instead of some other development area. We are fortunate in that we have all the advantages of a development area for the whole of Ulster and not for a restricted area as in some other parts of Britain. The Ministry of Commerce tries its best by additional incentives to get firms to come to the outlying parts of Ulster and this will continue to be the Northern Ireland Government's policy.[75]

Brian Faulkner, who was also to become a Northern Ireland prime minister, said:

Michelin had built one factory at the county town of Antrim and then decided to build another one in the Province. We specifically offered them one million pounds extra government assistance if they went to Londonderry in order to get more male employment there. In spite of this, Michelin decided that it was in their interests to site the factory elsewhere and built it at the predominantly Protestant town of Ballymena, in County Antrim. The Government was, of course, accused of not really trying to get the factory for Londonderry, a shallow political criticism which I deeply resented.[76]

Northern Ireland's principal strategy was to attract industries from outside the Province. Ulstermen had put an alternative plan to the joint Working Party under the chairmanship of Sir Robert Hall in 1962. Ulster industry should be subsidised to the tune of 10 shillings a week per employee at a cost of £5,600,000 a year to eliminate unemployment. This was rejected. O'Neill, who was then Minister of Finance, said: "The Hall Report is a great watershed in our affairs. It has given us a cold, impersonal look at ourselves. It has tested the Imperial Government to help us in certain areas and met a negative response."[77] Most of the firms who came were looking to sell their goods on the British Mainland or further afield and therefore favoured locations which were near to the eastern ports. Others preferred to produce near to the main markets in Ulster and two-thirds of the population lived within 30 miles of Belfast.

Londonderry itself had a number of other disadvantages. It was for much of the century a one industry town. Shirtmaking had been established in the 19th century, but by the end of the century was already coming under pressure from other manufacturers in England, Scotland and Belfast who were nearer to the main markets. By 1951 7,200 employees, 90% of whom were women, were selling 90% of their product to Great Britain. By the 1960s the number of workers in the industry was down to about 5,500.[78]

Now Londonderry was also facing competition from the Far East. (Frank Curran would certainly know about the problem which British workers face from cheap labour in that quarter. His book was printed in Hong Kong.) Pre-war attempts to diversify industry had met with little success. A shipyard, which had once employed 2,000 people, closed in 1924 and could never be reopened. The city was too far from the sources of raw materials.

Belfast Lough was much deeper than the River Foyle and hence could take bigger ships. In 1960 B.P. located their refinery in Belfast for this reason. The port was going into decline, although several hundred thousand pounds were spent on improvements in 1960. Passenger services from Londonderry were also ailing and the Burns and Laird Lines announced the closure of their operation to Glasgow in 1966. People who used the ship do not remember the frequently very rough journey along Ulster's north coast with a great deal of affection. Making the trip via Stranraer-Larne was several hours quicker.

Londonderry also suffered because it had a predominantly rural hinterland which was thinly populated. This affected its prospects as a port and as a provider of goods and services to the region. Republican claims that the creation of the Northern Ireland state cut the city off from its Donegal hinterland and damaged its trade do not seem to be well founded. Statistics do not show any marked falling off in trade after 1921 and the port continued to import fertilizers, feeding stuffs and grain for Donegal. In the 1930s coal was sent from Britain to Eire via Londonderry. Into the 1960s 60% of the potato exports from the city were from the Irish Republic and the Londonderry oil storage depot supplied most of County Donegal.⁷⁹ However the amount of trade was always limited. The 1925 Boundary Commission found only one merchant in the city who depended on trade with Donegal for his living.⁸⁰ In so far as trade was inhibited by partition it was a result of initiatives by the Irish government. It developed Letterkenny and Ramelton in Co. Donegal to bypass Londonderry in the import of coal and export of potatoes, and imposed import duties in the 1920s which reached a peak in the mid-1950s.⁸¹

In the 1960s the British government did not seem to be helping matters in Londonderry. It announced in 1968 that HMS Sea Eagle, an anti-submarine training school, was to be transferred from its home at the former Ebrington Barracks in Londonderry to Portsmouth. David Owen, then Parliamentary Under Secretary of State for Defence, visited the base in July and explained that the transfer would reduce costs.⁸² At the same time the British government was planning the closure of the RAF station at Ballykelly near Londonderry. The establishment employed more than 300 civilians and 1,000 service personnel and injected about £1,500,000 into the local economy. The Londonderry Trades Council backed the fight to save Ballykelly and an 18,000 signature petition was presented to Parliament by the local Westminster MP, Robin Chichester-Clark.⁸³

Local Republican politicians were, however, quite indifferent. Eddie McAteer, the Stormont MP for Foyle, said "I do not regret the departure of the British forces." At the Corporation meeting in January 1968 the Unionists voted for a motion supporting Limavady Rural District Council's efforts to retain Ballykelly. On a recorded division the Nationalist Party members abstained.⁸⁴

Babies Galore

One chronic problem in Londonderry, which magnified the city's housing and employment difficulties, was the very high Catholic birth rate. In 1964 Londonderry's birth rate was 31.8 per 1,000 compared with 23.1 for Northern Ireland as a whole, 17.6 in England and Wales, 19.5 in Scotland and 21.3 in the Irish Republic.⁸⁵ When this fell to 26.9 in 1966 a Londonderry Republican councillor remarked how regrettable this was. The city's birth rate was up to 27.5 in 1968.⁸⁶

In 1961 Catholic adults, who outnumbered Protestants by less than 2:1, had 4 times as many babies. Alan Robinson thought that such birth rates were more typical of a tropical underdeveloped country than a temperate West European nation.[87]

This had some extraordinary results. Nearly 40% of the South Ward's population was under 15, compared with 23% in England and Wales. Londonderry's natural increase in population was almost 5 times the rate of England and Wales. It meant that over a 10 year period Londonderry built enough houses to meet its immediate requirements as calculated in 1951, and it should have been able to eliminate sub-tenancy, but by 1961 so many new families had appeared that there was a big shortfall.[88]

Thus it was that Protestants often accused Catholics of being irresponsible in having such large families and overstretching the resources of a state they were often quick to repudiate. It was pointed out that the structure of family allowances encouraged such irresponsibility, but on the one occasion reform was proposed it had to abandoned.

The Northern Ireland government usually kept in step with the British government in implementing changes in state benefits so that there was uniformity throughout the United Kingdom. But in 1956 there was a debate when the British government announced increases in family allowances. It is often said that the Ulster administration wanted to reduce allowances. This is not so. At the time the family allowance stood at 8 shillings for the second and subsequent children. The Westminster proposal was that the allowance for the third and subsequent children be increased to 10 shillings. The Northern Ireland Minister of Labour and National Insurance, Major Neill, proposed that in Ulster this be amended so that families got 9 shillings and 6 pence for the second and third children and 8 shillings for subsequent children.

Neill said in Stormont:

> *Family allowances are not required here with a view to bringing about any increase in our population. Such an increase could only make our position more difficult to solve and create major problems for the future. As it is, the high rates of insurance have been a major cause of the chronic under-employment which has for so long been a feature of our economy. In these circumstances the proper aim of a family allowance scheme in Northern Ireland should be to increase the standard of living for as many families as possible.*[89]

The Westminster proposal would have given no increase at all to families with 2 children and 20% more to those with 6 children. Richard Rose found in his survey that 31% of Catholic families had 6 or more children compared with 8% of Protestants.[90] The Ulster proposal would have given the 2 child family 18.8% more and the 6 child family 7.5%. The British government scheme would have benefitted only 57,000 families and the Ulster scheme 104,000 families. Critics thought that the Stormont amendment would be seen as anti-Catholic. They did not stop to think whether the denial of any increase at all to 47,000 2 child families might not be viewed as anti-Protestant.

The Northern Ireland government dropped its idea and gave up its attempt to deter irresponsibility. The continuing high Catholic birth rate meant that enormous numbers came on to the job and house markets, making the Stormont government run very fast just to stand still. It also contributed to high Catholic unemployment. Those on the dole were often the young who could not get onto the first rung of the ladder. The percentage of unemployed Catholics therefore often mirrored the very high percentage of the younger population which they represented rather than their percentage of the population as a whole, which was much lower.

Turning the Tide

The Mathew Report had decided Londonderry should be a growth centre, but action did not have to wait until the Area Steering Committee reported. Efforts to bring jobs to the city and otherwise promote its development were being made throughout the 1960s. Indeed they had started much earlier.

BSR (Birmingham Sound Reproducers) had occupied a government advance factory in Londonderry in 1951; Dunlop opened a rayon factory at Pennyburn in 1953; and Dupont started production in 1960. Dupont was to establish a complex at Maydown which included the British Oxygen plant and the Coolkeragh power station. Here a port facility was established which could accommodate bigger ships than the city docks.[91] Altnagelvin Hospital had opened in 1960 at a cost of £2,500,000. It was the most modern in the United Kingdom.[92]

The strength as well as the weakness of attracting large, footloose projects was shown in the 1960s. In 1960 the BSR factory had closed but had reopened a year later trading as Monarch Electric with further government assistance. A second and third factory were opened and by August 1966 the firm employed

1,800 people. In March 1966 unemployment in the city stood at 10.1%, little higher than the Northern Ireland average. By January 1967 Monarch Electric had folded and the February unemployment total leapt to 20.1%. The firm later set up operations in East Kilbride, Scotland, another development area.⁹³

Nevertheless the Northern Ireland government ploughed on regardless. Earlier in 1966 the Milanda Bakery began operations with 120 new jobs in Glen Road, and Dupont announced it was to commence production of orlon and lycra with hundreds more jobs.⁹⁴ In 1967 an airport was opened at Eglinton. In 1968 there were a string of successes, including 2 new firms at Maydown. Deyong, Golding Ltd. from Sussex would start up in September making light clothing and lingerie employing up to 250 after 2 years, and Plastic Capacitors Ltd. would have 50 workers making electric components.⁹⁵ In June the Minister of Commerce, Brian Faulkner, announced an expansion by Molins Machine Co. Ltd., which was increasing its job target from 300 to 800, and in the same month the Arntz Belting Co. Ltd. said they would take over the old Monarch technical training college at Pennyburn, eventually employing 130. Saracen Ltd. would take over 30,000 square feet of the Monarch premises in Bligh's Lane with up to 200 people making lingerie and nightwear.⁹⁶

There was no lack of advance factory space as some had claimed, said Brian Faulkner at Stormont. "It will on the contrary require a great deal of effort to find suitable tenants for the existing large amount of factory space available or being provided in the area."⁹⁷

A couple of weeks later he confirmed that the clearance, levelling and preparation of the site at Springtown (an old army camp being converted into an industrial estate) would be completed by mid 1969. Part of the site was already useable and an 18,000 square feet factory was being built for Thomas French and Sons Ltd. and another of 7,000 square feet for West Ulster Studio Industries Ltd. would be started soon. Work would begin on further advance factories of 30,000 and 18,000 square feet by the end of the year. Later in July 1968 the British Shoe Corporation confirmed they were starting recruitment so that they could begin operations in temporary premises in the Autumn with the intention of occupying a factory at Springtown a year later.⁹⁸

The effect of government policy was to reduce the number of unemployed from 5,567 in February 1967 to 4,401 in February 1968 and 3,720 in July 1968. By October 1968, the month of the first "civil rights" march in Londonderry, there were 3,483 on the dole (12.5%), the lowest since 1966.⁹⁹ Terence O'Neill told the Hon. Irish Society in London that in 1968 2,200 jobs had been negotiated for Londonderry, one third of all the new jobs in Northern Ireland. Minister of Commerce, Roy Bradford, stated that since 1 April 1967 £11,000,000, amounting to 30% of government expenditure on factories, grants and loans, had been devoted to the North West of Ulster.[100]   Brian Faulkner wrote:

We were quite successful in our efforts on behalf of Londonderry and 'the West'. Between 1964 and 1969 7,000 new jobs negotiated by the Government were brought to County Londonderry. As early as 1966 we were anticipating full employment in the city of Londonderry within a few years through industries already established or in the pipeline.[101]

It would probably have come about without the closure of Monarch Electric.

What is clear is that by the time of the first "civil rights" march in Londonderry the employment situation had vastly improved. After the trauma of the Monarch closure, unemployment was down from 20.1% to 12.5%, an achievment which was all the greater in view of the large numbers of young people coming on to the job market as a result of high birth rates. New projects were being announced all the time as a consequence of what can only be described as a massive programme of positive discrimination in favour of Londonderry by the Northern Ireland government. The Londonderry Area Steering Committee had recommended a complete programme of planned development. By 1968 no-one could reasonably believe that the development of Londonderry was being held back. But it would be well to bear in mind the words of Lord Stonham, the Labour government Minister of State at the Home Office with special responsibility for Northern Ireland, and as such the only man with any great knowledge of Ulster.

In June 1968 Lord Stonham paid a visit to Londonderry. He said: "The Northern Ireland Government is building advance factories and offering them on terms which I do not think could be bettered anywhere else in the world." Its creation of new jobs in the area had been "spectacular".

Provided there is good will and irrelevant questions are not allowed to cloud the issue and if they concentrate on getting these factories filled with happy, busy workers, I believe that when I return in two or three years time, the situation will be very radically improved.[102]

But irrelevant questions did cloud the issue and Lord Stonham did not return as a minister. When disorder broke out, power passed to those who knew nothing about the situation and he was ushered out the back door.

Part II

The Civil Rights Movement

We have looked at some of the "civil rights" complaints, but what of the organisations doing the complaining? I suppose the first organisation to come to mind is the Northern Ireland Civil Rights Association (NICRA), but there were in fact a whole series of bodies which made up the wider movement. NICRA had no branch in Londonderry until 1970 and thus its role in the major events in the city was limited. John Hume was never a member. There were 3 main groups of "civil rights" activists who operated through a number of organisations.

    a. The Moderate Middle Class Catholics

    b. The IRA

    c. The Socialist Revolutionaries.

By the "civil rights era" we usually mean 1968 and 1969, the years of the "civil rights" marches. It can however be argued that the era in question lasted for 6 years, from the beginning of 1964 to the end of 1969. In the case of Londonderry it is even possible to argue that it lasted just 6 months, from October 1968 to April 1969. You can make your own choice after studying the facts.

Moderate Beginnings

The IRA campaign of 1956-62 ended in defeat. Only a year after it commenced the campaign began to wind down, and although it stumbled on for a few years the Catholic community knew that it was a waste of time. An IRA communique in February 1962 formally brought an end to hostilities and referred to an Irish public "whose minds have been deliberately distracted from the supreme issue facing the Irish people - the unity and freedom of Ireland."[1]

It was hoped that this defeat would put an end to Irish Republican agitation. A greater realism and growing materialism would turn the Northern minority's attention to social and economic matters and away from the constitutional issue. Later it would be claimed that the "civil rights" movement was prepared to accept improved conditions in Northern Ireland as an alternative to a united Ireland.

There was at least some change of attitudes, but these were principally about the question of participating in the affairs of the Northern Ireland state. In 1964 a journalist with the Dublin based *Irish Times,* Michael Viney, visited Ulster to write a series of articles. In writing about the "New Voices" in the Catholic community Viney cited the example of J. J. Campbell, a senior lecturer at St. Mary's College (a Catholic teacher training institution), and Brian McGuigan, a solicitor.² They had appealed to the Northern Ireland government to make greater efforts to get Catholics to accept nominations to public boards because they felt there was now a greater willingness to serve. A few years earlier Dr. G. B Newe had urged his fellow Catholics to allow people to participate in public life, from which they had previously excluded themselves.³

The reaction to the latest initiative of Campbell and McGuigan by the Catholic establishment was very negative. A *Derry Journal* editorial said that "Mr. J. J. Campbell and Mr. Brian McGuigan of Belfast have been amongst the most assiduous exponents of a policy of appeasement of the Stormont Government, to the limit of the obsequious and even, as many must have felt, beyond it." ⁴

Michael Viney also found that they had been called "Castle Catholics begging crumbs from the Government table" and commented:

It seems to me nonsensical to complain on one hand of discrimination and non-representation and then to belittle with nods, winks and sighs the gesture these two men have made. If it is dishonourable, as a Catholic, to sit on a statutory committee, then why complain of non-representation?

(*Irish Times* 5 May 1964)

A couple of weeks later John Hume was invited to write a two-part article for the *Irish Times* under the title *The Northern Catholic.* This was an important piece which is worth considering at some length because of the light it throws on moderate Catholic attitudes. Hume deplored the bitterness of the attacks on Campbell, McGuigan and Newe and bemoaned the fact that "Disagreement with, or criticism of, the nationalist approach - or lack of it - inevitably brings down upon one's head a torrent of abuse. 'Obsequious', 'Crawling', 'Castle Catholic', 'West Briton', are samples of the terms used."⁵ He also urged Catholics to play "a fuller part in public life".

This was, in political terms, the least successful part of his article. The crime of Campbell, McGuigan and Newe had been to suggest that the Catholic community might have been in some way to blame for their poor representation on statutory bodies by vilifying any Catholic who allowed himself to be nominated. It was politically unacceptable to suggest that anybody but the Unionists was at fault. By identifying himself with much an approach Hume had made a political mistake, which he was soon to rectify. 1964 saw this self-critical argument buried without trace. In future "discrimination" was to be the key word.

But Hume dealt with other important matters. In remarks directed at a liberal Protestant audience, he said of the Nationalist Party: "In 40 years of opposition they have not produced one constructive contribution on either the social or the economic plane to the development of Northern Ireland" and "It is this lack of positive contribution and the apparent lack of interest in the general welfare of Northern Ireland that has led many Protestants to believe that the Northern Catholic is politically irresponsible and therefore unfit to rule."

Apart from providing the Unionist Party with valuable ammunition in the emotional times of an election, their attitude to the Constitutional position has lost the Nationalist Party the sympathy of liberal Protestants and has prevented themselves and their followers from playing a fuller part in the development of the Northern Community.

He went on:

The position should be immediately clarified by an acceptance of the Constitutional position. There is nothing inconsistent with such acceptance and a belief that a thirty-two county republic is best for Ireland. In fact, if we are to pursue a policy of non-recognition, the only logical policy is that of Sinn Fein. If one wishes to create a United Ireland by constitutional means, then one must accept the constitutional position.

Hume thought that a united Ireland would have to come "by evolution, ie, by the will of the Northern majority." And in similar vein:

Catholics of all shades of political thought are expected to band together under the unconstructive banner of nationalism. This dangerous equation of nationalism and Catholicism has amply contributed to the postponement of the emergence of normal politics in the area and has made the task of the Unionist ascendancy simpler. Worse, it has poisoned the Catholic social climate to the extent that it has become extremely difficult for the Catholic to express publicly any point of view which does not coincide with the narrow nationalist line.

What did this all mean? Well it certainly meant that even the early John Hume had not renounced the goal of a united Ireland. It would now, however, be achieved by constitutional means and with the consent of the Northern majority. It therefore followed that what characterised "nationalism", or even "narrow nationalism", was not the pursuit of a united Ireland, but the pursuit of a united Ireland in an unconstructive way. Thus Hume's rejection of "nationalism" did not represent a rejection of Irish nationalism, merely that variety of it pedalled by the Nationalist Party.

Acceptance of the constitutional position did not imply an acceptance that Northern Ireland should remain a part of the United Kingdom. It could only have meant an acceptance that Northern Ireland was at that moment a part of the United Kingdom. All that was being abandoned was the idea that the only effective way of opposing the Union with Britain was to refuse to acknowledge its existence.The issues involved are somewhat reminiscent of Sinn Fein's agonizing in the 1980s about whether fighting elections and taking seats was in some way letting the side down by acknowledging institutions not operated by an all-Ireland government.

Republican politics are full of such oddities. A decade before Hume wrote his article, the British government had agreed to provide training for members of the Netherlands Naval Air Squadron. The training happened to take place at the Eglinton Royal Naval Air Station near Londonderry.The Anti-Partition councillors in Londonderry (later to be organised as the Nationalist Party) were furious. Councillor J. Hegarty talked about "this Dutch invasion."⁶ They had nothing against the Netherlands but they were upset that the permission of the Irish Republic had not been sought by the Dutch government before sending airmen.

The controversy can only be explained by reference to the Constitution of the Irish Republic. Article 2 defines the "national territory" as "the whole island of Ireland, its islands and the territorial seas" and Article 3 asserts "the right of the Parliament and Government established by this Constitution to exercise jurisdiction over the whole of that territory."⁷ As good Republicans, the opposition councillors were symbolically asserting the territorial claims of the foreign government to which they owed their allegiance. After the coronation of Queen Elizabeth II, the Republican Stormont MPs and Senators and the 2 Westminster MPs issued the following proclamation:

Whereas we, the undersigned, are the elected representatives of the greater

portion of Ireland over which the British Crown and Government claim
sovereignity and jurisdiction ..... and whereas Queen Elizabeth of England
has been crowned with the title of Queen of Northern Ireland ...... now we,
in the name of the people we represent ...... hereby repudiate all claims now
made or to be made in the future by or on behalf of the British Crown and
Government to jurisdiction over any portion of the land of Ireland or her
territorial seas.[8]

John Hume's giant step forward on the constitutional issue amounted to an
acknowledgement that Ulster was actually governed by the United Kingdom
with the help of the Northern Ireland government. Hume's biographer, Barry
White, seemed to think his man was looking forward to "the emergence of a
third force in politics, between unionism and nationalism." This was not so.
Hume wanted a more efficient form of Irish nationalism. He said:

The necessity for a fully organised democratic party which can freely
attract and draw upon the talents of the nationally-minded community is
obvious. It is to be hoped that the new Nationalist Political Front will create
such an organisation.

This body, also referred to as the National Political Front was set up in
Maghery, Co. Armagh on 19 April 1964. The meeting was attended by,
amongst others, all the Republican MPs and Senators, and Councillors on the
Londonderry and Belfast Corporations. It aimed "to stimulate the growth of
Nationalist constituency organisations" and to create an organisation "with all
the machinery of a normal political party in such areas where these do not
already exist." It was for those "who support the national ideal " i.e. a united
Ireland.[10]

The argument about efficient opposition was very important. The Nationalist
Party had no national headquarters. Until 1966 it held no annual conference.
There was no formal constituency organisation. One Londonderry oppostition
councillor said: "Constituencies were like dioceses and the MPs like bishops,
answerable to no one and answering to no one."[11] According to Hume's
biographer "the usual process for selecting candidates in nationalist constituencies
was that the local clergy called a convention, with every Catholic oraganisation
qualifying for two delegates."[12] There was a strong demand for more efficient
and more formal party organisation controlled by the membership. Others
were questioning the effectiveness of the policy of non-participation in the
affairs of the state.

There was a growing Catholic middle class which had benefitted from the 1947 Education Act with its provision for secondary education regardless of means. In his article Hume said:

There exists in the North at the moment a greater wealth of talent - young business men, professional men and graduates - than ever before and there is a growing desire among them to get together, to pool these talents and to tackle community problems.

The traditional Republican policy of non-participation in public affairs was depriving this emerging Catholic middle class of power, influence and career opportunities. On the grounds of pure self- interest many of them wanted a change. The more political among them began to see that a united Ireland might in the long term be more easily achieved by playing a role in the public life of the Province. It would be a policy of opposition through participation.

An organisation called National Unity had been formed in 1959. Michael Viney thought that "It seems increasingly to be the focus of middle-class Catholic discontent with the calibre and electoral effectiveness of most of the Nationalist MPs." It was dedicated to a united Ireland with the consent of a majority of Ulster's population. Later the National Democratic Party ploughed a similar furrow. The Nationalist Party finally accepted the role of official opposition at Stormont in 1965. The Campaign for Social Justice in Northern Ireland (CSJ) was launched in January 1964 "for the purpose of bringing the light of publicity to bear on the discrimination which exists in our community against the Catholic section of that community representing more than one-third of the total population."[13] Essentially a middle class organisation, it published most of the selective, misleading and often simply false information which was to create the English guilt complex about Ulster's minority in the 1960s.[14] The CSJ's argument was much more acceptable than that of Messrs. Campbell, McGuigan and Newe. Catholics were under-represented on statutory bodies and in the civil service simply because of discrimination. Those who actually came to participate in the affairs of the state could therefore be represented as people who were heroically breaking down the barriers of discrimination; the promoters of Catholic group interests rather than traitors to the cause. The political necessity to find a way to get the Catholic middle class into positions of influence meant that the discrimination argument had to be brought to the fore. It provided the political cover necessary to allow a change of tactics to take place within the Catholic community.

There was a similar mixture of middle class self-interest and political insight behind the change of tactics on the housing issue. Upwardly mobile Catholics were often pursuing more individualistic goals than the great majority of their community. Many resented the stifling control and intrusions of the Catholic Church in the "ghettos". (Priests traditionally visit their flock with or without invitation in their homes and even today it is not unusual in Londonderry for priests to demand to know why a married woman is not pregnant. The implication being that the couple may be using contraceptives disapproved of by the Catholic Church.) These people wanted to move to Protestant or mixed areas. They were the forerunners of that minority of individualistic Catholics who are today rebuked by their Church for not sending their children to Catholic schools. These members of the middle class were untypical. Most of their co-religionists wanted to live in Catholic areas. Other more politically conscious Catholics realised that concentrations of their people in certain areas were politically inconvenient and, as we have seen earlier, advocated the allocation of houses to Catholics in Protestant areas while avoiding any suggestion that Catholics should give up any of their houses to Protestants. The proposed outward movement from the "ghettos" was effectively sold as a form of Catholic colonisation so that the Catholic middle class would not be seen as deserting their communities.

Arguments about discrimination and gerrymandering were not new. They had been going on since the formation of the Northern Ireland state, but there was something of an upsurge after 1945 with the election of a Labour government and the formation of the Anti-Partition League, which produced a series of pamphlets. Meetings were held on the British Mainland in co-operation with the Friends of Ireland, which was supported by a number of Labour MPs. It was always felt that a Labour government was more likely to grant Republican demands, but they got no change out of Attlee and a nation that had just emerged from a war in which the Irish Republic had remained neutral.

Now, with the election of another Labour government in 1964, there were new hopes of making progress. A year later the Campaign for Democracy in Ulster became the modern equivalent of the Friends of Ireland. The idea of appealing to the hated Brits rather than to their fellow Ulstermen was also not new to Republicans. Cahir Healy, the Anti-Partition League Secretary, told Stormont in 1949:

> *This house is not going to determine when partition will end. The Irish people and Westminster will determine that question and when that hour*

comes they will not give a tinker's curse what you think about it.[15]

But there was a change of tactics in 1964. The old guard argued: 'There is discrimination and gerrymandering, therefore we need a united Ireland'. The new wave was saying: 'Let's get fairness and justice in Northern Ireland'. There was, however, no evidence in these early days of the "civil rights" era that any of the new Moderate Middle Class Catholic groupings had renounced the goal of a united Ireland.

The Role of the IRA

We have seen that the IRA gave up its military campaign in 1962. There seems to be a popular belief that its members then went to sleep until the end of the decade, leaving the political stage free for the new "civil rights" politicians to pursue politics totally at odds with IRA objectives. Not so. The failure of the 1950s campaign caused the IRA to reassess its tactics.

The secret prison paper Saoirse (Freedom) published an article by Eamon Timoney, 'Quo Vadis Hibernia' , urging the Republican Movement to be concerned with day-to-day local government, with co-operatives, with economic and social issues. By the autumn of 1962, this was the new direction that attracted the [Irish Republican] Army and, perhaps to a lesser degree, Sinn Fein. [16]

Timoney had been the IRA's commanding officer in Londonderry until he was arrested in March 1957.[17]

The Wolfe Tone Society was then formed in 1963 with branches in Belfast, Dublin and Cork. Gerry Adams described it as "a republican-orientated discussion group" which became "a meeting point for republicans and socialists, for Irish language enthusiasts and communists."[18] Meanwhile Roy Johnston, a Marxist who had been active in Republican politics in London, had returned to take up a lecturer's job at Trinity College, Dublin, and had joined Sinn Fein. Johnston was to have a profound influence on IRA thinking in the 1960s and by 1968 had become Director of Information on its Army Council. He formulated " the stages theory".

It envisaged workers in the Six counties conducting a civil rights campaign that would establish equality for the Catholic minority. In the process, the sectarian barriers between the two communities would be broken down, enabling the proleterait to recognise their communal class interest. At that point Sinn Fein political agitation in the South would transform the working classes' ingrained conservatism into a progressive non-sectarian attitude.[19]

The bourgoisie would then oppress all workers who would combine together to overthrow capitalism by violent or peaceful means.

Such left wing views were by no means alien to the Republican tradition. James Connolly, founder of the Irish Socialist Republican Party in 1896, leader of the Irish Transport and General Workers Union and a prime mover in the 1916 Easter Rising, has long been the inspiration of the Republican left. The IRA Army Council's manifesto of Easter 1933 stated that "the reorganisation of Irish life demands the public ownership of the means of production, distribution and control"[20]

The IRA's monthly journal, the *United Irishman,* campaigned on social and economic issues in the 1960s: the housing situation and ownership of ground rents in the Dublin area, and privately owned fishing rights elsewhere in the South. The IRA also sponsored the Dublin Housing Action Committee, which won good publicity. In the North, Gerry Adams helped set up the West Belfast Housing Action Committee. He said:

By the mid-'60s the movement had shed most of its militaristic leanings and a small, politically conscious organisation was developing and beginning to examine critically the role of republicanism and the task of finding a strategy towards the goal of an independent republic.[21]

The idea was not to abandon the goal of a united Ireland, but to find a new way of achieving it. Michael Farrell, one of the Socialist Revolutionaries, thought they were adopting "a more flexible policy of working within the system to bring it down."[22] Republicans "needed to enlist mass support, or at least the maximum possible support, for the republican cause" wrote Adams. "We could not free the Irish people. We could only, with their support, create conditions in which they could free themselves." "These kinds of conclusions resulted in people like myself becoming involved in housing and the other agitational activities which the movement had begun to promote." "There was a realisation that one could not organise politically as an illegal organisation". Therefore there was " a conscious decision to leave the back room conspiracies and come out into the open."[23]

The Wolfe Tone Society enabled contacts to be made with trade union officials, socialists and communists, who were needed to launch a broader based campaign.

In 1965, says Adams

> *republicans attempted to set up 'One Man, One Vote' Committees. However, largely because of their lack of political acumen, allied to the hostility of the NILP, that initiative foundered, but only temporarily. Within the Wolfe Tone Societies, the question of civil rights in the 6 counties had become a recurring theme. In August 1966 they hosted a conference on civil rights in Maghera, County Derry and another in November in Belfast where republicans were enjoying a rise in local support.*[24]

The celebration of the 50th anniversary of the 1916 Easter Rising had created a reawakened interest in Republicanism. According to the *Irish News* (Ulster's daily Catholic/Republican newspaper) 20,000 marched to Casement Park in Belfast on 17 April 1966 with 50,000 more lining the route. Most of the crowd "sported the national colours or waved miniature Tricolours."[25]

A week earlier, Londonderry saw a local celebration of the anniversary on a smaller scale. About 1,000 people paraded to Celtic Park to listen to Sean Keenan give the oration. Keenan had been interned as an IRA man during the 1950s campaign. He told the crowd:

> *This two nation idea must not be accepted by the Irish people. Was it for a Republic whose boundaries terminated at Carrigans or Bridge End that Pearse and Connolly died? In recent years there has been a well organised outcry against the use of force as a political weapon. Many public men on both sides of the Border are joining in, and they raise hypocritical hands in horror at the use of force to remove the unjust and vile thing that is Partition, but they continue to use force to maintain it.*[26]

The national spirit seemed to be at a low ebb at the moment, he said, but it was low before Easter 1916. "We appeal to you as Irish men and women to break the connection with England."[27]

And so it was that the Wolfe Tone Societies of Dublin and Belfast met on 13 August 1966 at Rathlure House, Maghera, the home of Kevin Agnew, a

Republican solicitor. Agnew was the election agent of Tom Mitchell (who had been convicted of terrorist offence in 1954 and had been the IRA commanding officer in Crumlin Road jail) when he fought the Westminster seat of Mid Ulster.[28] The meeting had been at the suggestion of the Dublin branch, dominated by IRA men Roy Johnston, Tomas MacGiolla and Cathal Goulding (the IRA Chief of Staff). On the second day it "voted to start a civil rights crusade" and "The last act of the gathering was to decide that in future they would operate as a civil rights group and that the banner of the Wolfe Tone Society would be dropped."[29]

This IRA manoeuvring had been going on in secret, but one of its discussion documents had fallen into the hands of the Irish government. Brian Lenihan, the Minister of Justice, revealed part of its contents in the Dail and the *Newsletter* (Ulster's Unionist morning paper) published details relevant to the North on 21 May 1966.

> *The IRA document captured in Eire includes a lengthy plan to take over Northern Ireland with the aid of an 'armed stand' in the heart of Belfast, and an appeal to the United Nations, it was disclosed in Dublin last night....*

> *The document is alarming to the Eire Government as it envisages the people of the Republic forcing the Government to intervene to save their fellow countrymen in the Northern outbreak....*

> *The successful tactics to date in the Republic of roping in students to act as pickets in strikes and demonstrations such as protests against lack of proper housing facilities, is to be emulated in the North....*

> *Well-meaning people who join debating organisations like the Wolfe Tone Society and students' debating societies are to be used to the advantage of underground movements.*

The Republican Publicity Committee in Dublin, which handled the IRA's press relations, did not deny the document's authenticity, but said that it represented "only suggestions for a plan of campaign". We shall see to what extent any of these ideas were put into practice.

The Birth of NICRA

Following the endorsement of the idea of a "civil rights" campaign by the

Wolfe Tone Society and the IRA, the Northern Ireland Civil Rights Association was formed. Its meeting at the International Hotel, Belfast, on 29 January 1967 to elect an executive committee and agree a constitution is normally regarded as the occasion on which it came into being.[30] Fred Heatley and Frank Gogarty, Wolfe Tone Society members and NICRA national officers, agreed that the Society exerted "the main pressure" resulting in the formation of the Association.[31]

Four people who had been at the Maghera meeting, Fred Heatley, Jack Bennett, Michael Dolley and Kevin Agnew were elected to the NICRA Executive. None were IRA members. The others were quite a mixture. Noel Harris (Chairman of NICRA and member of the Draughtsman and Allied Trade Association), Derek Peters (Secretary of NICRA) and Betty Sinclair (Secretary of the Belfast Trades Council) were all members of the Communist Party. Dr. Joe Shearer was from the Belfast-based Republican Labour Party formed in 1964 by Gerry Fitt, Dr. Con McCluskey had founded the Campaign for Social Justice, Paddy Devlin was then in the NILP, J. Quinn was from the Liberal Party, and there was even the Chairman of the Queen's University Young Unionists, Robin Cole.[32] This is what Gerry Adams had to say about the inaugural meeting:

The meeting to establish NICRA was well attended and was packed by republicans, who wielded the biggest bloc vote.

Contrary to later claims by the Unionists that republicans took over the civil rights movement, we were there from the very beginning. Republicans were actually central to the formation of the NICRA and far from using it as a front organisation those of us who attended the inaugural meeting were directed to elect only two of our membership to the executive.[33]

He is probably referring here to the two Wolfe Tone Society members, Heatley and Bennett. Elsewhere Adams wrote:

We republicans were there in strength. We were acting on instructions not to pack the executive; it was sufficient to have an influence. We were also instructed to vote for Communist Party nominees....A backward glance over this first NICRA leadership shows how the republican voting strategy assured a nicely rounded leadership for the parent Civil Rights Association.[34]

The IRA, operating from a position of weakness after the failure of the 1950s campaign, was initially prepared to take the long view. Short term "civil rights" objectives would be more likely to be won with a respectable NICRA Executive. It would be much more likely to impress the Labour government and liberal Protestants. Once the marches started, the IRA soon realised that the ability to win votes at committee meetings was of little importance. Power lay on the streets and that is where it concentrated its limited resources. It does, however, seem that not everyone at the inaugural meeting realised the value of being discreet about their Republican aspirations. Senator Nelson Elder attended the meeting as a Unionist Party observer and later told the Northern Ireland Senate:

> *They were not interested, even at their first meeting, in civil rights. A member from the Wolfe Tone organization - someone referred to him this afternoon - and various other people made contributions, all for a United Ireland.* [35]

NICRA had an original membership of 70, but by the end of the first year this had fallen to 27. There were no street protests during this year and the organisation concentrated on helping alleged victims of the Special Powers Act, itinerants amd squatters.[36] By the time the Cameron Report was published in 1969 membership was 240.[37] It is perhaps a testimony to the power of the media that such a tiny organisation became so well known.

The first "civil rights" march was reluctantly sponsored by NICRA and organised by Austin Currie on 24 August 1968 from Coalisland to Dungannon. Cameron says that about 2,500 took part and that police identified 70 Republicans (by which they meant those in the Sinn Fein tradition), of whom 10 were IRA members, among the stewards.[38] The Cameron Report said:

> *There was hope among many participants that something new was taking place in Northern Ireland, in that here was a non-violent demonstration by people of many differing political antecedents and convictions, united on a common platform of reform. Miss Sinclair [now Chairman of NICRA] closed the proceedings by leading those present in singing 'We shall overcome'. The marchers thereafter dispersed.*[39]

Bernadette Devlin saw things differently:

> *The marchers were interspersed with various bands, playing* Who fears to speak of '98 *and* Faith of our fathers. Faith of our fathers *is a Catholic hymn which has been degraded by frequent playing at Nationalist gatherings and*

is one song I hate to hear at a political meeting, because it betrays the old mentality that equals Irish and Catholic. But we had a bash at Faith of our fathers *anyway; so much for non-sectarian...*

Betty Sinclair, chairman and leading light of the Civil Rights Association in those days, got up, fearing the movement would be discredited if a fight broke out. 'This is a non-political, peaceful demonstration. Anyone who wants to fight should get out and join the IRA,' she said. And the crowd roared back, 'Where do we join?' Betty then realised that without any forethought at all she had organized a march in Coalisland, a town which was ninety per cent Republican; [40]

It is true that the organisers tried to close proceedings with a rendition of "We Shall Overcome" but

By the time we'd got to the end of the first verse of our anthem, Betty and all her friends had scuttled into the lorry and driven off, leaving the population of Coalisland outside the town of Dungannon.

After that we sat down in big circles all over the road and sang rebel songs till midnight. [41]

For the uninitiated a rebel song is an Irish Republican song.

The march had been to protest about the allocation of houses in the Dungannon Rural District. Most books record that the problem was highlighted when a 19 year old single Protestant girl was given a council house in Caledon.

Two houses were the centre of controversy: numbers 9 and 11, Kinnard Park. Both had been taken over by Catholic squatters with the encouragement of the local Republican Club. These clubs had been set up by the IRA to try and get round a ban on Sinn Fein, but they were themselves banned as an IRA front. The McKenna family in number 9 left voluntarily and the house was subsequently let to a Protestant housing applicant, Miss Emily Beattie, who happened to be the secretary to a solicitor who had stood as a Unionist Parliamentary candidate. The controversy reached a peak in June 1968 when Miss Beattie took possession of her empty house on 13 June, and the Goodfellow family had to be forcibly evicted from number 11 by the police on 18 June. Austin Currie, Nationalist Party Stormont MP for East Tyrone occupied 11, Kinnard Park for a few hours in protest on 20 June.

It seemed a cut and dried case, but things are never that simple. Emily Beattie was engaged to one of the dwindling number of Co. Monaghan Protestants, Bill Crawford. He wished to move to Co. Tyrone and marry Miss Beattie, but as a resident of the Irish Republic was having difficulty getting a work permit in Northern Ireland. Once he married a United Kingdom citizen he would get automatic exemption and would be free to work in Ulster. However, they had nowhere to live. The home of Emily Beattie's parents was hopelessly overcrowded already. They therefore decided to apply for a council house. The application had to be in Emily's name only as her fiancee, as a non-resident of Northern Ireland, had no right to have his name on the list. Marriage plans in March 1968 had to be put back as their application had not been successful by that time.

When number 9, Kinnard Park became vacant the council considered the poor conditions the Beattie family was living in just outside Caledon (as well as the fact that the applicant was unable to marry until she had a home) and took part of the family out of those poor conditions by reaching an understanding that Emily Beattie's two brothers and a sister would sleep at the newly allocated council house. She was married in September 1968, and Bill Crawford was able to move to Ulster. Thus the home allocated to "a single Protestant girl" actually housed 5 people.

What of the Goodfellows, whose claim to housing was assumed to be so much stronger? They had been living outside the district near Markethill, Co. Armagh until October 1967. The family then moved to live with Mrs. Goodfellow's parents at Brantry in the Dungannon Rural District. In November they started squatting at Kinnard Park. It is therefore clear that they had come from outside the area and expected to be accommodated immediately. Under modern English housing standards they would have had no claim to be housed as homeless persons because they had left their previous accommodation voluntarily. As normal housing applicants they would be lucky to get on a housing waiting list because of their lack of a residential qualifications in the area.

The reason why they were evicted was that the council had allocated the house, on the recommendation of the local Unionist councillor, to a Roman Catholic, Mr. Alexander Brady and his family of 5. Mr Brady and Miss Beattie had not only lived within the Dungannon Rural District for some time, they had both lived within one and a half miles of Caledon. On grounds of both housing need and their local connection they merited houses in Caledon. The Goodfellows, by squatting at number 11, were merely keeping out a Catholic family more deserving of a house.[42]

The Background to Civil Rights

Before we look at the October 1968 march in Londonderry, which marked the start of the violence, it will be useful to examine the nature of the "civil rights" demands to help us understand the nature of the movement they produced. Max Hastings wrote of the "civil rights" movement:

The reforms which they sought - basic democratic rights for every Ulster citizen - were so patently reasonable that one might imagine that no civilized man of any religious belief could oppose them.[43]

Bernadette Devlin spoke of "the civil rights movement's demand for simple justice".[44] Tim Pat Coogan said of the period after the Second World War: "Henceforward, Northern Catholics began to seek an end to gerrymandering and discrimination in housing and jobs, rather than a reunion of the country under a Dublin parliament."[45] Gerry Adams thought the movement was seeking "the elementary demands of western democracy" and organised "a modest campaign for reasonable, basic and just demands."[46]

The civil rights movement looked for the democratisation of the 6 county state, but the state made it abundantly clear that it would not and could not implement democratic reforms. The civil rights movement had not demanded the abolition of the state, nor a united Ireland. The civil rights struggle had not raised the constitutional question.... [47]

It was fashionable at the time to use phrases like "the Border is not an issue" or "the Border is irrelevant ". Some writers thought the movement was "neutral" on the issue. "Constitutional issues," wrote Sarah Nelson, "were no longer supreme. Civil rights activists demanded reform of the regime rather than Irish unity. They called not for Britain to be rejected as Ireland's enemy, but for the regime to conform more closely to British standards." Those who were "traditionally anti-British, called 'for full British rights - full British standards'."[48]

While the "civil rights" movement seemed at times to be demanding "Fairness for All" it was never concerned with Protestant grievances. The real demand which came across on the streets was for Protestants to stop being unfair to Catholics. As Catholics were supposed eg. to have less houses, it was pursuing a claim for more houses for Catholics. It was a Catholic movement promoting Catholic group interests. Conor Cruise O'Brien said of NICRA: "It was 'non-secretarian' meaning, as ususal in Northern Ireland, Catholic-based with a few Protestant sympathizers."[49]

A close examination of the situation in Londonderry, supposedly the worst example, shows that Protestants weren't being noticeably unfair to Catholics. Certainly they were not depriving Catholics of any British rights which they as Protestants enjoyed. Where people were worse off than on the Mainland - in terms of housing conditions for instance - both communities were affected. Protestants were being portrayed as guilty when they were not, and it was this fact, reinforced by a belief that Catholics must have known they were distorting the truth, that influenced the Protestant reaction to the "civil rights" movement.

If Catholics were not being denied their rights and were thus using mere propaganda, they must be pursuing other objectives through "civil rights" agitation. The suspicion was increased when Ulster Protestants (but not British politicians) realised that many of the pronouncements about the Border and the Constitution not being in question were based on semantic deception.

One of the most important deceptions concerned the question of demands and objectives. It is true that the "civil rights" movement did not demand the abolition of the state nor a united Ireland. It is true that it did not campaign for these things. The movement definitely did not want to make the Border an issue and preferred that the Protestants and British politicians should regard it as irrelevant. The tactical aim of the "civil rights" leadership was to focus attention on non-constitutional issues to try and convince as many gullible British politicians and liberal Protestants as possible to support them. They therefore chose to exclude from the stated aims of their organisations any mention of their views on the constitutional question ie. whether Ulster should remain a part of the United Kingdom. It did not follow that because they were not openly espousing Republican objectives or making a public issue of them that they were not pursuing such objectives.

The Moderate Middle Class Catholics believed that

1. Acceptance of the constitutional position did no imply support for the constitutional position, simply a recognition of the current reality.

2. Acceptance of the constitutional position and participation in the affairs of the state were not incompatible with a belief in a united Ireland.
3. The pusuit of intermediate demands which would promote reconciliation was a good way of bringing about a united Ireland by consent.

The IRA theoreticians also thought that the pursuit of social and economic objectives (and in particular a "civil rights" campaign) would unify the Protestant and Catholic working class, eventually bringing about a united Ireland. Therefore a significant portion of the "civil rights" movement (later I shall argue it was most of it) was deliberately pursuing "civil rights" as a means of achieving a united Ireland. However on tactical grounds they had chosen not to turn a united Ireland into a "demand". Protestants were wholly justified in being suspicious about statements claiming disinterest in the constitutional question.

On the other hand it could be argued that "reconciliation" and "the unity of the working class" were fairly harmless objectives and should not have given rise to concern. A united Ireland would take a long time to achieve by this route. I think the answer is that Loyalists doubted the sincerity of theorists like John Hume and Roy Johnston when they outlined the way in which social and economic campaigns could lead to a united Ireland. Having had some experience of the kind of theories that middle class intellectuals can come up with, I can well believe that Hume and Johnston may have been sincere in the early 1960s. They were writing in the wake of a crushing IRA defeat and there seemed no immediate hope of achieving a united Ireland. Both therefore looked at very long term strategies aimed at winning over Ulster Protestants. However, as the decade progressed, Republicans came to see that their best hope of achieving their objectives lay in persuading the British government to overrule Ulster's elected representatives, rather than in bringing their fellow Ulstermen round to their way of thinking. By 1970 it was the dominant Republican view that it was possible to get the hated Brits to unify Ireland, if necessary against the Loyalist majority's wishes.

At some time in between, certainly after October 1968, "civil rights" leaders saw that the real value of their campaign was to convince the British government of the moral superiority of the Catholic position, win changes which would be of symbolic importance, undermine Unionist self confidence, and open the way for further demands. "Civil rights" became a way of defeating Loyalists, rather than a way of bringing about reconciliation with them. Those leaders were not averse to bending the truth. The Wolfe Tone Society member Jack

Bennett, who was to go on to work as a sub-editor on the *Belfast Telegraph*, told James Thompson: "one could exaggerate and the measure of exaggeration in civil rights allegations was justifiable and necessary in order to achieve the aims of the movement."[50] Tim Pat Coogan had to admit that "the climate created by the build-up of agitation by such fiery socialist orators as Eamonn McCann both heightened unionist fears of being thrust out of the Union and kindled republican hopes of catching a tide that would sweep away the Union altogether."[51]

The "civil rights" movement could not be said to consist merely of a few leaders with novel theories, nor of the few hundred who actually joined a "civil rights" organisation. These people were often outnumbered by more than 10:1 on marches by those who had joined no organisation and were not subject to the control of NICRA or anyone else. It was this great mass of people which created the impression of strength. These ordinary members of the Catholic community, just as much as their Protestant counterparts, could scarcely believe that Loyalists would come to support a united Ireland through policies of "reconciliation" or "uniting the working classes". Their approach was more pragmatic. The "civil rights" movement was showing itself to be a useful and effective vehicle for promoting Catholic group interests. As long as it was effective it was immaterial what rationale the leaders put forward as a justification for its activities. Conor Cruise O'Brien seems to have shown rather more insight on this point than most writers.

> *So Catholic youth came into the streets against the Protestant State. And the tricolour, the flag of the Catholic State, came with them. This was a negation of what had been the essential doctrine of the civil rights movement - that it was a movement for equality in the area itself, and for the rights possessed by other citizens in the United Kingdom, and not a nationalist movement demanding constitutional or territorial change. But the people of the ghettoes were not committed to civil rights doctrine. They were interested in the relationship between 'us' and 'them', and in what promised a change in that relation: new tones of voice, new movements of feet.*[52]

They were not averse to one of "them" helping "us".

> *What Catholics wanted, in 1969, were militant champions of the Catholic community. Since Parnell's day - and before, in different conditions - they had known that such champions might be all the more effective for being Protestant in religion, provided they were 'Catholic in politics'.*[53]

What become important was to "learn the liberal language" to appeal to the Brits.[54] When, at the end of 1967, a *Belfast Telegraph* poll showed that only 16% of Catholics "preferred the existing constitutional position to an independent united Ireland" it revealed how little attitudes had changed. [55]

Believing Makes it So

The Cameron Report said that one of the causes of the disorders in Ulster was

> *A rising sense of continuing injustice and grievance among large sections of the Catholic population in Northern Ireland, in particular in Londonderry and Dungannon....*[56]

Londonderry Unionist, Major Gerald Glover, said of this statement: "Of course there is a rising sense of injustice, but should there be? Is this feeling justified?" [57] I suppose the short answer was no, it was not, especially as one of the things about which Cameron said there was a feeling of injustice was the supposed absence of a points system for allocating houses in Londonderry. But this is to assume that the British and Northern Ireland governments were only concerned with justified beliefs.

While I was reading the First Annual Report of the Housing Executive (1971-72) I came across a section headed "Why we were established" (p.10-11). The report noted that Cameron had said "grievances concerning housing were the first general cause of the disorders" but remarked that Professor Richard Rose's survey found that there was no evidence of systematic discrimination. In fact an examination of Rose's full findings (not given in the Housing Executive report) shows that in Unionist controlled local authorities 21% of Protestants and 23% of Catholics lived in council-owned property. In "Nationalist" controlled areas 15% of Protestants and 39% of Catholics occupied council houses. Rose's conclusion was that

> *the survey found no evidence of systematic discrimination against Catholics. The greatest bias appears to favour Catholics in that small part of the population living in local authorities controlled by Catholic councillors.*[58]

But then the Housing Executive report says something quite extraordinary:

> *Perhaps the shortage of good housing rather than systematic religious bias was the main reason for complaints about housing allocations. Whatever*

the cause the administration of housing policy in Northern Ireland did not inspire confidence throughout the community. In Community Forum No2 1972, Derek Birrell and Alan Murie, of the New University of Ulster, wrote 'Such a situation does not arise necessarily because of overt or extensive maladministration or mismanagement but through the conviction that such malpractice exists. Such a conviction need not be an accurate representation of objective evidence and may simply represent a loss of confidence in administrative agencies.'

Having seen their country torn apart by Catholics who had been supposedly badly treated in the allocation of houses by wicked Protestants, it was really no comfort to the Loyal majority to be told that Catholic beliefs were unfounded, but the relevant thing was that they had those beliefs. The whole moral basis of the Catholics' case was that they had justified grievances about housing. Take away the factual justification and their agitation becomes a hollow sham. The Protestant community is vindicated and we English can all get rid of our feelings of guilt.

To say that Catholics had "a loss of confidence in administrative agencies" is to say no more than that, since the secession of Southern Ireland from the United Kingdom, the greater part of the Northern minority has lacked confidence in any aspect of a state which it has wanted to overthrow. The statement of Birrell and Murie does however point to an important aspect of Irish psychology, which has been difficult for the English to grasp: the ability to believe something not because it is true but as an expression of Irish feelings about the state. In this respect Ulster Protestants are definitely British rather than Irish.

We English tend to be rather literal in our modes of thought, but the liberal Unionist, Patrick Riddell, rightly thought that "the Irish in the main are an emotional race, addicted to myth, unloving of disenchantment."[59] He also said, in a remark which was equally applicable to Ulster Catholics:

The Southern Irish are surprisingly and formidably expert propagandists but not so expert at looking inside themselves and assessing fully and honestly what they find there. They are intellectually astigmatic, strongly flawed by a capacity for self-deception, unversed in the truth about their country and their race and unwilling to be made aware of it, opting for romanticism, perhaps afraid.[60]

Sometimes it is an Irishman's patriotic duty to believe something and he does so. Once he has decided to believe, and committed the initial act of self-deception, then his belief is entirely sincere. English liberals, in approaching the problems of Ulster, seemed to assume that the only way someone could unjustifiably state something in the face of all the facts would be by means of a cynical lie which he did not believe. Detecting a sincere belief in the hearts of Northern Catholics they thought this was a good reason for assuming those beliefs were justified. But, putting it as charitably as possible, the Irish are good at telling stories because they usually actually believe what they are telling you.

Arguments about discrimination in housing had always been identified with the Republican movement. They had always been a good way of getting at the Prods. What is more the accusations had always previously been linked with a demand for a united Ireland. When new Catholic politicians revived the complaints, no-one in the Bogside needed to be drawn a diagram. When someone said 'Stop discrimination against Catholics', everyone knew where he stood on the question of a united Ireland. A.T.Q. Stewart once wrote:

> *The great strength of Catholic criticism of government is its ability to carry over into the local situation of today the inherited Catholic consciousness of the entire Anglo-Irish struggle since it began.* [61]

It was undoubtedly good for the cause to believe certain things about housing, and they were believed. The English would probably do this as a cynical exercise in deception. The Irish can do it as an idealistic exercise in self-deception.

The whole discrimination and gerrymandering campaign was a very important exercise. In talking about an analysis of electoral registers, including the one in Londonderry, Tim Pat Coogan said: "the electoral figures may not justify but they help one to understand the bombing statistics." Commenting on the low percentage of Catholic nominees on public boards the same author said: "Out of such percentages are gunmen made." [62]

The traditional approach to the "civil rights" movement is to regret that it was "taken over by extremists" but to concede that its initial complaints were justified. They were not, and I have spent some time showing why. Once this is established the nature of the "Ulster problem" is transformed. We need an alternative explanation of why we have bombers and gunmen. I shall return to this later.

Meanwhile perhaps we should reinterpret Terence O'Neill's famous televised address to the nation on 9 December 1968 in which he said "Ulster stands at the crossroads".

> *In Londonderry and other places recently, a minority of agitators determined to subvert lawful authority played a part in setting light to highly inflammable material. But the tinder for that fire, in the form of grievances real or imaginary, had been piling up for years.*[63]

There can be little doubt that O'Neill did believe that imaginary grievances were part of the inflammable material which led to the explosion of violence in Londonderry and that he had a duty to react to such grievances. It was a fatal error. To react to the romantic fantasies of the Irish was to fuel hopes of achieving the ultimate dream of a united Ireland, and to unleash the violence which Republicans had always been prepared to use.

The Cameron Report

Throughout the "civil rights" era there was considerable Loyalist frustration that their leaders did not do more to refute the allegations made against Unionism. The editor of the *Londonderry Sentinel*, Charles Buchanan, said of a society of Labour Lawyers report in September 1968:

> *What those Labour members do not appear to be aware of is that the vast majority of Unionist supporters in Northern Ireland are so disgusted - and amazed - that any attention at all has been paid to the Nationalist Party's campaign, that they would, in fact, welcome an investigation - provided that it was completely neutral and unbiased and prepared to sift for the truth.*
>
> *On the question of house allocation alone, such an investigation could not fail to confirm that local authorities that are Unionist controlled give a far higher percentage of homes to their political opponents than many of the Nationalist controlled authorities.*[64]

A month later he complained that

> *The Unionist Party which is being blamed by so many organisations for conditions in the city - indeed, in the whole country - has uttered not a word.*[65]

As the chorus of criticism grew deafening, Buchanan wrote:

Few Ulstermen or women will disagree with the declaration at the weekend by Mr. Roy Bradford, that the Government must act now 'to clear our name of any allegations of injustice'.[66]

The Sentinel therefore welcomed the setting up of the Cameron Commission in January 1969 in an editorial headed SET THE RECORDS STRAIGHT.

The decision by the Northern Ireland Cabinet to ask the Governor to set up an inquiry into conditions in the Province that have led to unrest is one that has received widespread support because in this way, the true picture of events - and, possibly, the background to them - will be investigated and an assessment of the overall picture made by an impartial and reputable body....

On several occasions over tha past few months we have urged that the Government should have set up such an inquiry because we felt that, when all matters are taken into consideration, many of the allegations that have been made against Northern Ireland, and the conditions that exist, will fall very much short of their targets....

Unfortunately the depth to which the inquiry will go has not yet been revealed, but we believe that, if it is full and fearless, faults will be found in many places, particularly in the recruitment of labour and the numbers which employers of one persuasion engage from another. There can be little doubt of what the outcome of an examination of those figures in Londonderry will reveal.[67]

Unfortunately we didn't get a full, fearless and unbiased report which was prepared to sift for the truth. Instead we got a superficial and shoddy piece of work which was hopelessly one sided. William Craig, who had been sacked by O'Neill from his post of Minister for Home Affairs for taking too hard a line, was sceptical from the very beginning. After the report appeared in September 1969 he said:

Cameron has been a sort of referee in a political game - the equivalent of a referee with no knowledge of soccer being asked to referee a football match.[68]

Nevertheless the Cameron Report's findings on discrimination and gerrymandering were taken to be of monumental importance. John Hume claimed

The report of the Cameron Commission completely vindicates the civil rights movement. I find it most fair. It proves the injustices which the civil rights movement had complained of. [69]

Michael Farrell said of the report:

It confirmed and documented the existence of discrimination and gerrymandering against Catholics and vindicated the Civil Rights movement. [70]

Max Hastings got quite carried away:

the Cameron Report was, and will remain, the textbook of the Ulster crisis. Brilliantly constructed, articulately written, forcefully expressed, it clarified almost every criticism of the Protestants and the Unionist Party made since time immemorial. [71]

A senior Unionist figure in Londonderry admitted to me that he and his colleagues were "lazy and lax" in compiling information to counter Republican allegations. But there was a more serious problem. O'Neill and those who supported his liberal line wanted a guilty verdict from the Cameron Report. They were therefore not keen to challenge many of the complaints. O'Neill himself wrote about Cameron:

His report became one of the text books upon which reform could be based. [72]

A guilty verdict was necessary to bring in the reforms which would solve everything. Unfortunately they were only successful in creating problems rather than solving them. In his "Ulster stands at the crossroads" speech on television in December 1968, O'Neill asked

What kind of Ulster do you want? A happy and respected Province, in good standing with the rest of the United Kingdom? Or a place continually torn apart by riots and demonstrations, and regarded by the rest of Britain as a political outcast? [73]

As we shall see, O'Neill got his reforms and the rioting which they were designed to avoid.

The Socialist Revolutionaries

This very important group did not become prominent in the "civil rights" movement until the late 1960s. It consisted largely of New Left Marxists or Trotskyites, although many would be difficult to classify. The best known figures from this tradition were Eamonn McCann, Michael Farrell and Bernadette Devlin. They operated principally through People's Democracy, an informal organisation lauched at Queen's Unviersity, Belfast in October 1968. It had no presence in Londonderry, where the local Socialist Revolutionaries grouped around McCann worked within the local branch of the Northern Ireland Labour Party, which they preferred to call the Derry Labour Party. This was to become a maverick body set apart from the rest of the NILP, which wanted Ulster to remain part of the United Kingdom. McCann & co. preferred to co-operate with left-inclined Republicans, particularly those in the local Republican Club.

This loose local alliance formed the Derry Housing Action Committee (DHAC) which worked on similar lined to the body sponsored by the IRA in Dublin. It campaigned on local housing issues, disrupted meetings of the Londonderry Corporation and in June 1968 blocked Lecky Road with a caravan in support of a family's application for a house. [74]

The NILP as a whole had been pushed steadily leftwards by the participation of the young Socialist Revolutionaries, although outside Londonderry they tended to desert it in the late 1960s. Michael Farrell, for instance, canvassed for the NILP at the 1965 Stormont elections and was a member of the NILP Executive in 1967, but later tended to be more interested in non-party agitation. Cyril Toman (later of People's Democracy) was Chairman of the NILP Young Socialists. They and McCann were also members of the Irish Workers Group, a revolutionary body which published *Irish Militant*. All had been at Queen's University together in the early 1960s. [75] Farrell became Chairman of the Irish Association of Labour Student Organisations (IALSO) and gave a good indication of the Socialist Revolutionary philosophy at its first conference in 1967:

> *IALSO by virtue of its all-Ireland character can play an important part in creating a single all-Ireland Socialist Party which is a vital prerequisite for the establishment of a worker's Republic as only a socialist party can unite the working class of both parts of Ireland in the struggle against their common capitalist master.* [76]

The NILP was induced to support a number of conferences on "civil rights" and this was doubtless very important in mobilising the British Labour Party. It did however alienate the Loyalist working class, who saw it as complaining about insubstantial or ill-founded grievances and hence assisting Republican agitation.

The NILP was a declining force by the time the "civil rights" campaign reached its peak in 1968-69.

The 5 October Revolution

The previously little known revolutionaries hit the headlines with a bang on 5 October 1968 on the occasion of the first "civil rights" march to be held in Londonderry. The nominal organiser of the parade was NICRA, but it had little control over proceedings.

The initiative had been taken by the Derry Housing Action Committee. Eamonn Melaugh wrote to NICRA inviting the organisation to march in the city. His letter said: "It would not be unreasonable to expect 10 or 15 thousand people to support your association in a protest in Derry."[77] Eamonn McCann, who organised the march, estimated that about 400 actually took part. *The Londonderry Sentinel* said 350. It is interesting that later accounts all seem to inflate the figure to over 2,000. This prompted McCann to say: "Had all those who now claim to have marched that day actually done so, the carriageway would have collapsed." [78]

NICRA agreed to be named as the organiser of the march but as it had no branch in the city, an ad-hoc committee was set up to make the necessary arrangements. It had representatives from the Republican Club, the James Connolly Society, the DHAC, the Labour Party Young Socialists and the NILP. The committee didn't function so McCann and Melaugh took charge. This meant that the revolutionaries stamped their identity on the parade.

> *None of the placards demanded 'civil rights'. We were anxious to assert socialist ideas, whether or not the CRA approved. We used slogans such as 'Class war, not Creed war', 'Orange and Green Tories Out', 'Working Class Unite and Fight'. The intention was to draw a clear line between ourselves and the Nationalist Party, to prevent pan-Catholic unity.* [79]

It was a naive hope in the context of Northern Ireland. Those who attended were almost to a man (and woman) Catholics and Irish Republicans.

The NICRA representatives who met the Londonderry organisers were unfamiliar with the geography of the city and agreed to a route which started in the Protestant Waterside and proceeded across the river via more Protestant areas to the Walled City, from which Republican marches were traditionally excluded. It soon became clear that the Apprentice Boys, a Protestant and strongly Loyalist organisation, had made plans some months earlier to walk over a similar route on 5 October.

It was later said that the Apprentice Boys parade was invented after the announcement of the NICRA march in an effort to get it banned. This was not so, and to its credit the Sunday Times Insight Team did acknowledge this.[10] The Loyalist parade was in fact an annual event about this time of year. To become full members of the Apprentice Boys association people have to attend a ceremony in Londonderry and a party from Liverpool had been doing this on an annual basis since 1964. They would arrive at the Waterside railway station and then march across the river. Cheap fares on the Liverpool-Belfast ferry were not available until October and hence the first Saturday of that month was chosen for the trip. The Liverpool Murray Club was able to produce correspondence with the Belfast Steamship Co. Ltd., Northern Ireland Railways and Belfast Corporation Transport referring to the 5 October visit - all dated well before the NICRA parade was announced. National officials had granted permission for the visit to the Apprentice Boys headquarters in the Walled City in a letter dated 17 March 1968. [11]

The Northern Ireland government was therefore faced with a situation where NICRA wanted to march along a similar route and at a similar time to a Loyalist organisation which (rightly) perceived it as being mainly composed of Republicans. There was also the problem that NICRA wanted to walk through predominantly Protestant areas. The tradition was that each community walked through its own areas to avoid conflict. NICRA's protestations that it was "non-sectarian" could not conceal the fact that almost all its members supported Irish Republican objectives and this was well understood by Ulster Loyalists. There was therefore a danger of conflict.

The Minister of Home Affairs, William Craig, therefore banned all parades in the Waterside and the Walled City on 5 October. This meant the Apprentice Boys could not walk at all and they complied with the ban. NICRA at least had the option of marching elsewhere on the west bank of the Foyle, which was after all where most of the local marchers lived. NICRA, as the official organiser, was served with the order placing restrictions on its route. Its officers advised compliance at a meeting with local activists on the day before the march.

For two hours the CRA representatives explained to us that it was their march, it was they who had formally notified the police, and that they, therefore, were the only people with authority to decide whether or not it should go ahead. We explained that we were marching anyway. It was some time before the Belfast delegation grasped the central point that they had no means of stopping us marching. Their opposition collapsed when one of their number, Frank Gogarty, broke ranks and announced that 'if the Derry people are marching I'm marching with them'. [12]

Gogarty was one of the ex-Wolfe Tone Society members. Lord Cameron was tremendously impressed with the NICRA Constitution and the nice responsible people associated with the organisation. But he knew nothing about street politics. When it came down to it the nice NICRA people who voted on committees were totally impotent. They could not stop marches and real power resided with those with influence out on the streets. Resolutions were all very well but it was the marches which hit the headlines and were the power base of the organisation. The Cameron Report did manage to conclude: "we think it is established that members of the Irish Republican Army were present and represented among the stewards" on 5 October. [13] Gerry Adams was later to say of NICRA:

The leadership was cautious, perhaps rightly so, but the initiative never lay with it anyway. The initiative was on the streets and any campaign which involves street politics needs its leadership on the streets also; otherwise it ceases to lead. [14]

Having put the NICRA leadership in its place the local militants gathered in Duke Street on 5 October in an attempt to defy the ban. Some British Labour MPs were there and John Hume and Eddie McAteer turned up after initially being unsure about the wisdom of the exercise. They marched up to the police line and stopped. Betty Sinclair, the NICRA Secretary, climbed on a chair and advised people to go home.

'There must be no violence,' shouted Miss Sinclair, to a barrage of disagreement. [15]

Michael Farrell recalls that the bus carrying members of the Young Socialists Alliance (YSA) from Belfast was half an hour late and when they arrived Betty Sinclair was already into her speech. [16] The YSA was a non-party organisation composed of militant Socialists, whose exploits on 5 October were its main claim to fame and it was dissolved by the end of the year. The Cameron Report (which was stronger on finding out what happened when than it was at political analysis) found that the YSA

threw their placards and banners at the police, and that some stones were thrown at the police from the crowd. After about five minutes, many of the police. having drawn their batons individually, the County Inspector ordered them to disperse the march. [87]

The *Londonderry Sentinel* reporter observed that "There was a surge of youngish people towards the police and marchers broke their placard sticks to use as weapons against the police." [88] Batons and a water cannon were used and the crowd was dispersed very quickly but rioting broke out over the next 24 hours on the west bank, shops were looted and young hooligans attempted to build barricades. On the Sunday afternoon Frank Curran observed that "a mob of about eight hundred" assembled. "The young men were better prepared than the Duke Street marchers. Steel rods and bricks were in plentiful supply; petrol bombs made their first appearance, hissing like blazing arrows into the police ranks." [89]

Back in the City Hotel, on the evening of 5 October,

In a corner Miss Sinclair was loudly denouncing the 'hooligans and anarchists' who had provoked the police and 'ruined our reputation'. [90]

Betty Sinclair was not unsympathetic to the Republican tradition. She had, after all, participated in the Easter Rising 50th anniversary celebrations in Belfast in 1966. [91] But in terms of tactics she and the Communist Party were regarded as moderates by the new breed of Socialist Revolutionaries. Eamonn McCann said that by July 1968

our conscious, if unspoken, strategy was to provoke the police into over-reaction and thus spark off mass reaction against the authorities. We assumed that we would be in control of the reaction, that we were strong enough to channel it. [92]

Some leading figures like Gerry Fitt and Eddie McAteer received minor injuries. According to Gerry Adams

The republicans decided that if there was going to be trouble the people who should get hit should be the visiting MPs who had been invited to attend as

observers. As the late Liam McMillan recalled in a pamphlet:

'The Belfast republicans had been instructed in the event of the parade being halted by police cordons to push leading nationalist politicians or any other dignatories into police ranks. This they did to such effect that one became the first casualty of the day of violence, receiving a busted head.' [93]

The marchers' injuries were slight, Two policemen were detained in hospital but no protesters. A hospital spokesman said that an analysis of the injuries to marchers showed that minimal force had been used. Many of the injured had been struck by stones thrown by people in the crowd. [94]

The confrontation in Duke Street was fairly minor although the rioting afterwards was not. But compared with the violence in Paris in May 1968 when the CRS riot police hit everything in sight, the October march barely justified a couple of column inches in the international media. Liam de Paor, a Dublin lecturer who was certainly no Unionist sympathiser, wrote: "The conduct of the RUC in Derry on 5 October 1968 was no worse than that of any police force in similar circumstances acting on similar instructions." [95] It was certainly absurd to suggest that it put in question the whole basis of the Northern Ireland state as some people have suggested. The suppression of the Paris riots did no such thing in a French context, even though the force used by the police was so much greater. When the Eire police used their batons to disperse a sit down protest on O'Connell Bridge organised by members of the Dublin Housing Action Committee in January 1969, the event went unnoticed. Allowing the October march to proceed would have been an unsatifactory option as it might have led to anarchy. If you do not permit the dispersal of an illegal and violent parade by force then you must accept that people can march where and when they like regardless of the consequences, and those consequences would be much more severe than in the Surrey stockbroker belt.

However, the details of who did what on 5 October were not important. The march was far more significant in showing that a group of organisers had emerged who were prepared to engage in confrontation if necessary, and that this was a tactic which had made Terence O'Neill's government consider concessions to the minority community. Immediately after the confrontation the Moderate Middle Class Catholics (including John Hume) formed the Derry Citizens Action Committee (DCAC) on 9 October 1968, committed to peaceful protest. Eamonn McCann refused to support it. The Catholic community therefore had a choice between potentially violent confrontation and reasonable, non-violent action. In effect it chose to keep both options open. The Socialist Revolutionaries had made the initial assault but now influence passed to the sweet reasonable people so that they could act as the recipients of concessions. Such people operated best in the shadow of violence. The turn of the revolutionaries would come again within a few months. In the meantime the IRA men played out their role as impeccably behaved stewards, more cautious than the militant Socialists, happy to bide their time.

A DCAC march on 16 November 1968, skilfully designed to assert the right to walk anywhere it wanted by sheer force of numbers, taught the Catholic community valuable lessons about the inadequate resources of the Royal Ulster Constabulary. The police were unable to cover all the approaches to the Walled City and the marchers, some 15,000 strong, made a detour around the police cordons, swept through an unguarded gate and did as they pleased. The ban was made inoperable. Protestant residents did protest and there was a violent confrontation but they were hopelessly outnumbered. It was a Catholic victory over the Unionist population and the occupation of the Walled City, where 10,000 Protestants had died in the Siege of Londonderry to secure civil and religious liberty throughout the United Kingdom, was a symbolic prize. Later "Group after group spread upon the streets until it seemed that a competition was in train to see how many times the Craig parade ban could be smashed." Curran's perception of the situation was that "the police abdicated, leaving the city to the celebrating multitude." [96]

The irony was that the alleged "police state" of Northern Ireland had too few policmen to enforce controls on large marches. There were only 3,000 RUC men to police 1,500,000 people, and only about 90 of them were permanently based in the City of Londonderry. As they worked 3 shifts, only a third of them were available at any one time. In Londonderry 30 of the 90 policemen were tied up in administrative jobs so at any time there were usually only 20 RUC officers available to oppress 30,000 Catholics. [97] Jim Callaghan noted that it would often take 3,000-4,000 policemen to control a large march on a Sunday afternoon in London. The anti-Vietnam War demo at Grosvenor Square in October 1968 saw 8,000 police on duty. [98]

The Spirit of 1968

Was there any particular reason for the upsurge in street activity in 1968? There was undoubtedly a combination of factors. One of the most important was the worldwide pattern of protest in that year. Violent demonstrations, occupations and rioting quite suddenly became commonplace, particularly in West Germany, France and the United States. Large anti-Vietnam War demonstrations were held in London. This was a student-led, and hence middle class, revolt. In Britain only 25% of students were from working class families, in France the figure was 16% and West Germany 5%. [99]

Looking back 20 years later a *Times* editorial correctly stated: "In any systematic way, the events of 1968 were participated in, watched, and read about largely by the richest, most comfortable, most bored, most spoilt." It concluded "1968 was not a revolt of the masses, but a revolt against the masses." [100] Even in 1971, when I went to university, those of us who were from the working class minority were expected to conform to middle class attitudes. We would be lectured by middle class revolutionaries about a working class which only existed as a kind of Marxist theoretical construct. Many working class students were absorbed into this trendy milieu.

Given that the 5 October march was controlled by the Socialist Revolutionaries, the pattern of events on that day was wholly explicable in terms of what was happening elsewhere. The form of protest - a march followed by rioting - was an approved method of expressing dissent. The organisers would have also hoped that middle class liberals in Britain, in reading about the unrest, would interpret events as favourably as they had done elsewhere. Michael Farrell said of the Londonderry march: "The effect was electric, especially among students. This was our Paris, our Prague, our Chicago." [101] What was different was the composition of the marchers. Although students and ex-students were well represented, most of the protestors were ordinary Catholics. The rioters in the Bogside were local youths.

This brings us to the second important feature of the worldwide events of 1968, the expectations of the protestors. Some of the slogans used in France summed up the mood: "Everything is Possible", "Take Your Dreams for Reality", "Power to the Imagination". The French tend to be a little poetic, but the message was clear. In 1968 there was a feeling that everything could be changed. It was this mood which was caught by ordinary Catholics. Their revived hopes were not for "civil rights" but for more substantial changes. The idea of persuading the Protestants of the need for a united Ireland, which was born out of the defeat and hopelessness of the early 1960s, came to be seen as far too timid. The Labour government, which had withdrawn from Cyprus and Aden, might instantly turn Irish dreams into reality.

The revival of Republican aspirations had been taking place for some time. Far from witnessing a willingness to accept that Northern Ireland was part of the United Kingdom and a movement away from Republicanism, the "civil rights" era actually saw a move in the opposite direction. Christopher Hewitt has shown that votes cast for parties committed to a united Ireland at Westminster elections went from 26% in 1956 (shortly before the opening of the IRA's campaign) to 14.5% in 1959 (with the IRA effectively defeated) to 18.2% in 1964 and 21.1% in 1966. There was a similar trend in Stormont elections.

To conclude, all indicators of nationalist sentiment among Catholics show an increase in the period just before NICRA became active. The low point comes in the late 1950s or early 1960s, thereafter nationalist support increases steadily. Immediately prior to the NICRA agitation nationalist sentiment was at a peak comparable to what it was just before the IRA campaign started in 1956. [102]

In October 1968 the more militant tactics (but not the revolutionary politics) of the Socialists suited the younger Bogsiders. But the doctrine of non-violent direct action also had its supporters and was part of the worldwide pattern of protest. The Derry Citizens Action Committee was for a few months part of that tradition with its more or less peaceful marches and sit down protests.

The O'Neill Factor

If in 1968 there was a general hope of making dreams come true, the extent to which these hopes persisted depended on the perceived willingness of those in government to give in to pressure. The Labour government at Westminster seemed to be a soft touch, but the existence of a liberal Northern Ireland government under Terence O'Neill, who had taken over as Ulster's prime minister in 1963, also played a role in shaping events.

O'Neill spent the first years of his life living in London's Mayfair in a house with 10 servants including a nanny and a Swiss governess. He was educated at a preparatory school in Winchester and at Eton College. His grandparents had inherited Shanes Castle in Northern Ireland and members of his family lived there, but O'Neill only visited Ulster in his holidays. After school he went to France and Austria to learn languages, worked on the English Stock Exchange and then was the civilian ADC to the Governor of South Australia. He joined the Irish Guards during the war and married an Engishwoman. O'Neill finally took up residence in Northern Ireland in 1945 when he was in his 30s and he was elected unopposed to the Stormont Parliament a year later. His father had been an Ulster Westminister MP and had drilled the Ulster Volunteers in the Ballymena area during the 1912-14 crisis. Unfortunately O'Neill seems to have taken after his too trusting grandmother, whose Shanes Castle home was burnt down by Sinn Fein.

She was strictly impartial in her employment policies because she pleaded that with her London and Scottish background she knew nothing about Irish affairs. It was a terrible shock to her when the house was burnt. I can remember in her old age she would often say to me: 'After all that kindness they burnt down my home.' Many other large houses in Ireland had military guards at that time, but she refused to have one. At the crucial moment of the fire the head forester, a Catholic, refused to ring the fire-bell - kindness did not seem to count in those terrible days. [103]

Many would argue that O'Neill also knew little about Irish affairs. Bernadette Devlin may well have been right when she said: "With his lack of warmth, and with his Eton-and-guards-regiment background, his main problem as Prime Minister of Northern Ireland was that at no stage did he ever belong." [104]

When Terence O'Neill became prime minister his policies were expressed in rather woolly terms. He wanted to "improve community relations"; he was against "religious bigotry"; he sought "justice and fairness". They were lovely warm sounding phrases much loved by middle class liberals. O'Neill in many ways embodied the worst aspects of the English middle class at the time. He gathered around him a group of liberal Unionists: journalists, academics, civil servants and businessmen who came to dominate the Unionist Party. Grass roots Loyalists lost control of their own political movement. O'Neill spent much of his time as prime minister jetting around the globe trying to meet world figures. In his autobiography the people he met were typically described as "pleasant", "nice", "charming" and the meetings were "cordial". There was little mention of the moral or political virtues of the individuals concerned. He was most at home amongst cosmopolitan people engaged in polite conversation.

O'Neill was a typical 1960s materialist who believed that rising standards of living would solve most political problems. He also rejected historical tradition, as did most of 1960s man. There was a vague feeling that material and technical progress was the most important consideration and as there was unparalleled material prosperity at the time then we had somehow reached the highest stage of civilisation to date. As the development of technology and the wealth it brought did not seem to depend on the study of the past but on the study of totally new methods, history was irrelevant. Completely new and improved standards applied. The past was a burden, full of the ignorance and prejudice which the new rational materialism would banish. If we could all be nice to each other and get plenty of consumer goods, all would be well. O'Neill was to say in a 1969 radio interview:

The basic fear of the Protestants in Northern Ireland is that they will be outbred by the Roman Catholics. It is as simple as that. It is frightfully hard to explain to a Protestant that if you give Roman Catholics a good job and a good house, they will live like Protestants, because they will see neighbours with cars and television sets.

They will refuse to have 18 children, but if the Roman Catholic is jobless and lives in a ghastly hovel, he will rear 18 children on national assistance.

It is impossible to explain this to a militant Protestant, because he is so keen to deny civil rights to his Roman Catholic neighbours. He cannot understand, in fact, that if you treat Roman Catholics with due consideration and kindness they will live like Protestants, in spite of the authoritative nature of their church.[105]

I tend to agree with Richard Rose that such arguments would be unlikely to make Catholics "exchange their religion, nationality and politics for all the cars and television sets that Stormont can offer".[106] Hooked on consumer society individualism, he could not see that most people in Ulster were motivated by non-materialistic political values. Catholics were never going to give up their aspirations for a united Ireland in return for the good life. They would take the financial benefits of being part of the United Kingdom and still retain the dream of their forebearers. For a united Ireland was not a goal pursued as a result of conducting a cost-benefit analysis. It was and is a dream, an objective with an almost mystical attraction.

O'Neill told the Irish Association in February 1968:

The people of England have a considerable sense of history, and a varied chronicle to which they can apply it, but who seriously imagines today that the Sussex farmer or the plater on Tyneside dwells upon Nelson or Wellington, Magna Carta or the Reform Bill? They are far more concerned with the value of their take-home pay, with job stability, with the education of their

*children. I think the idea that people on this side of the Irish Sea have some
different motivation is a myth which ought to be exposed. If the publicists
and the politicians and the propagandists were to mute their historic
trumpet calls, who would call for a reprise when the last note had died
away?*[107]

He was right to think that the English had temporarily turned their backs on
their history, but he was wrong about the people of Ulster. The Battle of the
Boyne and the Siege of Londonderry were honoured historical events because
they taught valuable lessons about the present: that civil and religious liberty
was only secured at an enormous price and is only maintained by vigilance, and
if necessary by sacrifice. Goethe once said that those who do not learn from
history are doomed to relive it. O'Neill was about to relive a historical conflict
he did not understand.

For Captain Terence O'Neill the problem of Catholic agitation could be solved
by removing the alleged causes of their stated grievances and by ensuring a fair
allocation of material resources. His aim was to commit Catholics to Ulster's
membership of the United Kingdom by being nice to them. Like most middle
class liberals in Britain he desperately wanted to believe in the validity of the
"civil rights" complaints (without ever examining them in detail) so that his
preferred "solution" to Ulster's problems would be relevant. Prejudice in the
market place was economically inefficient, so all he had to do was banish
prejudice and ensure the rational functioning of economic mechanisms. The
Protestants of Londonderry would be prevented from hogging all the houses
and the Bogside Catholics would see that a nice car and television set were
preferable to a united Ireland.

Hence after the events of October/November 1968 in Londonderry O'Neill
took the opportunity to force a number of changes past a reluctant Unionist
Party. The Londonderry Corporation was suspended and replaced by a
Development Commission. On 22 November 1968 it was announced that there
would be a housing allocation scheme (points system) for all publicly owned
houses. A Parliamentary Commission for Administration was to be set up to
examine allegations of maladministration or discrimination by public bodies.
Local government reorganisation would be completed by 1971. The company
vote in local government elections was to be abolished. In April 1969 the
introduction of a universal franchise for council elections was announced, and
in July the same year it was confirmed that electoral divisions in the new
council areas would be drawn up by an independent statutory commission.

There can be no doubt that it came as a complete surprise to O'Neill that this programme of reforms, which substantially met the demands of the "civil rights" campaigners, did not solve the problem. Unrest in 1969 only seemed to get worse.

As he did not seem to understand the context in which he was operating, O'Neill had little grasp of how his actions would be interpreted. This got him into trouble early in his prime ministerial career. As we have seen, the written Constitution of the Irish Republic claims jurisdiction over Northern Ireland. Successive prime ministers of the Republic had refused to renounce this claim. Lord Brookeborough, who was O'Neill's predecessor, had refused to meet his opposite number in the South until the territorial claim was withdrawn. O'Neill endorsed this view on taking office in 1963 and again in July 1964.[108] Then in January 1965 he suddenly met Eire premier Sean Lemass at Stormont without informing his own cabinet.

O'Neill's idea was that by taking the initiative and showing he was prepared to be nice, there would be an improvement in relations and a recognition of Ulster's constitutional position. He probably thought that Eire would see a contradiction between their aggressive claims to Northern Ireland and their stated desire for better relations. Eire saw no such contradiction. Eamon de Valera said in 1957 that the best way to end partition was "to have as close relations as they could with those in the six counties and try to get them to combine on matters and interests common to them both".[109] This strategy has been pursued in modern times through the Anglo-Irish Agreement. Talks therefore did not indicate a loss of interest in a united Ireland, merely an interest in pursuing this goal by different means.

O'Neill was soon to realise that his action, without any removal of the South's claims to govern Ulster, was interpreted as a sign of weakness. He met Lemass's successor, Jack Lynch, in 1967 only for Lynch to say shortly after the October 1968 march in Londonderry: "Partition is the first and foremost root cause of such demonstrations and partition arose out of British policy."[110] Later in the same month Lynch told the Anglo-Irish Parliamentary Group at Westminster that "the clashes in the streets of Derry are an expression of the evils which partition has brought in its train."[111]

The "civil rights" agitation was taken at face value by O'Neill. He was keen to win the support of the Moderate Middle Class Catholics. It really did not occur to him that even these moderates only saw "civil rights" as a means to an end and hence that once their initial demands were met they would soon be keen to press on towards a united Ireland. O'Neill was certainly dismayed that once he had conceded the "civil rights" demands the concessions were dismissed by the campaigners as being of little value. Some writers have said the reforms were "too little too late". In fact the reforms gave the "civil rights" movement what it said it wanted just 3 months after NICRA's first march. But it was also true that they were too little, because the movement always wanted more than it demanded.

If the "civil rights" complaints were insubstantial and the concessions made were dismissed as being of little value by the movement (thus rather confirming the Unionist interpretation of events), what was the point of the "civil rights" agitation? Straightforward demands for a united Ireland had got nowhere. Neither the British nor the Northern Ireland government was in the least bit interested. Worse than that, the Loyalist majority in Ulster had occupied what might be called a position of moral superiority in the eyes of the British people for much of this century. Firstly they were in a majority and hence the demand of a minority to overthrow the Constitiution was seen as inherently undemocratic. Secondly the Loyalists were pro-British and the Republicans anti-British, and prior to the 1960s there was a preference for those who supported us rather than those who hated us.

The "civil rights" campaign was designed to blacken the Protestants' name. They had done such wicked things that the oppressed Catholics - guiltless and vulnerable - should be seen as morally superior. To a large extent it worked, helped by the general mood of the 1960s with a guilt-ridden middle class looking for oppressed people everywhere (particularly those the British were alleged to have oppressed) so that they could make restitution and feel a little less guilty. The mood also afflicted part of the Protestant middle class in Ulster and Terence O'Neill was their hero.

The most important aim of Catholic politicians was to get some movement in positions which had been fixed for some time. They needed to create some forward momentum and get the Unionists pedalling backwards. The ancient power struggle required "us" to find a way of putting one over on "them". The IRA's Tomas MacGiolla said the "civil rights" movement "has succeeded in moving what was considered hitherto to be an immovable object".[112] "Civil rights" did get O'Neill back-pedalling, keen to make concessions based on English assumptions about politics which had no validity in the very different Ulster situation. The reforms were seen as an admission of guilt and displayed

O'Neills willingness to make concessions in the face of violent protest. They were an open invitation to see how far the cycle of agitation and concessions could be pushed. As the Unionist leadership had admitted its community's guilt, the reforms also established the idea of concessions as a kind of restitution for past wrongs, which still plagues Ulster politics today.

It was really not until 1974 that the O'Neillite section of the Protestant middle class was expelled from the Unionist political scene and the Loyalist grass roots finally reasserted control of the organisations operating in their name. Hence at the time that it was most needed the Protestant case against the "civil rights" movement went largely unstated because O'Neill had no wish that the movement's central demands should be questioned. His reforms would bring about Catholic support for Ulster's position as part of the United Kingdom and this could not happen if the grievances which were the reason for the reforms were submitted to any substantial challenge.

O'Neill gave to Unionism's opponents a series of symbolic prizes. They had little intrinsic value but they meant a great deal. Let us take the example of the universal franchise in local government elections. When this was granted it made very little difference to election results. In itself it was neither a significant gain for Catholics nor a significant loss for Protestants. Most Unionists had come to the view that, on the general merits of the case, a universal franchise should be introduced. However the context in which they were being asked to grant this reform was important. Catholics claimed that the restricted franchise greatly disadvantaged them. This was not so. But the claim was that Unionists had deliberately withheld the universal franchise as a way of oppressing them. The concession of "one man, one vote" was therefore seen as an admission of guilt and a Catholic victory.

Sometimes we may see 2 dogs fighting over a bone. One puts the other to flight but then contemptuously abandons the bone, in which he has lost interest. The important thing is the victory, not the prize. Or to put it another way, the real prize is the victory and the psychological edge it gives over the vanquished. Catholics, in forcing the concession in those particular circumstances, did gain a psychological edge. The Protestant leadership lost self-confidence and had suddenly become predisposed to make further concessions. On the Catholic side there was no great celebration at achieving a universal franchise because it was of little value, even though it had previously been of fundamental importance according to "civil rights" propaganda. Unionist resistance to this change was based on an argument that it would not stop the street agitation and this was entirely the wrong time to be announcing another concession. It became a big issue simply because it was a bone of contention. Both sides knew that in Ulster you really shouldn't give up a bone in these circumstances. Better to wait until the controversy blows over.

Students and Protestants

People's Democracy had been formed at Queen's University in the immediate aftermath of the October march in Londonderry. Before the end of the year it organised some events, particularly in Belfast, but over in Londonderry that period was dominated by the moderates in the DCAC. The new year brought big changes.

The O'Neill reform package of November 1968 encouraged the cautious DCAC to agree to a suspension of marches to allow the package to be implemented. But Peoples's Democracy, in particular Michael Farrell, felt the need for further confrontation. The organisation initially turned down the proposal to hold a march from Belfast to Londonderry but finally the idea was pushed through a poorly attended meeting at Queen's during the Christmas vacation. The march was due to arrive in Londonderry on 4 January 1969. All the leading moderate Catholics opposed the march. John Hume thought it would lead to sectarian violence.[113] When the marchers stopped overnight near Maghera, Kevin Agnew arranged for armed IRA men to guard them.[114] The march aroused hostility in Loyalist areas as it traversed the patchwork of Protestant and Catholic villages along the route. On the final day of the march on the approach to Burntollet Bridge the police warned that there was a crowd of Protestants up ahead and the marchers safety could not be guaranteed.[115] The organisers insisted on going ahead and they came under a violent attack in which many of them were injured. Later as they straggled into Londonderry stones were thrown at them as they passed the Protestant Irish Street estate. Catholics rioted in the city that night.

It was not pretty. All we can do is to try and understand why there was this Protestant response. The previous night Ian Paisley had held a religious meeting in the Londonderry Guildhall. A Catholic mob gathered outside and attacked men, women and children as they left the meeting. A car belonging to someone at the meeting was burnt by the mob. The Burntollet incident was a Protestant backlash against this violence aimed at those who were seen as stirring up trouble so soon after a series of concessions had been made to the "civil rights" movement. Militant Protestants perceived in the pattern of events the Republican violence which was to come, long before the academics and journalists. Their reaction on this one occasion was unfortuantely to try and put events into reverse by the use of violence.

Farrell certainly saw the value of martyrdom and was happy to march into the confrontation against the advice of the police. Many of the non-revolutionaries in People's Democracy were alienated and it lost its broad appeal. Protestant support disappeared, and this was to worry Eamonn McCann and Bernadette Devlin. They were concerned at the religious polarisation their activities had created. This process was further advanced by another People's Democracy march in Newry on 11 January. Marchers attacked the police and burnt a number of their vehicles. Farrell and 12 colleagues occupied the post office and Cyril Toman was said to have "attempted to organise local teenagers into a 'People's Army".[116] John Hume was present but he was simply swept aside by the mob.

In February 1969 People's Democracy contested a number of seats in the Stormont general election. In places where there was a straight fight with the Unionists they simply got the Republican vote, perhaps to the disappointment of those who still naively hoped that the Protestant working class might support them. For instance, the South Londonderry seat of Major James Chichester-Clark was contested by Bernadette Devlin and she was beaten by 9,195 votes to 5,812. There had been no contest in the constituency since 1949 when a Unionist beat a Nationalist candidate by 9,193 voters to 5,909. Little had changed. Elsewhere People's Democracy members took votes from the more traditional Republican candidates. This showed that there was support from part of the Catholic community for the organisation's militant tactics. Michael Farrell wrote that

Even at this stage the PD candidates argued that the only real solution to the Northern problem was the creation of an Irish Socialist Republic.[117]

This explained the lack of Protestant votes. It was no consolation to Protestants that this was to be a different form of united Ireland. They preferred to stay within the United Kingdom.

In Londonderry John Hume, standing as an independent, replaced the Nationalist Party's Eddie McAteer as the Foyle constituency's MP. This was another vote of confidence in the new "civil rights" tactics, which were clearly more effective. Eamonn McCann, the NILP candidate, got 12% of the vote, mainly from the young militants.

Meanwhile People's Democracy concentrated more of its efforts on working within NICRA. The Secretary of NICRA in the early part of 1969, John McAnerney, saw this as a process of infiltration and thought Michael Farrell and Frank Gogarty were the main figures behind it. McAnerney was told a month before the NICRA AGM that Betty Sinclair would be removed as Chairman and replaced by Gogarty. He noticed a significant influx of young members from the university area before the AGM. The predicted change did take place and Farrell and Kevin Boyle of PD were voted onto the NICRA Committee.[118]

Bernadette Devlin said the Socialist Revolutionaries successfully forced out the Communists because they were "as reactionary as the Unionists".[119] In March 1969 Heatley, McAnerney, Sinclair and Shearer resigned from the NICRA Committee and issued a statement saying:

> *We have been taken over by people preaching the most extreme form of revolutionary socialism, the sort of politics that have been causing trouble in France, Germany, Japan and many other parts of the world.* [120]

The IRA was more content to bide its time and Dr. Con McCluskey of the CSJ even went so far as to

> *point out how correctly republicans have adhered to the spirit of our movement, never at any time trying to promote their own political views.*[121]

Catholics and Revolutionaries

By virtue of the make up of its supporters the "civil rights" movement quickly became Catholic and Republican. The moderates and the IRA were not unduly disturbed by this, but some of the Socialist Revolutionaries were. They were far less pragmatic than the other groups. For many of them it was important that the Protestant working class should be cultivated to achieve the kind of workers republic they desired. To other sections of the "civil rights" movement the end was more important than the means. There were several routes to a united Ireland and in the final analysis any form of united Ireland would be acceptable.

The Socialist Revolutionaries believed that the capitalist system was to blame for social problems such as poor housing. People were being oppressed because they were workers, not because they were Catholics. Catholics and Protestants were both being exploited and had a common class interest. The enemy was the Tories of both religions. What was needed was a class based revolution.

The basic problem they had was that there was no political market for their product. The Catholic community, even though it was happy to resort to revolutionary methods from time to time to "free Ireland", was basically very conservative and did not agree with the Socialist political analysis of the situation. The only way the revolutionaries could play a significant role was by promoting very similar aims to the rest of the "civil rights" movement in relation to discrimination and gerrymandering. Their militant methods made them popular as a "civil rights" ginger group. But the problem was how to get back to the basic Socialist analysis, oppose the Catholic employers and attract Protestant working class support.

Eamonn McCann noted that when the 16 November march had occupied the Walled City there were many speeches attacking the Unionist Party.

No attack was made on any political philosophy accepted by any section of the Catholics. No mention was made of Frank McLaughlin, slum landlord.

Because by that time the movement, now led by the Citizens Action Committee was a mass Catholic alliance, uniting Catholics of all classes and all non-unionist political parties.

It had become impossible to criticize a Catholic on a Civil Rights platform without being denounced as a 'wrecker'.[122]

Bernadette Devlin had similar concerns:

Over the months the CRA has moved in a natural progression from demanding something for the minority (that is, the Catholics); to demanding Catholic equality; to demanding Catholic power. This has been better appreciated by the Paisleyites, who are in no doubt that it is a Catholic movement, than by the civil rights supporters. [123]

She complained that

you had Catholic slum landlords marching virtuously beside the tenants they exploited, Catholic employers marching in protest against the Protestants they excluded from their factories.[124]

Bernadette found it difficult to take the anti-Protestant line because of an incident in her childhood. Her mother had married the son of a roadsweeper, which angered her snobbish grandmother, who ran a pub, forge and stables in Cookstown. So influential was this woman that when Miss Devlin's parents sought references to apply for a Housing Trust property, no Catholic could be found who was prepared to risk offending grandmother. In the end 2 Protestant councillors provided the references.[125] This was all the more noteworthy because Bernadette Devlin felt that her father was probably in the IRA.

McCann thought

It is perfectly obvious that people do still see themselves as Catholics and Protestants, and the cry 'get the Protestants' is still very much on the lips of the Catholic working class. Everyone applauds loudly when one says in a speech that we are not sectarian, we are fighting for the rights of all Irish workers, but really that's because they see this as the new way of getting at the Protestants. [126]

Operating within a Catholic movement had brought great benefits.

since October 5th, we have found that we have an audience listening to us and applauding us, of tens of thousands of people. We got carried away by this, and submerged the Young Socialist Alliance in the PD; we submerged our politics into the Civil Rights movement. All that we managed to get across was that we were more extreme than the Civil Rights people.[127]

It was then difficult to promote left wing Socialist principles.

we have been frightened of scaring off our mass audience. We thought that we had to keep these people, bring them along, educate and radicalize them. It was a lot of pompous nonsense and we failed absolutely to change the consciousness of the people. The consciousness of the people who are fighting in the streets at the moment is sectarian and bigoted. [128]

Bernadette Devlin found that "the more socialist and more determined PD grew, the fewer its numbers became."[129] Both Devlin and Farrell talked about attempts to change the "civil rights" demand for a fair allocation of jobs and houses into a demand for more jobs and houses for everyone.[130] The Derry Labour Party took up this line and in October 1969 (by then far too late) was demanding "An end to the concentration on religious discrimination. Instead a programme to end the shortage of jobs and houses."[131]

There were differences about the idea of embarking on an unpopular but ideologically pure road to Socialism. Bernadette Devlin summed up the situation thus:

There is no denying that my personal position is much closer to Eamonn than it is to Michael. This is not a personality clash. There is a difference in tactics. It depends on whether one accepts that you have a base in the Catholic working class and that you then proceed to radicalise them, leaving the door open for the Protestants to join or whether you move completely out and take very few people with you, standing on a clear, socialist basis, taking only part of the Catholic working class and definitely cutting off the Catholic middle class and thereby beginning to get more of the Protestant working class to stand with you. These are two different approaches. That is why in some cases Michael Farrell might be seen as a militant Catholic. I don't mean that he is sectarian but he is using Catholic militancy as a base on which to build his socialist movement rather than using the fundamental principles of socialism.[132]

Michael Farrell stated his own position as follows:

I do not want to be represented as an advocate of 'Catholic Power', but I do insist that we have to explore the radical possibilities of the base that we do have, at this moment, among the working class, and that base is the Catholic section of the working class.[133]

Given that Farrell was less concerned about being part of an essentially Catholic movement, it is surprising that he was the most opposed to working with other Catholic organsations. Bernadette Devlin was chosen as a Unity candidate to contest the Mid Ulster Westminster by-election in April 1969. She was a compromise candidate chosen by a meeting of Catholic organisations after Austin Currie of the Nationalist Party, Kevin Agnew, and ex-IRA prisoner Tom Mitchell agreed to stand down. Farrell and People's Democracy refused to help but Eamonn McCann stood by her. For Devlin the important thing was to campaign on the right programme. "I fought the election honestly on the non-sectarian, radical socialist politics I believed in", she said, "but too many

Catholic Conservatives came out in support of what they saw as 'the pan papist candidate'"[134]

Several thousand of my votes were definitely dishonest. They came from Nationalist sympathizers who told themselves, 'We don't agree with one solitary word she says, but better a Catholic we don't agree with than a Unionist.' [135]

It underlined the fact that whatever the small group of Socialist Revolutionaries said or did, the Catholic population would simply ignore the bits they didn't like and bestow support on a purely pragmatic basis. The revolutionaries were for the moment useful, no more than that. In particular young Catholic youths

we're not interested in the theories of the People's Democracy, or in the socialist doctrines of Eamonn McCann, Michael Farrell or Bernadette Devlin. The idea of class solidarity with Protestant workers was so foreign to them that it did not even offend them. But the tone and the air of civil rights militants - the sheer you-be-damned style of things - impressed them.[136]

The likes of McCann and Devlin were less concerned about the Republican nature of the "civil rights" movement, as long as it was the right sort of Republicanism. McCann said: "we must try to set up some sort of radical socialist front between republicans and ourselves."[137] He would not have wanted a united Ireland dominated by "Green Tories" (middle class Catholic conservatives). But the ultimate goal of the Socialist Revolutionaries was always clear. Devlin was able to say of her position at the end of 1968:

I had moved from traditional, mad, emotional Republicanism to socialism in the context of Ulster; now I was joining my new-found socialism to my old belief in a united Ireland. Only in a thirty-two-county Ireland could socialism even begin to work.[138]

In April 1969 Michael Farrell was repeating what for him had been a consistent position:

the border must go because it is a relic of imperialism, and in order to root out imperialism we have to root out the neo-imperialist set-up in the South and the neo-colonial one in the North.... The unification of Ireland into a socialist republic is not only necessary for the creation of a viable economy, it must also be an immediate demand, because only the concept of a socialist republic can ever reconcile Protestant workers, who rightly have a very deep-seated fear of a Roman Catholic republic, to the ending of the border.[139]

In fact the greater emphasis on a united Ireland cut the Socialist Revolutionaries off completely from the Protestant working class.

It would be only fair to also draw attention to another honest, but suicidal, attempt by the Socialist Revolutionaries to maintain the kind of consistent position which the other Catholic groups never attempted to uphold. They decided to have a march to Dublin to expose conditions in the South. Arrangements were made by Socialist organisations in the Irish Republic to receive the marchers. The trek culminated in a rally outside the General Post Office in O'Connell Street on 7 April 1969. Michael Farrell criticised unemployment and poor housing in the South, which was no more than Southern Socialists and Republicans were doing, but by the time they reached Dublin the People's Democracy supporters were taking a pasting in the Irish press.

The trouble started at the border where Cyril Toman produced a copy of a novel banned in the South in protest against severe censorship laws there. On the way to Dublin marchers were asked about Irish laws which prevented divorce and the importation and sale of contraceptives. They replied that these things were a denial of civil rights to Protestants in the South. Irish Catholics were furious. It was all very well these people marching to Dublin to tell them how oppressed the Northern Catholics were, but to imply there was something wrong in the Irish Republic was going too far. When Farrell said that Jack Lynch and Fianna Fail only supported the struggle in the North to distract attention from their own slums and unemployment, it went down like a lead balloon.[140]

John Feeney, the Southern Socalist who co-ordinated arrangements for the march, claimed he had received assurances from PD that they wouldn't give prominence to the issues of birth control or censorship and said Toman's actions were "calculated to offend the rebublican socialist feelings of a large section of the Twenty-Six Counties."[141] Fergus Woods (who had been a PD Stormont candidate in South Down) dismissed the Dublin march as "a gimmick for Protestant support".[142] In looking back at this event Michael Farrell said recently:

*We had a lot to learn about the dynamics of Southern society. One thing
we learnt quickly enough, however, was how a movement that was
lionised when it challenged the Unionist regime in the North could be
vilified when it turned its attentions to the South.*[143]

It was yet another lesson that the Socialist Revolutionaries would only be
supported by Catholics if they performed a clearly defined role which served
Catholic group interests.

April 1969: The End of "Civil Rights"

Terence O'Neill had called the Stormont general election of February 1969 to
gain support for his policies. In a number of constituencies pro- and anti-
O'Neill Unionists stood against each other. O'Neill did not get the unambiguous
result he wanted and almost lost his own seat to Ian Paisley, who stood as a
Protestant Unionist. He soldiered on for a while, just managed to get agreement
for a universal local government franchise and then resigned as prime minister
in April 1969.

"Civil rights" activists John Hume and Ivan Cooper had both been elected to
Stormont in February (for Foyle and Mid-Londonderry). They resigned as
Chairman and Vice Chairman of the Derry Citizens Action Committee in mid
March because their new "political" role conflicted with that of the "non
political" DCAC. About a week later Councillor James Doherty, the
Chairman of the Nationalist Party, resigned as DCAC Treasurer as he felt his
participation in the organisation was injuring the Nationalist Party.[144] This was
effectively the end of the DCAC's influence on events, which thereafter
spiralled out of control.

We have seen that by April 1969 the Socialist Revolutionaries were committed
to the idea of a united Ireland and not only saw their "civil rights" campaign as
consistent with this objective, but actually viewed it as a means of bringing the
objective about. This much they had in common with the Moderate Middle
Class Catholics and the IRA in the early days of the "civil rights" era. But how
had the thinking of these other groups progressed?

John Hume was by now writing in a newspaper article about a strategy which
involved the 3 Rs - reform, reconciliation and reunification.[145] That was
unambiguous enough as to where he stood on Ulster's position within the

United Kingdom.

Meanwhile Sean Keenan, who had been the main speaker in Londonderrry during the 1966 Easter Rising celebrations, and who was to become a member of the Army Council of the Provisional IRA, was also making his position clear.[146] On Easter Sunday 1969, 5,000 people marched on a Republican parade from Letterkenny Road to the Guildhall Square. The Irish tricolour was prominently featured on the march, which stopped in Great James Street for a rendering of "A Soldier's Song", which was also sung at the close of the rally. This is , of course, the national anthem of the Irish Republic "composed for the Republican movement in 1907 as a song to encourage guerrilla soldiers to fight against the Crown."[147] At the rally Keenan said:

People of Derry, this is indeed a proud day. Never in all the years I have been associated with the Republican movement, have I seen such a crowd present in Guildhall Square, and for no other reason than that they believe in the reunification of Ireland. From this day forward let no man - politician or otherwise, - say that the people of Derry are British, or that they want British standards. We want Irish standards. Our enemy is still England.[148]

Sean Keenan represented that wing of the IRA which was not content to keep quiet about the ultimate aim. He felt that people were ready for more than "civil rights" and was no doubt unhappy that they might think that "civil rights" was an alternative to a united Ireland. Keenan had read the situation correctly. The previous Saturday a DCAC march had also attracted 5,000, and apart from the organisers, most of those taking part would have been the same people. The inhabitants of the Bogside were equally happy to turn out for "civil rights" and Republican parades.

Just a week after the Easter Sunday march the Nationalist Party gave a dinner in honour of their recently defeated MP, Eddie McAteer. He told the dinner guests:

We will pursue our quest for a United Ireland without apology and without regard to the offensive bribes dangled before us.[149]

Neil Blaney, a leading Fianna Fail politician and member of the Irish cabinet, also spoke at the dinner. He advocated a Federal Council of Ireland to control an "all-Irish defence force" and foreign affairs.

What I am saying is that the Unionist people of the Six Counties and the
people of our neighbour isle should recognise the futility of the Irish Border,
the increasing frustrations which its continuance builds up, and the fact that
it has one day to end.[150]

When further rioting broke out in Catholic areas of Londonderry on the
weekend of 19/20 April 1969 with bricks and petrol bombs being hurled at the
police, the *Derry Journal* reported that:

Mr. Liam Cosgrave, T.D. , leader of the Fine Gael Party, in a statement
yesterday, said that while events in the North were to be deplored it must be
realised that as long as Partition remained genuinely peaceful conditions
would not be maintained. [151]

Thus by April 1969 the Socalist Revolutionaries, the new breed of moderates,
the old breed of moderates, IRA members, the Irish prime minister, an Irish
government minister and the leader of the Irish opposition were all saying they
wanted a united Ireland. Every significant group in the "civil rights"
movement was openly campaigning to bring about a united Ireland, and yet
English political observers still thought that these people were neutral on the
constitutional question. There are none so blind as those who will not see.

Meanwhile John Hume was learning important lessons about extracting
concessions when there was a threat of violence present. A policeman had to
fire 2 shots in the air to extricate himself from an angry Catholic mob. In a
protest which blamed the policeman rather than the rioting mob, the population
of the Bogside evacuated their area on 20 April 1969 and held a meeting in the
Creggan. John Hume presented an ultimatum to the police:

The residents intend to return at 5 pm this afternoon and if the police are not
out of the area by then we will not be responsible for the consequences.[152]

Frank Curran felt that "The police faced the prospect of thousands of men and
women descending on them, literally ready to come to grips with them."[153] Ten
minutes before the deadline the police were ordered to pull out by Minister of
Home Affairs, Robert Porter.

Many writers talk of the sense of power which Catholics gained from such
climb downs and concessions.

For many militants the nature of the ultimate goal was less interesting than the sense of power actually wielded in the present, as contrasted with the long powerless past. [154]

Of the November 1968 reform package:

What they did was to confirm to the Catholic masses that the power which they were beginning to feel was real. When on 16 November fifteen thousand people stood in a mass on Craigavon Bridge confronting the police they felt being there in those numbers, real power in their grasp. That was a heady thing to happen to people from the Bogside, something which no cabinet minister could ever understand. [155]

The Catholics were a little drunk on the heady sensations of revolt: they had made Ulster a focal point of English affairs, they had had their cause ring through every home in Britain. [156]

The Catholic minority therefore "caught the scent of blood, changed its objectives and embarked on a campaign to destroy the Ulster State." [157] Such a change of direction can be explained completely in terms of the feeling of power linked to a belief that anything was possible. "Civil rights" demands were fine as short term expedients at a time when the Republican movement was weak. Now that it was gaining strength it could look forward to getting what it really wanted.

Cathal Goulding, the IRA Chief-of-Staff, had told the Belfast Telegraph in February 1969:

The IRA has never gone out of existence, and we don't intend that it should ever go out of existence. The physical force movement is continuing and it will stay until the final goal has been achieved. [158]

Those who had engaged in military training wanted to put it to use and often became impatient but "Now we train them for political agitation in the meantime, and make them aware of what is necessary for successful revolution." South of the border the IRA had been able to combine violence with campaigns on social issues.

In May 1968, the IRA burned out £60,000 worth of buses used to take workers to a factory owned by an American company, the E.I. Company of

Shannon, during a dispute over union recognition. In the west, in Rossaveal on the Connemara coast, a £6,000 fishing boat owned by an American-financed company was wrecked in August by an IRA bomb, and in June, 1969, a number of buildings on farms owned by Germans were set alight.[159]

The Road to Rebellion

In late June and July 1969 some of the tensions within the "civil rights" movement came to the surface. From the platform after a march in Strabane on 28 June, Bernadette Devlin said: "You must stand for the Protestant working people as well as the Catholic working people, yet you march arm-in-arm with people who discriminate against Protestants"[160] and "You march for employment in Strabane but you march with employers who pay low wages in Strabane."[161] John Hume retaliated with a press statement:

I am convinced that the approach to our problems of people like Mr. McCann and the People's Democracy - which is today far removed from the large number of students who sat down in Belfast last October - is more likely to lead to sectarian strife than the approach we advocate. [162]

The Derry Labour Party hit back with a statement of its own:

The Civil Rights Movement is now undeniably a Catholic movement. A Catholic movement on the streets, as John Hume well knows, will not bring about normal politics in Northern Ireland; it will drive deeper the wedge between Catholic and Protestant;[163]

Strabane had been the scene of another controversy a few months earlier. The Republican controlled Strabane Urban District Council had decided to dispense with the services of their Protestant solicitors, Messrs. Wilton and Simms, who had served the council for 3 generations, and had engaged a firm of Catholics. In December 1968 Laurence O'Kane tried to raise the matter at a meeting of the Strabane Branch of the Civil Rights Association. He was prevented from putting a motion deploring the decision. The branch contained Republican members of the council concerned. Mr. O'Kane walked out in protest, denouncing the local authority's decision as "blatant discrimination". Later a Mr. James Duffy resigned from the CRA branch committee because debate on the issue had been suppressed. [164]

There was another "civil rights" march in Newry on 5 July 1969. Tom

Mitchell, who had been an IRA officer during the 1950s and was later their commanding officer in Crumlin Road Jail, seemed to echo Sean Keenan's concerns in his speech from the platform.

The movement is a means to an end. There was a danger that the overall objective would be lost sight of, but I think that most of those associated with the campaign stand for the reunification of the country. Without that ultimate objective it would not be worth pursuing. We must work for reforms within the context of a 32-county Republic. [165]

That evening about 70 People's Democracy supporters met in Newry to discuss the future. Cyril Toman read out a document which said:

Believing that capitalism and the misery it engenders knows no bounds, the People's Democracy links its struggle in the Six Counties with the struggle against exploitation and repression in the Twenty-six Counties. It cannot be denied that the majority of Civil Rights supporters in the North believe in a united Ireland. [166]

He asked his audience: "How long are we prepared to go along with this farce of walking with Green Tories?" and Tom McCourt of the Derry Labour Party noted that "There are some large employers in the Civil Rights movement in Derry; their precious bloody unity is destroying any chance of uniting the working class."[167]

Meanwhile on the same day as the Newry march a funeral was taking place South of the border. On 25 August 1939 the IRA had planted a bomb in a crowded Coventry street as part of a terror campaign on the Mainland. An 81 year old man and 15 year old schoolboy were among the 5 people killed. Two IRA men, Peter Barnes and James McCormack, were convicted of the crime and were hanged in 1940. Their remains were returned to Ireland in 1969 and they were reburied in Mullingar, Co. Westmeath. 5,000 people turned out to honour these men and IRA gunmen fired a 3 volley salute over their graves.[168]

There was more serious rioting in Londonderry on the weekend of 12/13 July. On the Sunday about 300 youths broke the windows of commercial premises and threw stones and petrol bombs at the police. Barricades were built and a community centre, the Rossville Hall, was set on fire and completely destroyed. During the weekend various "civil rights" and DCAC figures tried to control the mob. Those who intervened included Father Tony Mulvey, Claude Wilton,

Brother O'Sullivan (Principal of the Christian Brothers School) and James Doherty. None were successful. Scarman concluded that the violence was not provoked by Protestants or police. "Their behaviour was wanton aggression."[169]

Eamonn McCann was also out trying to avert inter-communal violence. Even he was worried by events in July.

This has nothing to do with Civil Rights. The old primaeval instincts have come to the surface. It is a religious war.[170]

The Socialist Revolutionaries' desire for confrontation had brought many aggressive young people to the fore who were now difficult to control. The revolutionaries were not in principle opposed to violence but many were disturbed that it might be directed against Protestants rather than the police. The working class alliance against the capitalist state seemed farther away than ever. At other times McCann was reluctant to condemn the "young hooligans" as they were the best material available to the New Left.

The moderates were not blameless either. They had raised expectations after October 1968 by taking people onto the streets in a series of marches which had been stopped in Londonderry when they began to degenerate into violence. Eamonn McCann made a valid point when he said:

The CAC died in Derry after the riots of 19 April. It was difficult after that to organise a demonstration which did not end in riot, and the CAC was not about to assume such responsibility. But by ending demonstrations the moderates took away from the youth any channel for expression other than riot.[171]

As he told the Scarman Tribunal:

The people were taken on to the streets and left there, and abandoned and this Committee [the DCAC] bears some responsibility for the sectarian strife.[172]

In an analysis that would be echoed by many Loyalists, the Derry Labour Party said in one of its publications:

In the context of Northern Ireland politics taking thousands onto the streets for a points system in housing is like taking a tiger for a walk on a leash made of thread - and then when the tiger gets loose, whining 'it's not my fault'. In passing we might say that quite the most sick-making aspect of it all is the limitless ability of the 'moderate' leaders to absolve themselves from all responsibility for anything distasteful. Some of them seem to be cultivating an air of positive saintliness. One of these days on television Mr. Hume is going to tip his halo to the interviewer before not answering the question.[173]

It might also be pointed out that taking people onto the streets for a points system was doubly irresponsible in view of the fact that the Londonderry Corporation had operated such a system for over 20 years. Having quite lost control of the situation the Derry Citizens Action Committee faded away by the end of July. It was eclipsed by a new organisation, the Derry Citizens Defence Association (DCDA), which McCann says was set up by the local James Connolly Republican Club.[174] Sean Keenan, the Chairman of the Republican Club, became Chairman of the DCDA. On the original DCDA committee, 7 out of 8 were members of the James Connolly Republican Club.[175]

August 1969

As the month began the only topic of conversation was the Apprentice Boys parade on 12 August. This is an annual event organised by a Protestant organisation to commemorate the Relief of Londonderry after the Siege of 1688-89, a historic sacrifice which ensured the success of the Glorious Revolution, secured civil and religious liberties throughout the United Kingdom, and marked the end of the absolute power of the monarchy.

The route of the parade was to take it through the Protestant streets of the North Ward and the commercial districts of the city centre. The Apprentice Boys had never marched though the Bogside and had never expressed any wish to do so. The parade was and still is made up of members of the Apprentice Boys association and their bands carrying banners bearing the name of their branches and depicting scenes from the Siege of Londonderry. There are no placards or banners bearing political slogans. The marchers do not sing or chant anything. They march in silence to the tunes played by flute, accordion or pipe bands. In August 1969 the parade had been held annually for many decades and had not caused any trouble. There was therefore nothing in the conduct of the marchers or in the selection of the parade route which could be deemed offensive.

The most popular Catholic words in the build up to the parade were "invasion" and "defence". Those who saw in violence a way of winning further political concessions started spreading rumours that on the day of the parade the Bogside was to be "invaded" by Protestant marchers and the police. No evidence was ever brought forward to support the rumours. They were just a cynical attempt to raise tensions. Catholic leaders came up with totally unfounded stories that the Apprentice Boys would try to march through the Bogside. Having manufactured a non-existent threat they then began to talk about "defence". At a meeting on 4 August Sean Keenan said the chosen weapons would be "sticks, stones and the good old petrol bomb".[176]

Apprentice Boys leaders met with Bogside representatives on 8 August and gave them every possible assurance.[177] On the day the parade was efficiently marshalled and passed off without incident. It should be noted that it was only after the parade was over and the visiting branches had left the city that the real trouble started. The event was therefore not the cause of the violence. What followed had been planned for some time, and because it emerged that the important thing was to defeat the police rather than confront the marchers, any denial of the civil liberties of the marchers to walk through Protestant areas would not have prevented the violence. The momentum of events meant that many Catholics were ready for a confrontation with the state and were just waiting for the opportunity.

By August Republicans had made what might be called territorial gains. The Scarman Report said of the RUC:

Their patrolling of the Bogside had been slight and occasional for many months; and after the July riots it was almost non-existent. [178]

Under the liberal Minister for Home Affairs, Robert Porter, the feeling was that if the RUC did not appear in Catholic areas the local residents would not engage in riotous attacks upon them. The effect of the policy was that residents of the Bogside were free to do practically anything they wanted, and that included the making of preparations for large scale violence on 12 August.

One dairy reported that few empty milk bottles had been returned from the Bogside on 10 August, and non on 11th or 12th.[179] One estimate was that 43,000 empties had been retained by the locals.[180] These were to form the basis of a petrol bomb arsenal. One milkman found a note on a doorstep which read: "No milk today but leave me 200 bottles."[181]

A large open air meeting was held at Celtic Park on 10 August which was addressed by all shades of Republican opinion. Eddie McAteer made an ominous speech, part of which was reproduced in bold type as part of the *Derry Journal's* main story on the morning of 12 August.

If a hand other than ours embarks on the terrible work which we all fear on Tuesday [12 August] or even later this week, then be sure that this means the raising of the curtain on the last terrible act of the age-old Irish drama.

If we are beaten into the ground in this city as an unarmed and defenceless people, I pray to God that our watching brethren will not stand aside any longer. [182]

In the unlikely event that anyone had not picked up the coded message, the *Derry Journal* printed a translation:

Mr. McAteer said that he hoped that the 26 Co. Government would intervene if the situation in the North came to the worst. [183]

The "last terrible act of the age-old Irish drama" would, of course, mean the transition to a united Ireland. McCann condemned the invitation as "the height of irresponsibility".[184] In reporting the testimony of Paddy Doherty (Deputy Chairman of the DCDA) to the Scarman Tribunal, the *Derry Journal* later said that

Before the Apprentice Boys' procession in Derry on August 12, the Derry Citizens Defence Association, which controlled the Bogside during the disturbances in the city, passed a motion that in the event of an attack on the Bogside they would call on the people of Ireland to come to their assistance. [185]

A messenger was needed to bear the news. Therefore

Mr. Doherty said he was appointed to visit Dublin and was directed to put the motion before the Irish Government. He went there on August 11 and talked to some people whose names he did not know but whom he knew were civil servants.

'they accepted the motion and said that they would pass the views expressed in it to the members of the Irish Government,' Mr. Doherty said. [186]

On 12 August itself a crowd of Bogsiders came down to Waterloo Place adjacent to the Strand Road, a city centre street which the Apprentice Boys marched along. For two and a half hours the police cordon facing this crowd endured what Scarman called "a constant hail of missiles" and it was not until 5.00 pm that they finally charged the crowd to disperse them.[187] The marchers never broke ranks and had cleared the area by 4.00 pm. It is interesting to note that

Long before any move was made by the police into William Street, at about 3.30 pm, Mr. Keenan, Chairman of the DCDA, had given the order to erect barricades. [188]

The Sunday Times Insight Team, whose book could never be described as pro-Unionist, noted that both sides had given undertakings to provide effective stewarding.

The Apprentice Boys kept their side of the bargain; the DCDA did not keep theirs...
When it came to the 'defence' of the Bogside in the event of attack, however, the Derry Citizens Defence Committee showed a professionalism markedly at odds with the amateurishness of its arrangements to preserve the peace. [189]

The Scarman Report concluded that

By 'defence' the DCDA, in fact, meant a fight to keep all comers (including the police) out of the Bogside. [190]

We have seen how the Bogsiders horded a huge supply of bottles for petrol bombs, but what about the petrol? When he was questioned about this at the Scarman Tribunal, Sean Keenan put forward the rather quaint suggestion that it had come from local people who allowed it to be siphoned from their cars.[191] In fact hundred of gallons had been stolen from a local Post Office depot. [192] Three Londonderry petrol stations lost over 3,000 gallons during the rioting.[193] Materials for the building of barricades had been accumulated over a long period. By the time the police moved against the mob which was attacking them the barricades were up and huge supplies of petrol bombs were available at key points.

As the police tried to control the totally unprovoked rioting they were pelted with stones, bottles, petrol bombs and steel reinforcing rods.[194] Paint bombs were used to obscure the view of the drivers of police vehicles and make them crash.[195] A steel cylinder with steel spikes welded on it was intended to wreck the tyres of the same vehicles.[196] During the night hundreds of people launched a full scale petrol bomb attack on Rosemount police station.

At the Scarman hearings the Secretary of the DCDA, Michael Canavan, was asked by counsel for the RUC if this attack was a defensive action. He replied

Numerous incidents took place throughout Northern Ireland in those few days. It was to our advantage that the police force was drawn off.[197]

Scarman himself asked Canavan:

Do you know there is a difficult element to control? You know petrol bombs can do enormous damage - and damage to human beings? Did you have these considerations in mind before you authorised the use of petrol bombs?

He simply said

These considerations were important but I suppose you can't have a cake without breaking eggs.[198]

A journalist, Mr Jones, testified that

The whole of the Bogside had been turned into a munitions camp....In many streets women and children were filling bottles with petrol and some other substance in order to make petrol bombs. They were filling the bottles from bath-tubs which were filled with petrol. Other children were ripping up paving stones, breaking them, putting them in wheel barrows and transporting them to where the main confrontation was.[199]

Buildings were set on fire and burning vehicles rolled down hills towards police lines. Some people occupied the gas works and threatened to blow it up.[200]

In a role he has all too often played, John Hume objected to the presence of police in the Bogside. Deputy Inspector-General Graham Shillington told him that they were only there to control the crowd. If anyone in authority could give an undertaking to the RUC that the crowd had no intention of breaking out into the city centre, he would withdraw the police. But Hume could not take up what was almost a foolhardy offer. He said he could not be responsible for the actions of the crowd. [201] Power had passed to the hard men.

Sean Keenan put out an appeal to "civil rights" organisations throughout Ulster to "come out to draw the police away from Londonderry". An appeal also went out, as planned, to "everyone in Ireland" to come to their aid. [202] A tape of Keenan's was played at a NICRA meeting in Belfast. He could be heard saying "For Jesus's sake, help". [203] According to Michael Farrell:

> *The Bogsiders appealed for help. NICRA and the PD arranged mass rallies for a dozen centres to stretch the RUC as far as possible. It was understood that they would end in riots.* [204]

And indeed they did. This was anticipated by the Stormont government which probably concluded that as peaceful demonstrations would not draw police away from Londonderry they would, of necessity, be of the non-peaceful kind. All public meetings and processions were banned for the rest of August in the early hours of 13th. [205]

This did not, however, stop those who wanted to support the Londonderry rioters. A "civil rights" meeting in Armagh on 13 August turned into a riot with stones and petrol bombs being thown at the police. [206] On the same day in Dungannon a crowd left a meeting on the steps of the old Technical College to build barricades to seal off the Catholic West Ward. Buses and cars were set on fire to block roads and mobs tried to burn down the Courthouse, a warehouse and the *Tyrone Courier* offices. Firemen who tried to tackle the blaze were attacked with stones and petrol bombs. [207]

Those who attended a meeting in Coalisland, a town with few Protestants, marched on the RUC station and hurled petrol bombs at it. The married quarters were seriously damaged. Barricades were set up on key roads to cut off the building. A mob advanced behind a large mechanical shovel. Fortunately a pincer movement with armoured cars and a volley of shots managed to scatter the crowd. [208]

There was a similar pattern of events in Newry. Members of NICRA had gone to Dundalk south of the border to seek help. Scarman had no doubt some IRA men came to help build and man the barricades. Heavy lorries were used to seal off the west and south of the town. A number of public buildings including those owned by the Electricity Board, Ulsterbus, and the Post Office were smashed up and set on fire. About 1,000 people manned the barricades.

However on the morning of 14th the leaders seem to have panicked and 2 lorries headed for the border. A Customs post on the Omeath Road was set alight as they journeyed south. Apparently an incendiary device had ignited prematurely and 7 people were said to have been treated for burns in Dundalk. A Colt automatic was found in the debris of the Customs post. [209]

At Dungiven the RUC station was also attacked with stones and petrol bombs and the Orange Hall and Courthouse were burnt down when the fire brigade couldn't get through the hostile crowds. [210]

The situation in Belfast was interesting. NICRA had decided not to hold a meeting in the city. Nevertheless there was a meeting at Divis Flats on the evening of 13 August. At the time it was not clear who organised it. Gerry Adams solved the puzzle some time later when he wrote:

On the second day at an emotional meeting of NICRA in Belfast we heard a tape-recorded plea from the Bogside for help. A proposal to draw the RUC out of Derry or at least to prevent reinforcements being sent in was enthusiastically endorsed. Rallies were to be organised throughout the 6 counties. On behalf of the West Belfast Housing Action Committee I informed the meeting that we would hold a protest march and meeting on the Falls Road... We left the meeting to make petrol bombs. [211]

The march was from Divis Flats to Springfield Road RUC station where some windows were smashed. The marchers carried the Irish tricolour and sang the Soldier's Song. They went on to Hastings Street RUC station. Three policemen, standing outside to receive a petition about the situation in Londonderry, were pelted with stones, pieces of grating and petrol bombs. At about 10.45pm a police vehicle in Malt Street on the Grosvenor Road came under gun fire and was attacked with a hand grenade. [212] A hand grenade had also been thrown at a police vehicle in Cyprus Street, West Belfast in July 1968. [213]

More shots were fired at an armoured car in McDonnell Street and Leeson Street. The vehicle had the bullet marks to prove it. A Protestant owned car showrooms on the Falls Road was petrol bombed, cars dragged into the street and set on fire, and the property was looted around midnight. A petrol bomb was thrown through the windscreen of a saloon car driven by a fire officer mistaken for a policeman. There were 2 further attacks on Springfield Road RUC station involving stones and petrol bombs. Two people fired revolvers at the building. [214]

Detective Inspector Cushley testified that police were withdrawn from the riot area. He was forced

to deploy the forces only in patrolling the border areas and to concede to the rioters that portion of the road which they were determined to wreck and destroy. [215]

In the Ardoyne, Catholic youths attacked a small group of police with stones and petrol bombs in Hooker Street. Reinforcements were called for. The Catholics barricaded the streets and used "improvised explosive devices made from six-inch pieces of copper tubing". [216]

Father Gillespie agreed that those engaging in riotous behaviour this night in the Ardoyne area were not motivated by a desire to defend the area. [217]

Scarman found that

there is no evidence of any sectarian clash on the night of 13/14 August. [218]

In fact apart from a handful of stones thrown by frustrated Protestants in Londonderry, the violence on 13 August consisted almost entirely of co-ordinated and politically inspired attacks by the Catholic population on the forces of law and order. This was not a problem of 2 groups of people not being able to get on with each other, nor was it defensive action.

How did the people behind the Bogside barricades see the situation? One thing that was certainly important was the belief that the Irish government would intervene militarily. We have seen that the DCDA had resolved to make an appeal to those south of the border if things got difficult and that Eddie McAteer had expressed the hope that "our watching brethren" would not stand aside. Paddy Doherty had delivered the message to the Irish government on 11 August and Sean Keenan had issued an actual appeal for help on 12 August. The following day the Irish prime minister, Jack Lynch, addressed the nation on television. He did not criticise the Bogsiders for launching unprovoked assaults on the police and burning down property. Instead he said he had

asked the British government to see to it that police attacks on the people of Derry should cease immediately....the Irish Government can no longer stand by and see innocent people injured and perhaps worse. [219]

The Irish Army was to set up field hospitals in Co.Donegal and elsewhere on the border, which seemed to many a good excuse for troop movements. He then introduced the constitutional question yet again.

Recognising, however, that the re-unification of the national territory can provide the only permanent solution for the problem, it is our intention to request the British Government to enter into early negotiations with the Irish Government to review the present constitutional position of the 6 counties of Northern Ireland. [220]

Conor Cruise O'Brian, who visited Londonderry about this time, said of Lynch's speech:

Catholics interpreted it as meaning that the hour of their liberation was at hand. Irish troops or U.N. troops, or both together, were coming in, the walls of Jericho as well as of Derry were coming down. [221]

According to Michael Farrell

It seemed as if, for the first time since 1922, a Southern government was prepared to intervene in the six counties, and the longer they could hold out the nearer they would be to Irish unity. [222]

County Inspector Mahon of the RUC testified that on 13 August Irish Army trucks were seen patrolling from Bridge End to the Customs post on the border just outside Londonderry. [223] It is therefore not surprising that the broadcast, according to Frank Curran (then editor of the *Derry Journal*) "was hailed in Derry as an indication that Irish troops were on the verge of crossing the Donegal border to guarantee the safety of the Derry Catholics." [224] Eamonn McCann recalled that "News that 'the Free State soldiers are coming' spread rapidly." [225] John Hume remembered people spilling onto the streets shouting "The Irish Army's coming! The Irish Army's coming!"[226] What this meant for most Bogsiders was that the constitutional status of Northern Ireland was being put into question and few doubted that Irish troops in the Bogside and elsewhere would not leave until Ulster's British connection had been permanently undermined.

There had been sabre-rattling on the question of Irish Army intervention for some time. Back in April 1969, Mr. L. Cunningham, a member of Donegal County Council and an Irish TD (Member of Parliament) said: "The Irish government cannot stand idly by and allow the situation to develop." [227] This foreshadowed the words of Jack Lynch whose script said "stand idly by", but it came out as "stand by" due to an error on the teleprompter.[228] Also in April Senator B.McGlinchey from Donegal said that Irish troops should be withdrawn from peace-keeping duties in Cyprus and placed around Ulster's border. If the situation got worse they should enter Northern Ireland. [229]

The *Derry Journal* on 22 April 1969 had reported that:

Earlier yesterday the Taoiseach [Irish prime minister] met Northern Ireland Civil Rights leaders who appealed for Irish Government support for their suggestion that a joint peace-keeping force composed of British and Irish army personnel be stationed in areas such as Derry.

They were said to want "a physical military presence."

Inside the Irish cabinet, Charles Haughey, Neil Blaney and Kevin Boland were sympathetic to the idea of invading Ulster. Many years later in a radio interview, Blaney was asked how close the Irish Army came to going across the border in August 1969.

I think extremely close and in fact it was the belief of a number of us certainly that we were going across and I still regret very much that we didn't go across. [230]

Dr. Donal McDermott of the supposedly more moderate DCAC told the Scarman Tribunal that he had hoped that Irish troops would have entered the whole of Northern Ireland, including Belfast. [231]

Behind the Bogside barricades the rioters were beginning to get nervous by 14 August. For 2 days they had run amok and prevented the police from restoring order, but with no sign of the Irish fifth cavalry they feared they would soon be called to account. It was necessary to consolidate the gains already made through some kind of agreed cessation of hostilities which would provide a platform for further political demands. The RUC had inadequate forces to contain the violence and most of those on duty in Londonderry were exhausted. They had suffered dreadful casualties and of the 700 officers available in the city on 12 August, only 447 remained on duty at 11.00 am on 14 August and by 5.30 pm this number had fallen to 327. [232] Head Constable Thomas Hood testified that when his men went off duty at 2.00 pm on 14 August they had been working for 21 hours non stop and almost all had been injured. [233] Due to administrative incompetence on the part of the Northern Ireland government no arrangements had been made to feed the police in Londonderry. With little hope of relief the police on the west bank were forgotten men. If the Protestant housewives of the area hadn't fed them they would have been left to starve. Some of these local people were warned that they were under observation by the rioters and hence in the interests of their own safety should stop bringing food.

Troops belonging to the Prince of Wales Own Regiment were deployed in Londonderry at 5.00 pm on 14 August. They were part of the 2,000 strong permanent garrison in Northern Ireland. Soldiers were therefore not, strictly speaking, "sent" to Ulster in August 1969. They had always been there, although over the coming months and years reinforcements were required. John Hume had been one of the first to call for British troops to be deployed.

I spoke to the Home Secretary's private secretary in London by telephone on the Wednesday morning, August 13 and told him the only solution of the trouble that was going on was to send the British troops immediately. [234]

Roy Hattersley, then in charge at the Ministry of Defence in the absence of Denis Healey, who was in hospital, recalled a telephone coversation with Bernadette Devlin.

She said that if there weren't troops sent across the bridge in Derry, a large number of Catholics would be killed. And in a sense that was conclusive: if the leader of the Catholics was saying that, we really had little choice. [235]

The threat assessment was ludicrous. Catholics greatly outnumbered Protestants in Londonderry and the police were exhausted. It was, however, effective in persuading the gullible English, who were impressed by the argument that Catholic violence was purely "defensive". The political value of British troops on the streets controlled by sympathetic British politicians was enormous. Bernadette Devlin remembered the events well.

I vaguely saw the soldiers coming with barbed wire, but my most vivid memory is a crowd gathering around John Hume and other civil rights leaders.

They were jubilant. They were declaring that Northern Ireland was finished, Stormont was finished and we were on our way to a united Ireland because the troops were in.[236]

Eamonn McCann's feelings about the troops were that

Their appearance was clear proof that we had won the battle, that the RUC was beaten. [237]

Frank Curran confirmed that

The Catholics welcomed the British troops to Derry, because their arrival signified the Bogsiders' victory over the police. It was also effective proof of the proposition that Stormont's writ no longer ran in large areas on the west side of the Foyle.[238]

The reason the British troops' arrival was treated as a victory was that they had not come to help the police apprehend law breakers in the Bogside, or wrest control of the streets from the rioters. On the contrary, they were used to prevent these objectives being achieved. Although it is claimed that troops were acting in support of the civil power, they were doing no such thing. It is true that the Northern Ireland government had finally asked for troops to be sent in, but it had no say over what soldiers did and neither did the police.

After a meeting with Bogside representatives such as Paddy Doherty and Michael Canavan the battalion commanding officer, Lieutenant Colonel Todd, "agreed to withdraw the police behind the army lines, thereby modifying his original plan for a joint police-military operation." [239] He told the Scarman Tribunal about a meeting with Doherty and Canavan a few days later:

I tried to persuade them to let me send the military in, and asked who they were prepared to have in Bogside. But at that stage they were not prepared to have anybody, without it causing trouble. [240]

They told him they considered themselves to be "in a state of war". [241] The approach was to ask the rioters if they would kindly let the forces of law and order re-establish control of the Bogside. There was no question of them being compelled to abide by the law in that area or of their being brought to book for their past actions.

A DCDA press statement on 14 August said:

At a meeting tonight of Derry Citizens Defence Association Committee the agreement reached earlier between Colonel Todd (Officer Commanding the Troops in Londonderry) and representatives of the committee were ratified.

Details of this agreement were 1. All 'B' Specials to be withdrawn from the area governed by Londonderry Development Commission; 2. The RUC to be restricted to normal police duties; 3. The Derry Citizens Defence Association would help in keeping peace. [242]

Towards the end of August a new commanding officer, Lieutenant Colonel C. Millman was asked at a press conference under what circumstances troops would enter the Bogside. He said:

My orders are not to enter the area. We are trying to get back to normality of life. I have no orders to arrest anybody. [243]

How a no-go area controlled by petrol bomb throwers could be described as normal he did not say. Undoubtedly what he meant was that the Army was happy with the fact that fighting had stopped when it marched into Londonderry and was little interested in achieving anything else at that time. Violence had always been only a means to an end and for those behind the barricades this was a time for consolidating their gains. They had carved out an area where neither the police nor the Army exercised any authority. The liberal *Belfast Telegraph* journalist, Barry White, described it as "an area that had virtually seceded from the state" and the DCDA "was the effective government". [244]

The British Army was not just standing back, it was preventing the police and members of Ulster's majority from entering the area. It was therefore holding a defensive line which enabled the Republicans to build up their power unhindered by state authority or a popular backlash. The welcome given by Catholics to the Army was therefore conditional upon its acting as a defender of Republican interests. When it later tried to enforce the law in such areas, it outlived its welcome. For the time being fighting stopped because the British Army did not seek to interfere with the substantial territorial gains made by the rioters.

The early no-go areas were also a platform from which to press further demands. At a very early stage the rioters' spokesmen were outlining political objectives which went well beyond "civil rights" or "defence". During the night of 12/13 August NICRA issued the following statement:

> *A war of genocide is about to flare across the North. The CRA demands that all Irishmen recognise their common interdependence and calls on the Government and people of the Twenty-Six Counties to act now to prevent a great national disaster. We urgently request that the Government take immediate action to have a United Nations peace-keeping force sent to Derry, and if necessary Ireland should recall her peace-keeping troops from Cyprus for service at home. Pending the arrival of a United Nations force we urge immediate suspension of the Six-County Government and the partisan RUC and B Specials and their temporary replacement by joint peace-keeping patrols of Irish and British forces. We urge immediate consultation between the Irish and British Governments to this end. Time has run out in the North.* [245]

Bernadette Devlin and Eamonn McCann made a statement of their own:

> *The barricades in the Bogside of Derry must not be taken down until the Westminster Government states its clear commitment to the suspension of the constitution of Northern Ireland and calls immediately a constitutional conference representative of Westminster, the Unionist Government, the Government of the Republic of Ireland and all tendencies within the civil rights movement.* [246]

The *Barricade Bulletin* produced under the name of the Derry Labour Party said in August 1969:

> *Major Chichester-Clark [the Northern Ireland prime minister], as he knows very well, is in no position to say that the barricades must and will come down. We do not recognise his authority. His law does not run in our area. When we take down the barricades it will be on our terms and in our good time and not one second sooner.* [247]

Two days later it announced

> *The barricades come down when the government falls - not one minute before.* [248]

Paddy Doherty, the DCDA Vice Chairman, stated rather improbably that he had no political objectives in mind before 14 August. However he thought that

It was after they had arrived at the situation where the Army were outside protecting us, that personally, I thought we were on to a winner. [249]

Scarman asked Doherty: "did you think this was a fine opportunity to stake future political objectives?" and he replied "It was".[250] The demands put forward by various groups in Londonderry and Belfast were very similar. The *DCDA Newsletter* listed them as

1. *Abolition of Stormont*
2. *Disarming and disbandment of 'B' Specials*
3. *Disarming of RUC*
4. *General amnesty for all those who defended their homes behind the barricades.*
5. *Immediate release of all political prisoners*
6. *Repeal of Special Powers Act* [251]

They were testimony to the degree of sophistication which the "civil rights" movement had imposed on Republicanism. Among most groups there was now a realisation that there would have to be a step by step approach to a united Ireland. But they had all moved on from "civil rights" to more wide ranging intermediate political demands which would pave the way for the ultimate ideal. Many of the demands reflected IRA influence on the defence committees in that they sought to remove the traditional obstacles in the way of terrorist campaigns such as the B Specials, the armed police force and the power to detain terrorist suspects contained in the Special Powers Act. The abolition of Stormont would of course transfer authority to the more gullible and guilt-ridden British politicians who were far more likely to agree to a united Ireland than the majority of Ulster's citizens.

Meanwhile over in Belfast troops had not been deployed until 15 August. We have seen that the Loyalist community endured the events of 12/13 August without retaliation even though the use of guns, hand grenades and petrol bombs by Rebublicans was inexplicable except in terms of an attack upon the state. On 14 August a Catholic crowd gathered in Divis Street and at about 9.00pm was seen breaking up paving stones and throwing petrol bombs.[252] At around 10.30-11.00 pm this crowd, carrying the Irish tricolour and singing the Soldier's Song, entered the Catholic end of Percy Street armed with stones, sticks and petrol bombs and charged towards the Protestant end of the street, which led on to the Shankill Road. They used corrugated iron sheets stolen from a builder's yard as a screen, from behind which they threw petrol bombs at Loyalists.[253] At 11.00 pm they launched a similar attack down Dover Street, which also led on to the Shankill.

About midnight 4 shots were fired at the RUC from Divis Street and a gunman in Gilford Street shot dead a Protestant, Herbert Roy, and wounded 3 policemen.[254] After 1.00 am a Republican fired a machine gun from Derby Street into Dover Street.[255] Police also came under fire from the Falls Road end of Cupar Street and 3 Protestant civilians were hit in this area. Scarman found that

> *There is no evidence of any firearm in the hands of a Protestant civilian.*[256]

More shots were aimed at police in Conway Street around midnight and a constable was wounded. [257]

What is clear is that it was Republicans who started the trouble on 14 August by their attacks in Dover Street and Percy Street and it was only after this that Protestants reacted in like fashion, and police had to return fire against Republicans. Having seen large scale violence aimed against the state, Loyalists had had enough and were determined to put down what they saw as an insurrection. The use of guns by Republicans was widespread in Belfast before there was a Protestant backlash, and it had nothing to do with "defence".

In the Ardoyne Scarman reported that

> *The Tribunal is satisfied that the Hooker Street crowd began the night's rioting, and that a gun battle developed between Catholics and police.... there was no gunfire by the Protestant crowd.* [258]

Previously the police policy had been to saturate a riot area with a large number of vehicles but this was not possible in August because their forces were dispersed to deal with trouble elsewhere.[259] With the police overstretched Loyalists had to look to their own defence and that of the state. When they counterattacked, houses were burnt by petrol bombs which had been manufactured after Catholics had used this weapon against them and the police. On 15 August most of the houses in the Catholic Bombay Street were burnt in such a retaliatory attack, but Scarman found that

> *There is no evidence of any military-style planning behind the Protestant*

mobs. The explanation that fits the facts and the mood of the Shankill on the night of the 15th is one of communal anger against what they believed to have been a Catholic assault on them and the established order of the province.[260]

The order of events should be noted. It is a popular myth that after the 12 August 1969 there was a Protestant "pogrom" against Belfast Catholics. Certainly the Bombay Street incident on 15 August is much more famous than the Republican aggression on 13/14 August. But the facts are clear. Belfast Loyalists only retaliated against intolerable provocation, which included the Republican use of firearms. It was then, after the backlash had begun on 14 August, that Catholics pleaded for the troops to be deployed in Belfast. They realised that they had gone too far and craved the kind of defensive cordon which would prevent them being called to account. Gerry Fitt remembered

The crowds - there must have been 300 or 400 - were screaming 'Gerry, get the Army in, for God's sake get the Army in'.[261]

Fitt therefore rang the Home Secretary, Jim Callaghan, from a bookmaker's office off the Falls Road. [262]

On 16 August Belfast Catholics formed a Central Citizens Defence Committee (CCDC) modelled on the DCDA. Its Chairman was Jim Sullivan, who for many years had been the IRA's second in command in the city.[263] When the top man, Billy McMillen, was detained under the Special Powers Act on 15 August, Sullivan assumed command of the Belfast IRA and it was he who was left to search for guns, which had been in short supply.[264] The CCDC consisted of about 30 delegates.

Most of the delegates were ordinary men with standing in their areas, but republicans were strongly represented and the local clergy were also there in force. [265]

The CCDC also had the support of the Catholic diocesan bishop.[266] None seemed concerned about serving under the IRA's local commanding officer. The CCDC was necessary, not so much because people needed to be defended (the British Army would soon take care of that), but because the example of Londonderry had shown that Army officers preferred to talk to an identifiable body of rioters' representatives so that they could ask permission to do things. The CCDC would become a negotiating body pressing similar political demands to the DCDA from the Belfast end of things.

As a sign of things to come, the IRA drove a van containing 50lbs. of commercial explosives up to the Crossmaglen RUC station in Co. Armagh on 17 August. The main explosion was meant to be detonated by a hand grenade thrown at the van. The hand grenade went off but the commercial explosives did not.[267]

What Did It All Mean?

There is a fair agreement among the main participants and observers about what was going on in August 1969. Michael Farrell thought that "On 14 August the North was on the brink of war."[268] Father Tony Mulvey of St. Eugene's Cathedral in Londonderry observed that, after 12 August

Over the next few days the determination was so unanimous that I would only regard it as a community in revolt rather than just a street disturbance or riot.[269]

For Gerry Adams the events constituted a "spontaneous popular uprising".[270] Frank Curran said of the Londonderry violence that the police "must have known that this was no one-day affray but a serious attempt to wrest control of the streets from them."[271] Journalist Barry White saw it as "an uprising". Londonderry was "in a state of rebellion, by will of the people".[272]

Bernadette Devlin said that

According to Major Chichester-Clark, I'd incited Bogsiders to rebellion and plotted the overthrow of the State. But the situation in Northern Ireland was such that nobody cared.[273]

Chichester-Clark's view was that

This is not the agitation of a minority seeking by lawful means the assertion of political rights. It is the conspiracy of forces seeking to overthrow a government democratically elected by a large majority.[274]

Given the Republicans' own statements it is difficult to contest this view. From 12 August onwards events had little to do with "civil rights" or "defence". They had a great deal to do with trying to get the Northern Ireland government and Parliament abolished. On 19 August NICRA Chairman, Frank Gogarty, said

We still believe that this Government - the Stormont Government - has no moral right to continue in office and that it should be suspended.[275]

It also had a great deal to do with trying to get a united Ireland with the help of Irish Army intervention and in the meantime trying to create areas in Ulster where British authority could not be exercised.

Former British Army officer Robin Evelegh, quoting from a Manual of Military Law, gives a useful definition:

An insurrection, in short, involves an intention to 'levy war against the Queen', as it is technically called, or otherwise to act in general defiance of the government of the country.[276]

The Oxford English Dictionary defines an insurrection as

The action of rising in arms or open resistance against established authority or governmental restraints.

and as "an incipient or limited rebellion".

So defined it seems clear that there was an insurrection in August 1969. The violence throughout Ulster had a common political purpose and that was to overthrow the Northern Ireland government, and if possible end the rule of the British Crown. It is equally clear that the insurrection was not put down and that we are still paying the price for that failure today.

So was it all an IRA plot? Richard Clutterbuck came near enough to the truth when he wrote:

It would be a mistake to credit NICRA or the IRA with diabolical power of planning worthy of a chess player. Their philosophy was that expressed by Shakespeare's Mark Antony: 'Now let it work; mischief thou art afoot, take thou what course thou wilt.' [277]

To execute a plan it is necessary either to be in control of events or to be able to predict in advance the course of events so that plans can be made accurately.

Neither condition seems to be completely met in the case of the IRA. It was the grateful beneficiary rather than the instigator of the "civil rights" movement's success, and all the evidence seems to show that the extent of Catholic support for insurrection and the enormous gains of August 1969 were largely unforseen by all sections of Republican opinion. The IRA was caught out with its organisation still geared up to the pursuit of economic and social objectives and it had less guns available than its supporters would have wished. These shortcomings were to lead to a split in the organisation and the emergence of the more military minded Provisional IRA.

This is not to say that there was an absence of planning or that the IRA wasn't very influential. The strategy of the whole Republican community in the 1960s was to acheive as much as it could as quickly as it could. In the early 1960s there was a general perception that it was going to be a long haul to a united Ireland, which remained the ultimate objective of all the groups, be they the IRA, the Moderate Middle Class Catholics or the Socialist Revolutionaries. A "civil rights" campaign was therefore instigated to play on the guilt complex of British politicians and the liberal section of the Protestant middle class. Under the influence of John Hume more and more Catholics began to put their faith in the British government as an agent of constitutional change in Northern Ireland.

Implicit in this strategy was the idea that if circumstances changed and concessions could be won more rapidly than had been originally envisaged, then the demands of Catholic politicians should become more ambitious. Because "civil rights" was declared by all the main groupings to be a means to the end of a united Irish Republic, no dramatic change of direction would be required. It would simply mean taking a few more steps along the same road; from "civil rights" to the disbanding of the B Specials and the abolition of Stormont. When it seemed likely that the Irish Army was about to invade Ulster, the goal of a united Ireland appeared to be achievable within a very short period of time.

There were extensive preparations for 12 August with the accumulation of petrol bombs and materials for building barricades, and the rioting of 13 August to "take the heat off Derry" showed evidence of co-ordination. The DCDA also took some steps to try and set up Irish government intervention, The IRA had not controlled the "civil rights" movement, it had simply shared its objectives and built up IRA influence by the provision of stewards. When the Republican struggle entered a phase of street violence it was only natural that people should look to those who had stewarded the "civil rights" marches for leadership. Hence the IRA had an influential role in the defence committees which negotiated with the British Army.

Behind the barricades Socialist Revolutionaries such as Bernadette Devlin were important in Londonderry. Eamonn McCann saw her as the most influential leader and claimed the DCDA was "totally irrelevant to the fighting and defence of Bogside", although the latter claim is difficult to accept.[278] The Derry Labour Party issued technical advice to rioters:

Use of Petrol Bombs

1. *Try to throw bombs high in the air unless at very close range.*
    This causes more panic as well as doing more harm.
2. *Do not throw petrol bombs when the enemy is out of range.*
3. *One person has already been badly hurt when he threw a petrol bomb*
    overarm.
    Throw the bomb upwards, starting the arm movement low down. A
    petrol bomb should not be thrown by the neck. [279]

Paul Arthur, who had been a member of People's Democracy until April 1969, said of the situation in Belfast:

PD acted as a miniscule but important group behind the barricades. Both
Fergus Woods and Michael Farrell could only remember about ten of its
members being actively involved. It produced most of the literature and
manned Radio Free Belfast most of the time but it had to pass on its material
first to the Republicans who vetted it. [280]

(Here "Republicans" would be people from the Sinn Fein tradition). People's Democracy also helped to run Radio Free Derry. Regardless of the exact extent of each group's contribution it is clear that the IRA was not in complete control of the organisation behind the barricades, such as it was. But more importantly neither the IRA, nor anyone else for that matter, was in control of the local populations.

Conspiracies tend to be difficult to organise. Getting large numbers of people to do exactly what you want is not easy. That is why co-ordinated action is more often the result of a little bit of organisation introduced into a group of people who have shared values and shared perceptions of events. A common outlook often results in individuals making similar judgements about what should be done. Once the materials for making petrol bombs were made available in the Bogside, local residents needed little encouragment to produce them in large numbers and they hardly needed to be told who to throw them at. Doubtless most had only a vague impression of where it was all leading to, but it was leading in the right direction. It might mean the creation of a no-go area where they could do what they wanted; it might mean the overthrow of the Northern Ireland Parliament; or it might mean a united Ireland. All were steps along the same path, a victory for "us" over "them". Because insurrection was a result of a popular demand, all the politicians often had to hang on tight and watch events being dictated by local people over whom they had minimal control.

In a confused situation those with definite ideas tend to wield a disproportionate amount of authority. There can be no doubt that some of the ideas canvassed by the IRA in 1966, and contained in the captured document published in the *Newsletter,* did have some influence on events. The notion of an armed stand in the heart of Belfast linked to an appeal to the United Nations was modified somewhat by the actual course of events in August, when the centre of resistance became Londonderry. But appeals for intervention were made to the UN, not least by the Irish government. The idea of "the people of the Republic forcing the [Eire] Government to intervene to save their fellow countrymen in the Northern outbreak" did turn into an important political issue and very nearly resulted in a major IRA success. The parts of the document relating to the role of agitation on social issues, working through bodies like the Wolfe Tone Society, was pretty accurate. Loyalists who were familiar with the *Newsletter* article would have been justified in discerning a significant IRA influence on events during August 1969, and in reacting accordingly.

The kind of conflict was also influenced by the fashion for mass street protest elsewhere in the world. A.T.Q. Stewart is right in thinking that the Paris riots of May 1968 were important. Streets were barricaded and paving stones ripped up as students occupied the Latin Quarter on the west bank. For the Socialist Revolutionaries at least, the Bogside was their Latin Quarter. Leonard Green of the DCDA said that up to 100 foreign students assisted in the Bogside.[281]

In May 1968 Danny Cohn-Bendit told a radio reporter in Paris: "It'll be a massacre or police must withdraw."[282] A very similar message, in fact, to that which Bernadette Devlin conveyed to Roy Hattersley, who was convinced a large number of Catholics would be killed in Londonderry. The French government's response was very different however. Instead of forming a protective cordon around the rioters it sent in the CRS riot police. 367 demonstrators were injured, 460 were arrested, no-one was killed and the trouble was over within a month. *283* We, on the other hand, got 20 years of terrorist violence.

A T. Q. Stewart went on to argue

that once these contemporary pressures have operated, the form and course of the conflict are determined by patterns concealed in the past, rather than those visible in the present.[284]

It was an old battle and an age old struggle. Because of the power which these historical forces exercise over Irish Catholics, they do not need to be organised or incited to the extent that English people do. Given a recognisable pattern of events which provides an opportunity to weaken the British connection and undermine the Ulster Unionist position, Republicans do not necessarily need to be told what to do. Insurrections tend therefore to be more spontaneous, are based on grass roots support and have vague open-ended objectives. This is confusing for an Englishman, who looks for "grievances", an elaborate organisation and clearly formulated intentions behind such action.

The English assume that the mass of the people are fairly disinterested in politics and are rather apathetic. Politicians are more extreme than ordinary people, who only engage in political action if they are organised or incited. These assumptions lead Englishmen to provide explanations of events in which political organisations are the prime movers. Such explanations tend to understate the extent to which, in Northern Ireland, such organisations are prisoners of the populations they serve, and exist only because, and for as long as, the people have a use for them.

NICRA and People's Democracy had few members and would have been of little importance without the support of thousands of Catholic non-members who found them useful for a time. They were influential in so far as they were an expression of a popular need or an idea. Perhaps we could even go so far as to say that what they were could be partly defined not in terms of what their members and officers wanted them to be, but in terms of the use to which they were put by the Catholic population.

Some Unionist attempts at explanation have fallen into the English trap. To say that the "civil rights" movement was an IRA front is not strictly true because the organisation called the IRA was not in control of the movement. It was one of a number of small organisations which participated in formal structures which by themselves were of no great importance. Some Unionist explanations were not made in terms of organisations, however, and these were nearer the mark. Take, for example, a speech made by Ian Paisley in Londonderry in November 1968:

> *It is quite evident that all the talk about jobs and houses is the insincere cant, the cover, for subversive activity. Mark my words, it is but the prelude for an IRA upsurge.*[285]

Almost all of those involved in the "civil rights" movement, as members of organisations or just supporters, believed in a united Ireland and saw the movement as a way of subverting the Northern Ireland state with a view to its eventual abolition. Loyalists discerned in the popular mood of Catholics and in the pattern of events the conditions which were necessary for the launching of another IRA campaign. Part of this mood was expressed in a willingness of moderates to work with, and indeed under, senior IRA figures. Long experience had taught Protestants to recognise when another upsurge was on the way. Paisley's statement was therefore fundamentally accurate. Many Loyalists foresaw the current IRA onslaught and warned the English about it, but we took no notice.

Some Unionists' claims about the nature of the "civil rights" movement are not quite right and the problem is usually that they have been pressured into making explanations in terms of who controlled what organisation. It is far more productive to look beyond these tiny organisations and see what was happening in the mass movement. Here support for the use of physical force was growing. The IRA idea was therefore strong before the IRA organisation was strong. It might well be useful to consider that the IRA is just as much an idea rooted in the Irish Catholic conciousness as it is an organisation. The idea grew in strength as the possibility of a united Ireland grew, and as violence seemed to win concessions. The IRA idea had gripped the wider movement by August 1969 even if the IRA's organisation was not yet ready for the challenge.

Part III

The Politics of Security Policy

A. Counter-Insurgency for Beginners

Perhaps the most commonly asked question about Ulster is: 'How can we defeat the IRA?' or perhaps even 'Can we ever defeat the IRA?'. British security policy rests on a whole series of political assumptions about the majority and minority communities. These beliefs were acquired during the "civil rights" era. They gave rise to political policies which were formulated in the early 1970s. Since then British policy, regardless of the government in power, has changed very little. Security policy has not been allowed to conflict with this almost unchanging political strategy, to which it is subservient.

The legacy of this strategy has been 20 years of terrorism, death, destruction and broken lives. We can therefore say, at the very least, that one set of assumptions about Ulster has produced policies which have failed to prevent a generation of violence. But what if those assumptions are wrong? What if an alternative set of assumptions, producing different policies, could lead to a better future? After 20 years of violence it is perhaps time to re-examine our assumptions and find out to what extent the myths of the "civil rights" era still haunt English policy making and prevent us from defeating the IRA.

We have seen that when the British Army was deployed in August 1969 it was effectively used to prevent Irish Republican rioters from being brought to justice. It formed a protective cordon around them to keep the law enforcement agencies out of their areas. The political attitudes of Army officers at that time were highlighted by Eamonn McCann, who negotiated with them. He described a meeting with Brigadier Leng in Londonderry.

> *He said that the army had come to see that justice was done, that he knew of the injustices of the past, that things would be different now and that he hoped for a friendly relationship with us.*[1]

The Army, briefed by English politicians, was under the distinct impression that Catholics were rioting about injustices which had not been remedied. We now know this belief was absured, but it was nevertheless crucial in shaping security policy at that time. In particular it explained the failure to punish those who had engaged in insurrection, and the willingness to allow the rioters to consolidate their gains in no-go areas. The minority was seen as a community of innocents.

In September 1969 it became clear to what extent the Army had abdicated responsibility for law and order. In the presence of Army officers, Sean Keenan read a statement to a press conference:

> Following talks with the military authorities, the Derry Citizens Defence Association declares that the following position obtains: 1- Derry Citizens Defence Association will remove the barricades; 2- The military authorities guarantee the security of the people living in the present barricades area, in conjunction with the Defence Association, as far as is humanly possible; 3- Neither the RUC nor the USC will enter the barricaded area.

> *Until we see the specific proposals from Mr. Callaghan for the structure of a just society in Northern Ireland, a- the military authorities will not enter the present barricaded area; b- the Defence Association Watch Committee may request the presence of the Royal Military Police in specific instances where their presence would be to the public advantage; c- the military authorities will not take retrospective action in respect of activities dated prior to the possible entry of the Royal Military Police.*[2]

During questioning by journalists Brigadier Peter Leng said: "What goes on in Bogside at the moment is none of our concern" and "I am just here holding a peace line between rival factions".[3] Trying to put a better gloss on things the Army PR men issued the following statement:

> We wish it to be known that there was no agreement either in writing or verbally entered into with the Association in Derry.

> The Army only answered various questions put to them, and have explained that the military are there to keep the peace and to keep rival factions apart.

> *At this moment this does not extend to the Army entering the Bogside.*[4]

As the Army was not to enter the Bogside it amounted to the same thing. The only change was that the barricades were replaced by white lines on the road which the authorities could not cross. The idea that the Protestants, who were outnumbered by more than 3:1 on the west bank of the Foyle, were somehow a threat to the Bogside is simply amusing.

Robin Evelegh made some incisive comments about this period.

On 14 August 1969 the established civil law enforcement officers, the Royal Ulster Constabulary, had been thrown out of the Bogside by a riotous mob. It was the clear and unequivocal legal and constitutional duty of the military to use every weapon and resource necessary, whether lethal or not, to restore that civil authority to the Bogside on their own authorisation. Whether the civil authority in the shape of the Royal Ulster Constabulary was unpopular or partisan did not matter; the Royal Ulster Constabulary were the constitutional civil authority charged as constables under the Crown with enforcing the law. Yet the Army acquiesced in this defeat of the civil authority and permitted another regime to hold sway in the Bogside.

It is inconceivable in the era of telephonic and radio communication that Colonel Todd would have acted as he did without reference to his military superiors, or that they would have directed him as they must have done without reference to Ministers. Ministers must therefore have ordered the Army to ignore the law and to accept the overthrow of the civil authority by riot. [5]

The consequences were serious.

The people of Northern Ireland concluded that the enforcement of law, even by the military, was subject to political direction and therefore to pressure on politicians. Riots, demonstrations and uniformed marches produce this political pressure; therefore such activities pay off... The soldiers and policemen drew the conclusion that they could no longer be sure of the support of their professional or political superiors, or of the legal system, if they enforced the law impartially, without fear or favour. [6]

Political restraints on security policy have been a constant feature of the last 20 years. They are a symptom of the basic problem - the English perception of Ulster Catholics as a wronged and guiltless minority during the "civil rights" era. This has generated a huge reservoir of guilt, particularly among influential sections of the English middle class. From the very beginning Republican violence has been seen as understandable and possibly excusable in the light of the allegedly terrible things the Protestants did to the minority. It means, in particular, that the collective misdemeanours of the Catholic community have to be met with concessions to try and win them round, and not with punishment. Disloyalty has to be rewarded. We shall in fact see that the democratic process in Ulster has been effectively suspended to accommodate English feelings of guilt and the consequent desire to make endless concessions.

Counter-Insurgency Theory

It is often assumed that the political constraints on security policy are provided only by the politicians and that if the Army was given a free hand it would pursue a course based on purely military considerations. I am not totally convinced that this is the case, and my reasons will soon become clear.

After the Second World War it became increasingly apparent that military action was, in the future, more likely to be directed against guerrillas, terrorists and insurgents than against a full scale army. Operations in places like Malaya, Kenya, Aden and Cyprus produced a body of Counter-Insurgency Theory about how such military campaigns should be conducted.

Brigadier Frank Kitson wrote a very influential book called *Low Intensity Operations* in 1971.

In this connection it is worth pointing out that as the enemy is likely to be employing a combination of political, economic, psychological and military measures, so the government will have to do likewise to defeat him, and although an army officer may regard the non-military action required as being the business of the civilian authorities, they will regard it as being his business, because it is being used for operational reasons. [7]

Lieutenant-Colonel Julian Paget felt that

The first essential in any counter-insurgency campaign is that both the political and the military aims should be agreed by all concerned from the very start and should be clearly stated in a directive. As the military aim is dependant on political considerations, it is essential that the political directive should clearly state three points; firstly, the purpose and scope of military operations; secondly, the short-term political and military aims governing the campaign, and finally the long-term political aim which it is hoped to achieve when the military campaign is over. [8]

These aims, of course, have never been set out and this probably explains why many people see security policy in Ulster as being confused and lacking direction. For the moment it is sufficient to note that the theorists tend to agree that counter-insurgency involves a joint political and military campaign. Inevitably, therefore, senior Army officers have taken a close interest in the political aspects of the fight against terrorism. Most have formulated views about the nature of Ulster's political problems. Former soldiers such as Major-General Richard Clutterbuck and Lieutenant-Colonel Michael Dewar have, in their own books, swallowed whole the "civil rights" propaganda. It would be unusual if serving officers in Ulster had not arrived at some views on these issues, and if this had not influenced their ideas about the nature of sound political policies aimed at countering terrorism.

Frank Kitson told Bishop and Mallie:

> *The Army recognised that the trouble had arisen because there were injustices being perpetrated over the republican community. They thought that to merely knock the thing underground and wait for it to pop up in five years was a silly way of doing business, so they tried a totally different idea, which was to keep the two sides apart, try and put right their grievances and everyone would live happily ever after.*[9]

Kitson, writing in 1971, though it would be all over in 5 years.[10] This perhaps goes to show that senior Army officers with half-baked ideas about Ulster can be just as dangerous as British politicians. Having spurned the idea of 5 years of peace, they got 20 years of violence.

Political views can make or break a security policy. Because some senior Army officers have inherited odd views from academics and politicians I am not convinced that an Army free from control by politicians would necessarily do things differently. Some of the brass hats are carrying so much excess political baggage that they have probably come to similar invalid conclusions. I would also tend to the view that there is no purely military solution. Fighting terrorism certainly is about employing a combination of political and military measures, and using one without the other will not work. The key is to base campaigns on correct political assumptions and sound political policies. Then the military measures will begin to work.

We must remember that the IRA is not seeking to defeat the British Army militarily. It could never hope to do that. Its aims are similar to those of General Grivas, who led the EOKA terrorists in Cyprus. He wrote:

> *It should not be supposed that by these means we should expect to impose a total defeat on the British forces in Cyprus. Our purpose is to win a moral victory through a process of attrition, by harrassing, confusing and finally exasperating the enemy forces with the effect of achieving our main aim...*[11]

Paget said of insurgents:

> *Military success is not essential to them, for they can still gain their objective, if they can enforce a stalemate, in which the Security Forces finally decide that the cost of continuing an indecisive struggle is no longer worthwhile. Their purpose is to defeat the Government's will to fight on, and military action is only one factor in their struggle to achieve this.* [12]

The IRA's objectives are ultimately political. It wants a united Ireland. Any effective counter-insurgency campaign would therefore have to convince all concerned that the IRA has no hope of achieving this political objective. The British government has never been able to do this because of important reasons which I shall go into later.

Into the Bog

For much of this century the English have taken the view that it would be unwise for them to become involved in the day to day running of Northern Ireland. We instinctively felt that we would get into trouble if we did, and hence it was better to leave things to the Northern Ireland government.

After the First World War Edward Carson said he would prefer Ulster to be governed in exactly the same way as other areas of the United Kingdom. Instead the British government set up a local Parliament at Stormont under the 1920 Government of Ireland Act. One reason was that it hoped to persuade the South to accept a limited form of self-government within the United Kingdom and it wanted to offer the same kind of Parliament to both parts of Ireland. But that was only part of the reason. By 1920 many English politicians thought that all Irish affairs were a pain in the backside. They didn't understand them and they had very little idea about how to successfully govern either North or South. They therefore preferred an arms-length relationship, leaving local politicians to deal with matters which, to the English, were most mysterious. The South didn't like the deal, and went on to become an independent Irish Free State, but the Stormont Parliament flourished.

It had wide ranging powers to pass legislation but it was the subject of very tight financial control from Westminster. Only about 10% of the Northern Ireland government's income came from taxes which it controlled. Most revenue raised in Ulster (including that from income tax) went into Westminster's coffers. Stormont's share of this revenue was supposed to be returned to Ulster according to a set formula, but before long it became a bargaining process. If the Northern Ireland government wanted to increase spending it had to ask the British government for the money. Thus Stormont had extensive powers to do things which didn't cost money, but in financial matters it probably had no more autonomy than the average English county council. For nearly 50 years this arrangement suited the British government very well.

If matters relating to Ulster were raised at Westminster's House of Commons, the Speaker would normally stop the MP and tell him this was a matter for the Northern Ireland government. Thus by convention Ulster's affairs were not discussed at Westminster. Richard Rose calculated that in the 5 years 1964-68 the House of Commons "devoted less than one-sixth of one per cent of its time to discussions of Northern Ireland questions; most of this talk concerned matters of trade, not the matters that affected allegiance to the regime."[13]

In Whitehall Northern Ireland was dealt with by a division of the Home Office General Department which also looked after the Channel Islands, the Isle of Man and the Charity Commission. It had a staff of 7 and the minister responsible was Lord Stonham.[14] Central government involvement in Ulster was therefore minimal.

The "civil rights" agitation encouraged the Labour government to be drawn into the situation to save the oppressed Catholics from the wicked Protestants. Labour politicians were torn between mounting a crusade and keeping out of an area where they suspected they would get into a mess. It is interesting to see that Jim Callaghan, who became Home Secretary in December 1967, shared his predecessors' reluctance to become involved. He wrote:

The advice that came to me from all sides was on no account to get sucked into the Irish bog.[15]

I had no confidence that if the Ulster Unionist Government were replaced British intervention in Irish affairs would make the situation better in the long run. These are quicksands for the British and I adhered steadfastly to my view that the people living in Ireland had to come to terms with each other about the basis on which they were going to live together.[16]

The Press and others were warning us that Ireland was a quagmire and I needed no reminder.[17]

....the officials made it clear that the last thing I would want would be to take

over the Government of Northern Ireland. At that stage we knew little enough at first hand what was going on, and had few reliable means of finding out.[18]

Callaghan's immediate predecessor as Home Secretary, Roy Jenkins, said in 1967:

Despite the many attributes of the English, a peculiar talent for solving the problems of Ireland is not among them.[19]

Thus Ulster was seen as a bog, quicksands and a quagmire. The English knew little about what was happening there and had no great talent for solving the country's problems. And yet, showing neither prudence nor humility, they jumped in with both feet. Unionist politicians were pressured and threatened to try and get them to introduce totally inappropriate policies. Jim Callaghan confirmed that Harold Wilson threatened sanctions

such as reconsidering the financial arrangements or even changing their constitutional relationship....
He did not spell it out at the time but what he had in mind was cutting off Northern Ireland's representation at Westminster. [20]

When British troops were deployed in 1969 the Wilson government said that it had constitutional implications as the Army could only be controlled by the British Ministry of Defence and not by Stormont. The Westminster government would thus have to be more closely involved in policy making in Ulster. It was simply a rationalisation of its desire to meddle. British troops had helped in campaigns against the IRA in the 1920s and 1950s and during street rioting in the 1930s. This had always been a routine matter and the Army had worked with the police and the Northern Ireland government without any fuss being made. The difference was that in earlier instances the Army had simply been used to fight terrorism or put down disorder and the objectives of all the law enforcement agencies had been the same. In 1969 the Army was to be used to prevent enforcement of the law and thus was to be acting in opposition to the civil power. Its presence led to the British government taking over effective control of law and order from Stormont because only the Army was allowed to operate in certain areas and the police fell back into a secondary role. Terence O'Neill confirmed that

from that time Northern Ireland has, in fact, always been under at least semi-

direct rule from London. [21]

The deployment of troops had been requested by the Northern Ireland government because it had not been permitted to use the Ulster Special Constabulary (USC), better known as the B Specials. The crime rate in Ulster was low and this was reflected in the fact that it had only 3,000 RUC officers. The USC was an 8,000 strong part-time force, whose members were paid only a small annual bounty or honorarium. Its main role was as a counter-insurgency force, operating mainly at night. It guarded installations, carried out patrols and set up checkpoints to restrict the movements of the IRA. The USC was a localised force whose members had a detailed knowledge of their area and the people in it. The Southern Irish journalist and author, Tim Pat Coogan, wrote in 1970:

The B-Specials were - then as now - the rock on which any mass movement by the IRA in the North has enevitably foundered. [22]

Although in theory the British Army was responsible for defending Ulster's borders it had played a very minor role throughout the century. The IRA had been beaten in the past by the RUC and USC directed by the Northern Ireland government. Before any further IRA campaign could be attempted it would be necessary to get rid of the USC and transfer responsibility for security to British politicians who knew nothing about fighting terrorism in Ulster. One objective had been achieved. The other was accomplished by the Hunt Report. Harold Wilson confirmed that he wanted the B Specials disbanded and that Lord Hunt was his choice to draw up a report on the USC and the RUC.[23] It is therefore not surprising that Hunt did not disappoint Wilson.

Robert Mark, then Deputy Commissioner of the Metropolitan Police, was appointed to help Lord Hunt and he undoubtedly had a strong influence on his report. Mark had earlier visited Ulster as an observer with Douglas Osmond (Chief Constable of Hampshire) at Callaghan's request on 16 August 1969, just after the rioting.

Mark and Osmond were very critical of the fact that police stations were bolted and barred. This was a hangover from the IRA menace, which they did not believe was serious at that time, and seemed to be the traditional reaction to any new situation. [24]

The Hunt Report, published on 3 October 1969, showed a similar naivity in wanting the RUC to behave like English bobbies

Policing in a free society depends on a wide measure of public approval and consent. This has never been obtained in the long term by military and paramilitary means. We believe that any police force, military in appearance and equipment, is less acceptable to minority and moderate opinion than if it is clearly civilian in character, particularly now that better education and improved communications have spread awareness of the rights of civilians.[25]

The Hunt Report said that the IRA's capacity to mount terrorist attacks was not rated very high.[26] It therefore recommended that all "military" functions be transferred to the Army, the RUC disarmed and the USC disbanded (even though it could find nothing wrong with their conduct). The IRA was pleased to see the USC go, but reality soon encroached into Hunt and Mark's fantasy world, and when terrorist activities were stepped up the RUC got their weapons back. By 1977 the English bobby philosophy had been buried and "police primacy" had been introduced. This meant that the RUC took over the main responsibility for riot control and anti-terrorist activities in most of Northern Ireland, although it was still controlled by British politicians struggling to understand the realities of Ulster. It did mean that the rationale behind the abolition of the B Specials had been abandoned and Ulster's most effective counter-insurgency force had been sacrificed in vain.

But let us go back to the idea of "public approval and consent" for policing. This is an English concept born in a society where opposition to the state itself is insignificant. But in Northern Ireland a large part of the minority community had refused to give "public approval and consent" to the existence of the state. Although by law one third of the places in the RUC were, for most of the century, reserved for Roman Catholics they were never able to reach this quota. IRA intimidation was one factor but undoubtedly many Catholics see membership of a force which is often called on to defend the state as a thoroughly disreputable occupation. Opposition to the USC was even greater because of its counter-insurgency role against the IRA. Shortly after its formation a Catholic committee was set up in May 1922 to encourage recruitment to the USC from the minority community. Two IRA men and 3 Sinn Fein members were amongst those nominated to the committee by Michael Collins, just before the IRA launched a new military campaign against Ulster. One nominee was Frank Cromie, Intelligence Officer to the IRA's 3rd Northern Division.[27] Cromie and one of the Sinn Fein members were arrested soon afterwards because of their role in terrorist activities and most of the rest of the committee resigned in protest.[28] It had simply been a wrecking manoeuvre by people who were not serious about supporting the USC. Throughout the last 20 years

Republicans have exploited the naive English wish to obtain their "public approval and consent" in order to extract political concessions. We still have not received their consent, nor are we likely to as long as there are more concessions on offer.

In August 1969 it was said that the B Specials were not trained for riot control. But neither were the British soldiers who were deployed in Londonderry and Belfast. What influenced the Labour government was the notion that the USC was "unacceptable" to Catholics. It didn't occur to them that this was only because the force kept preventing Republicans from trying to overthrow the state. No security force can be both effective and acceptable to everyone in Ulster.

Michael Canavan, Secretary of the DCDA, was asked about the USC at the Scarman tribunal.

> Can you point out anything they did in Derry, which could give rise to that opinion [that they were a partisan, undisciplined and dangerous force] - in July or August?

He replied:

> *Nothing that they did in Derry in July and August. The inference would have been from what they were, rather than what they did.* [29]

They had done nothing wrong, but they were still terrible people. Even when the USC was hardly used at all, as in the late 1960s, Republicans still clamoured for its disbandment, indicating more than anything their fear of the force's potential effectiveness. Looking back on August 1969 in Londonderry it is easier to see now that what was required was not necessarily a highly trained riot squad but any brave body of men who were capable of subduing the Bogside rioters and re-establishing the rule of law. If we had known then that the result of throwing a protective cordon around the rioters would be 20 years of terrorism, would we still have failed to send in the B Specials to help the police?

We Never Learn

It is fair to say that English politicians learnt nothing from August 1969. All the main groups in the "civil rights" movement were pursuing the goal of a united Ireland. When all the "civil rights" demands were met they therefore changed their stated aims. In the August riots a large part of the minority community had supported insurrectionary activities. But there was practically no English reaction, no feeling that we had been conned. Having been told that it was all about getting British rights, we were now confronted with the old demand for the overthrow of the Constitution. But instead of revising our views about this so-called community of innocents, which was throwing petrol bombs all over Ulster, we rushed in and asked what we could give them to make them like us better. We gave them the USC's head on a plate and there followed the only IRA campaign this century which wasn't crushed in a few short years.

The Provisional IRA emerged in 1970 after a split in the organisation. The Official IRA continued military activities until 1972 and thereafter it gradually evolved into the Workers Party, a non-violent Marxist organisation. The split was said to be over a number of issues: the Officials were too left wing, too critical of the Catholic Church, too Southern-orientated, too concerned with politics rather than physical force. These issues are no doubt interesting but what led to the triumph of the Provos within IRA ranks had more to do with its success at meeting community needs. To the Catholic community the Official IRA came to be seen as out of date, a throwback to the "civil rights" era when the emphasis had to be on social and economic issues. But Catholics had gone beyond all that. Now they wanted a physical force option, people who could supply and use guns. In August 1969 the Belfast IRA was seen to have been found wanting. Guns were not made available in the quantities required. When the British Army started to enforce the law in certain areas, clashes with Catholics occurred, particularly at Ballymurphy in West Belfast during 1970. Guns were therefore now needed to use against the Army.

Many of the Provisionals were new to the IRA - men like Martin McGuiness and Gerry Adams, who were yesterday's "civil rights" rioters. The Provos were the voice of the new militant generation as well as a faction of the old IRA. Eamonn McCann went so far as to say:

> The Provisional IRA is entitled to see itself, and to demand to be regarded by others, as the legitimate inheritor of the struggle for civil rights launched in the North in 1968...
> *The men and women of the Provisional IRA today are the rioting children of a decade ago. To my knowledge there is no member of the command staff of the Provos in Derry whose first conscious political experience was other than attendance at a civil rights march or rally and, probably, whatever bout*

of stone throwing ensued.[30]

The new breed of IRA member was the main reason why the internment of terrorist suspects was not completely successful in 1971. Many exotic reasons have been put forward as to why internment did not stop the IRA in its tracks, but the plain fact is that most of the Provos were not picked up. For some time before August 1969 the police had been pressured into leaving alone the hard-line Republican areas where the IRA was to flourish. After August 1969 the Army kept the police out of those same areas. RUC intelligence was therefore out of date and related chiefly to the old IRA men, most of whom stayed with the Officials. Maria McGuire, who was in the Provos at this time, said of internment:

> it became clear that the Provisionals command structure in the Six Counties had been left largely intact....
> *But so many of the Provisionals were soldiers at street level, who had joined the movement to defend themselves after 1969, and here the British intelligence was obviously quite sparse.* [31]

Internment, which had been useful as part of previous anti-IRA campaigns, was made ineffective by the decision of the British government to allow no-go areas to develop. Fortunately intelligence has now greatly improved, and as long as we are aware of why internment was of only limited success in 1971 and we do not imagine that it could work on its own, we shall not be tempted to rule out its use in the future.

Some rather curious British attitudes to the Republican community were displayed after the Lower Falls Curfew of 1970. They are worth examining as they go to the crux of the problem. On 3 July 1970 the Army searched a house in Balkan Street in the Lower Falls following a tip off. They found 15 pistols, 1 rifle, a Schmeisser sub-machine gun and a quantity of explosives and ammunition.[32] A hostile crowd gathered in protest and a riot developed. Roads were blocked with hijacked buses. Grenades, petrol bombs and gelignite bombs were thrown at soldiers, and they had to open fire.[33]

The Director of Operations, Lieutenant-General Sir Ian Freeland had been exasperated by attacks on solders at Ballymurphy in April, and now, seemingly on his own initiative, imposed on the Lower Falls "a movement restriction on the civilian population of that area for the sake of their own safety and the safety of the soldiers" at 10.00 pm on 3 July.[34] It was to be known as the Lower Falls

Curfew. Through the night gunfire was directed at the Army but order was restored. The area was sealed off and all houses searched for weapons. Soldiers recovered 52 pistols, 35 rifles, 6 automatic weapons, 14 shotguns, 100 home made bombs, 21,000 rounds of ammunition and some explosives.[35] Estimates of the number of houses involved varied from 3,000 (Richard Rose) to 5,000 (Jim Callaghan).

Desmond Hamill saw it as a military success but

In political terms it was a disaster, not only alienating a whole community but building up within it an even more active resentment against authority.[36]

Jim Callaghan thought that

The adverse impact on the Catholic community was out of all proportion to the success of the Army's haul. [37]

Let us imagine for a moment that this incident had occurred in Bristol or Manchester and that the police or Army had gone to a house and found 15 pistols, a rifle, a sub-machine gun, explosives and ammunition. What would we say of the local community if it reacted by rioting against the forces of law and order? I suspect we would think their actions despicable. And then what if a general search of the area uncovered over 100 guns plus bombs, explosives and ammunition? If we were told the community was upset that the searches had been carried out, I rather think we would say that the weapons finds completely justified the searches and that the community should feel a sense of shame that such an arsenal had been concealed in its area. But the people of the Lower Falls felt no sense of shame. They attacked our soldiers with guns, grenades and bombs, and afterwards blamed the Army, not their own neighbours. I think we are entitled to ask: What sort of people are they, who react in this way? We English very rarely asked this question. We were still under the illusion that we were dealing with a community of victims and a community of innocents.

It is said that the Lower Falls Curfew was a turning point. After that the Army's honeymoon with the Catholic population was over. But strangely some political commentators seem to think the population of the Lower Falls should have been left alone to build up its arsenal in peace, and that the Army made some kind of error. In reality the incident only showed that Catholics would look kindly on the Army as long as it did not interfere with their illicit activities.

As soon as it became a law enforcing agency it was no longer welcome. Once it ceased to serve Catholic interests , support was withdrawn.

Talking With the Terrorists

Republicans had been agitating for some time for the abolition of Stormont. When they finally got their wish in 1972, it came in bizarre circumstances. In January of that year some paratroopers shot dead 13 people in Londonderry after coming under fire from a crowd of demonstrators. Lord Widgery's report exonerated the soldiers.

Although formally the Stormont government had responsibility for law and order, it had no control over the Army, which came under the British Ministry of Defence. It was therefore strange that the British government reacted to criticism of the Army by announcing that it was taking law and order responsibilities away from Stormont. The Northern Ireland government said it could not accept this - it was after all the English who were making a mess of security policy - and Stormont was abolished. Direct rule from Westminster became a legal reality.

Some politicised elements in the Army had been keen to bargain Stormont away. Frank Kitson suggested that internment in 1971 could have been used

To cheer up the Protestants while seeking a major concession on the Catholic side - getting rid of Stormont - and introducing direct rule.[38]

The British faith in negotiations and concessions was pushed to the extreme when the government arranged talks with the IRA in July 1972. By now the terrorist campaign was in full swing but the Heath government incredibly flew the IRA leadership to London on an RAF plane and kindly flew them back again without laying a finger on them. Sean MacStiofain, Daithi O'Connaill (David O'Connell), Martin McGuiness, Seamus Twomey, Gerry Adams and Ivor Bell were in the IRA team which met William Whitelaw at the home of his junior minister, Paul Channon, in Cheyne Row, Chelsea.[39] According to Tim Pat Coogan, Whitelaw told the IRA men:

The minority in the North have been deprived of their rights. I set myself the task of conquering this. You can give me some help in the matter.[40]

On 21 July 1972, on what became known as Bloody Friday, the IRA set off 22 bombs in Belfast's city centre. At the Oxford Street bus station 6 people were blown to bits. It showed that the English guilt complex about "civil rights" could even lead ministers to talk to murderers and give them free passage back to Ulster so that they could slaughter innocent civilians just 2 weeks later. They had learnt nothing and there were to be further meetings with the IRA over the years to come.

The IRA and the Catholic Community

Successive British governments have held, at one and the same time, two quite contradictory views about the IRA. They move from one to the other depending on which suits their purpose. The first view is that the IRA is a "gangster minority", a bunch of parasites hated by the rest of the Catholic community, which only keeps quiet out of fear.

The other view is that we have to be careful what measures we take against terrorism as we might "drive people into the arms of the IRA". Now if the first view were true the Catholic community would welcome us getting these parasites off their back. They would give us the names of all the terrorists through channels like the confidential telephone line in Ulster (where callers don't have to give their names). They would remain quietly in their houses when the security forces came to arrest and intern the IRA men and afterwards would welcome the police and Army like conquering heroes. It's a nice fantasy, but far removed from the truth.

In fact any moves against the IRA, such as house searches for weapons or internment, lead to innumerable complaints from Catholics and have often led to rioting. The second view, that Catholics might be "driven into the arms of the IRA" could only be true if their objectives are not completely at odds with those of the terrorist organisation. People who hate the IRA and want it off their backs do not run to it and give it support when the security forces take steps to remove the parasite. If someone is about to be driven into the IRA's arms by the slightest action against the organisation, then he or she must have objectives which are very similar or identical to those of the IRA.

It is not very often I agree with Gerry Adams but his analysis of the relationship between the IRA and the Catholic community is fundamentally correct.

Whether the people in the nationalist areas agreed or disagreed with the IRA and all its actions they recognised it as their army, knew for the most part which of their neighbours were members.[41]

Support for the IRA amongst the nationalist population of the 6 counties has been, as the tacticians of guerrilla warfare such as Mao and Che put it, the sea in which the people's army has swum and, like the sea, it has its tides, its ebbs and flows, but it is always there. [42]

Despite all the British propaganda stories it is obvious that the IRA exists and operates with the active consent of a sufficient number of people to finance, arm, clothe, feed, accommodate and transport IRA volunteers and in every way build up around them a voluntary political infrastructure.[43]

Very many people who disagree absolutely with the IRA nevertheless see it as a very important part of the political equation. They might deplore it, dislike it, have moral objections to it, but still have the feeling that if it did not exist there would be no hope of getting change. [44]

Barritt and Carter, writing just after the explosion of Catholic opposition to the internment of IRA suspects in 1971, said:

It was not realistic to suppose that the IRA, in the period after the introduction of internment, was a small band of evil fanatics with no convinced support from the Catholic population.[45]

Paul Arthur, writing in the 1980s, talked of the "Catholic ambivalence towards violence" and said that "there is no evidence of wholesale abhorrence in the Catholic community of what is being done in their name by their self-appointed protectors."[46] He saw the Provos as quite different from the "urban guerrilla" groups which emerged in the late 1960s. The IRA was "much more part of 'the people', deeply rooted in the community, and possessing historical precedents which went back at least to the mid-nineteenth century."[47]

The TV journalist Desmond Hamill pointed out that

It was a long time before soldiers realised that one of the fundamental problems was that people's views of what behaviour is acceptable is governed, very largely, by what they are used to. The 'respectability' of killing in the Republican cause goes back a long way, and as for stoning, the local view was often, 'Well the lad's doing no harm, he's just stoning the military.' [48]

The physical force tradition in Catholic politics is very well established. That is why I suggested that we might usefully regard the IRA as just as much an idea rooted in the consciousness of Irish Catholics as an organisation. The "civil rights" struggle showed that concessions were most easily extracted against a background of violence. The IRA continues to exist because it is useful to Northern Ireland Catholics. It provides the violence which is the cause of concessions. As Gerry Adams said, if the IRA did not exist there might be no hope of getting change; in other words progress towards a united Ireland, a goal which most Catholics share with the IRA. It is for the moment, and for the foreseeable future, providing useful means to bring about the desired end.

Passive support for the IRA is even resistant to the most horrible atrocities which it commits. One of these was the Abercorn Restaurant bomb of 4 March 1972. The explosion injured 136 people and killed 2 women in their early 20s. Jennifer McNern (21) lost both of her legs and her sister Rosaleen lost both legs, an arm and an eye. Richard Clutterbuck wrote a year later that the bombing

> was probably a major factor in sickening the remaining Belfast Catholics of violence.[49]

Unfortunately his remarks were premature. He underestimated the capacity of Belfast Catholics to stomach IRA violence.

On 8 November 1987 the IRA slaughtered 11 people as they waited to attend a Remembrance Day service. It became known as the Enniskillen Massacre. The tragedy moved the whole nation. Surely this would turn people away from the IRA. Later TV viewers witnessed the horror of 2 Army corporals being dragged from their car by a mob in West Belfast and murdered by the IRA.

In May 1989 Ulster held its local elections and Catholic voters had the opportunity to give their verdict on these atrocities. All Sinn Fein candidates are required to unambiguously support the "armed struggle" and so the choice was clear.

In the Enniskillen Ward of Fermanagh District Council, Sinn Fein once again outpolled the SDLP. Sinn Fein also got a higher total vote in Fermanagh District. In the 2 West Belfast wards of Upper and Lower Falls, the IRA's political wing again defeated the SDLP by a combined vote of 13,268 to 8,530. The victory was repeated in the Belfast totals. Media hype tended to disguise the fact that Sinn Fein's percentage vote throughout Ulster was virtually unchanged.

Northern Ireland's Catholics have always been prepared to support terrorist candidates. In 1955, with Republican sentiment on the upswing, Sinn Fein decided to fight all the Ulster seats in the Westminster general election. Many of these candidates were convicted IRA terrorists currently serving prison sentences. Two of the convicts, Tom Mitchell in Mid Ulster and Phil Clarke in Fermanagh and South Tyrone, were elected by narrow majorities in straight fights with Unionist candidates. Each Sinn Fein man polled over 30,000 votes. The entire Catholic electorate had backed them. Mitchell, who we came across earlier, had been convicted for taking part in an arms raid on the British Army barracks at Omagh in 1954. Another IRA prisoner reveived 19,640 votes in the Londonderry constituency.

In 1981 IRA men at the Maze went on hunger strike in support of "political status". Bobby Sands had been arrested on his way back from bombing a furniture store and was convicted of possessing a revolver which was found in the car.[50] He became the IRA Public Relations Officer in the H-Blocks and shortly before his hunger strike took over as its Commanding Officer.[51] In the middle of his hunger strike a Westminister by-election was held in Fermanagh and South Tyrone. The SDLP stood aside and Sands won the election on 9 April 1981, again with over 30,000 votes. Sands starved himself to death and in another by-election in August 1981 his election agent, Owen Carron, won the seat. The SDLP claimed it had been tricked in May, believing that another Republican candidate would stand against Sands, but it had no excuse for stepping aside in August. The truth is that the Catholic population of Fermanagh and South Tyrone did not want an SDLP candidate to stand against the IRA men and the party would have been vilified by ordinary Catholics if it had done so. All other explanations were just rationalisations of this fact.

Catholics also show their latent support for the IRA by their attendance at Republican funerals. In 1957 Sean South and Feargal O'Hanlon were killed whilst taking part in an IRA attack on Brookeborough RUC barracks in Co. Fermanagh.

When the bodies of South and O'Hanlon were carried across the border, their transmutation from young men to martyrs began. There began a week of all but national mourning. Crowds lined the route of South's cortege to Dublin. Larger crowds came to pay their respect. Mass cards piled up and overflowed. Town Councils and County Corporations passed votes of

*sympathy, in some cases not only for South and O'Hanlon, but also for their
cause....*

*At midnight on January 4, twenty thousand including the city mayor [of
Limerick] were waiting for the hearse.   The next day a great silent
procession of fifty thousand followed the casket to the grave.* [52]

Sands' burial in the North attracted an incredible 100,000 people.[53] The pope
had sent his envoy, Monsignor John Magee, to visit Sands in jail and present
him with a silver crucifix. Charles Haughey, leader of Fianna Fail, sent his own
emissary, Sile de Valera, granddaughter of Eamon de Valera.[54] The amazing
passion for Republicanism, even of the violent variety, lurks beneath the
surface, occasionally explodes into view, and sometimes makes the pope feel
that he has to pay homage.

We might again well ask of Ulster's minority: What sort of people are they?
Well they are certainly not innocents. They are quite comfortable voting for
convicted terrorists. It is quite certain that if the SDLP were to fold tomorrow,
then almost all its votes would go to Sinn Fein. Catholics would hardly bat an
eyelid. These are the same people whose loyalty we are expected to buy with
political concessions.

Lessons From the Colonies

We have seen that a body of Counter-Insurgency Theory emerged from the
campaigns in places like Malaya, Kenya, Aden and Cyprus. Militarily the
British Army did quite well in these places under very unfavourable conditions.
Many useful anti-terrorist measures were developed and then were seemingly
forgotten once we deployed troops in Ulster. On the other hand the political
aspects of counter-insurgency were inevitably shaped by the fact that in all of
the colonies our ultimate objective was to withdraw and bring British rule to an
end. Many bad habits were undoubtedly picked up by senior Army officers and
politicians alike, and much of the thinking about security policy is totally
inappropriate to a part of the United Kingdom which remains so in accordance
with the democratically expressed wishes of a vast majority of its people.

Our main aim in these colonies seems to have been to try and identify a group
of "moderates" to whom we could hand over power. In each country there was
a terrorist organisation trying to gain independence (or in the case of Cyprus,
union with Greece). The moderate politicians and the terrorist organisations
had the same ultimate objective. We British were for the most part not trying

to frustrate that objective, but we preferred to hand over power to nice, peaceful people rather than to terrorists. One of our main political weapons was therefore to give them what they wanted as a way of winning over the moderates and showing the people that violence was not necessary. Counter-Insurgency Theory talks of "winning the battle for hearts and minds". Soldiers familiar with the colonial campaigns came to believe that this meant making concessions to the population whose support the terrorists were trying to gain.

This worked in Malaya, for instance, where we promised independence and this cut the ground from under the Communist guerrillas. Malaya did not go Communist. But it was only possible to take this approach because the majority wanted British rule to end and we wanted to go. The equivalent policy in Northern Ireland would be to promise a united Ireland to the SDLP as a way of outflanking the IRA. As both organisations represent an anti-British minority, this is simply not relevant.

In the other 3 places - Kenya, Aden and Cyprus - the soldiers did a good job but the political strategy was a total disaster. In Kenya we faced the Mau Mau, who committed horrific and obscene atrocities. Their oaths included a pledge of loyalty to Jomo Kenyatta.[55] Kenyatta was sentenced to 7 years imprisonment in 1953 for managing the organisation. The Mau Mau was defeated militarily but Kenyatta became a government minister in 1962 and a year later was appointed as the first prime minister of a self-governing Kenya.[56] In 1964 Kenya became a one party state and the Mau Mau commander, "General China" (Waruhu Itote), became head of Kenyatta's personal protection squad.[57] Power had passed to the terrorists' leader.

In Aden our initial aims were to transfer power to a democratised federal government based on local tribal leaders and to resist Egyptian and Yemeni attempts to interfere in South Arabia. We were also to maintain our military base in Aden.[58] In the end we handed Aden over to the main terrorist organisation, the Egyptian-backed National Liberation Front, and abandoned our military base. [59]

Over in Cyprus Britain had to contend with an EOKA terrorist campaign aimed at bringing about Enosis (union with Greece). Archbishop Makarios was deported to the Seychelles in 1956 because he was implicated in the terrorist campaign.[60] However he had to be brought back in 1959 and was elected President of an independent Cyprus. Leading members of EOKA were appointed as ministers.[61] Markarios said in 1960:

The epic grandeur and glory of EOKA's liberation struggle has laid the foundation stone of national freedom.[62]

He saw independence as a stepping stone to Enosis and started dismantling safeguards for the Turkish Cypriot community built into the settlement with Britain. Terrorist leader George Grivas was brought back in 1964 to lead a military campaign against the Turkish Cypriots.[63] Makarios was later overthrown by another EOKA terrorist, Nicos Sampson, but he was stopped in his tracks when Turkey invaded the island, which was then partitioned in 1974.

My own impression of the colonial experience is that although we are quite good at physically fighting terrorists, neither the British Army nor British politicians have much experience of putting together a successful political package as part of a counter-insurgency campaign. They seem to have no experience at all of frustrating terrorist political objectives. On the contrary we seem to have conceded the political objectives from day one or ended up in complete disarray, actually handing over power to terrorist leaders.

Ex-Provo Maria McGuire confirmed that

The main examples followed by the Provisionals in deciding to hit British soldiers were the guerrilla campaigns against the British in Cyprus in the 1950s and Aden in the 1960s.[64]

Desmond Hamill summed it up thus:

The British, and some other colonial powers, had been seen to follow a pattern. At the start of terrorist activity there were always strong denials that the Government would give way to violence. After violence continued for a while it would be decided that the asset was not worth preserving and the colonial government would pack up and go. On this basis the Provisionals were to build their strategy.[65]

In the colonies we weren't very good at winning. On the other hand the RUC, the B Specials and the Unionist government had considerable experience of defeating the IRA. And yet it is a colonial-style policy of concessions that we are following, and we seem reluctant to learn anything from previous victories over the IRA.

The 1950s campaign ended in an IRA defeat. It is possible to cite many reasons for this, but I would say that the main consideration was that the Catholic community believed the campaign was a lost cause and hence gave little support to the terrorists. It simply did not believe the battle could be won. Neither the British nor Northern Ireland governments were prepared to consider IRA demands for a united Ireland. The defeat was caused by hopelessness, and the subsequent peace was also the product of a lack of hope. This in turn was the result of Unionist political policy, which was an essential part of their counter-insurgency strategy. It had nothing to do with making political concessions to Irish Republicans, but it had plenty to do with convincing your enemies that they could not win.

This successful policy was undermined during the "civil rights" era. Jim Callaghan could not grasp the political realities of Ulster in 1969.

From this time on we were engaged in a strenuous battle to win the hearts and minds of the Catholic population and to prevent them from falling into the despair that would give the terrorists their chance.[66]

In fact terrorism was born not out of despair but hope. It did not come because demands were frustrated but because they were conceded. In the 1950s no-one believed a united Ireland was possible in the foreseeable future; from the late 1960s onwards they did. All things were possible. Now a terrorist campaign made sense. Ever since, successive British governments have been reluctant to deny Republican hopes of achieving any of their political objectives. This has been a fundamental flaw in security policy.

The Role of the Irish Republic

The Irish government has always been tough on the IRA when it has threatened to disrupt Southern politics. In 1922 Michael Collins concluded a treaty with Britain which settled for independence in a 26 county Irish Free State. His opponents, the IRA Irregulars, thought this was a betrayal of the ideal of Irish unity and a civil war broke out. Collins didn't bother trying to win hearts and minds. By May 1923 he had locked up 11,316 men and executed 77 more.[67] On 7 March 1923, 9 Irregulars were tied together around a landmine at Ballyseedy Cross near Tralee. They were then blown up.[68] When a member of the Dail was murdered by Irregulars, the Free State government took out 4 senior IRA prisoners they were holding and had them shot.[69] The civil war soon ended.

Under the South's Public Safety Act 1931 the IRA was declared illegal, military tribunals were set up and powers of arrest and detention increased.[70] There were several executions without judicial trial and

> *No fewer than 513 persons were convicted by the Eire Military Tribunals between 1 September 1933 and 5 February 1935, while under the Northern Ireland Special Powers Act, it is worth noting that no special Court or Tribunal of Northern Ireland has ever executed anyone.* [71]

Eamon de Valera's government briefly lifted the IRA ban but reimposed it very quickly in June 1936.[72] The Offences Against the State Act 1939 brought in internment without trial and 400 Republicans were imprisoned during the Second World War.[73] In 1957, 60 were arrested under this same act and interned at the Curragh. Soon most of the leadership of Sinn Fein and the IRA was locked up.[74] Another military tribunal was set up in November 1961 and 25 heavy sentences were imposed on IRA men.[75]

During the current terrorist campaign, the Irish Republic established special courts in 1972 under the Offences Against the State Act which provide for trial by 3 judges without a jury.[76] In 1976, the Emergency Powers Act extended the period IRA suspects could be held without charge and Section 31 of the Broadcasting Act banned Sinn Fein and the IRA from radio and television, where they cannot even be quoted.[77]

It can therefore be seen that the South's legislation against the IRA has, if anything, been more extensive than that operative in Northern Ireland. This is a telling argument against those who accused the Stormont government of having oppressive legislation.

But we must not misunderstand Southern attitudes. The main motive for moving against the IRA has been fear of the disruption it can cause within the Irish Republic. IRA campaigns unleash strong passions which can sweep Southern governments out of power. Michael Farrell thought that the controversy surrounding anti-IRA measures brought down the Irish government in 1957.[78] Sinn Fein got 66,000 votes and won 4 seats in that election.[79] Bishop and Mallie saw disquiet over special legislation as contributing to Cosgrave's defeat in 1977. [80] Tim Pat Coogan believed that the intervention of H-Block candidates (IRA hunger strikers) cost Fianna Fail the 1981 general election.[81] In the 1950s

The Fine Gael government under John Costello had been prodded into

action by two considerations: the IRAs activities were threatening to propel the republic into a diplomatic confrontation with Britain, and it seemed that the IRA could mount a serious challenge to the state itself. [82]

J. Bowyer Bell felt that

Costello's fragile coalition, supported by the remaining three members of Clann na Poblachta, had to tread warily, fearful that the campaign might set off a patriotic orgy in the Republic. [83]

Cosgrave, in 1976, feared that the IRA campaign "if not checked would be spreading the same mayhem in the South." [84]

Once we understand the motivation of Southern governments, we shall not be tempted to have unreasonable expectations about the help they will be prepared to give in fighting the IRA in the North. These governments are after all still claiming jurisdiction over Ulster and still want a united Ireland. Thus the South will usually only move against the IRA when it considers terrorism to be a threat to the internal stability of the Irish Republic.

We have already seen how the Fianna Fail government sought to exploit Ulster's problems in 1968-69 by raising the constitutional question. Several senior politicians wanted the Irish Army to invade the Province. We can throw more light on Irish attitudes by taking a look at the Arms Trial scandal.

On 16 August 1969 the Irish government decided to make available financial aid to Northern Catholics. The precise sums involved and the methods of distributing the money were left to the Minister of Finance, Charles Haughey. He consulted an Irish Army intelligence officer, Captain James Kelly, who had been meeting people from the North and money was paid into a Belfast Fund for the Relief of Distress. According to Captain Kelly, 2 subsidiary accounts were opened at the Munster and Leinster Bank, Lower Baggot Street, Dublin on 12 November 1969 in the fictitious names of George Dixon and Ann O'Brien. The O'Brien account was to finance propaganda, the Dixon account was to buy arms. [85] In September 1969 James Kelly had seen Sean Keenan in Londonderry and on 6 October he met a number of representatives of the defence committees in Bailieborough, Co. Cavan. They included IRA men Keenan and Jim Sullivan. [86] It was through these people that arms would be distributed.

A key man was Northern IRA officer, John Kelly (no relation). He was to become Captain Kelly's main contact, and both ended up in the dock during the Arms Trial of 1970. John Kelly had led an armed IRA raiding party into the North on 30 December 1956. He was apprehended by the RUC near Dunamore, Co. Tyrone and was given an 8 year sentence.[87] This fact was known to Captain Kelly.[88]

A deposit was paid for a shipment of arms from the Continent. Captain Kelly consulted the Director of Irish Army Intelligence, Colonel Hefferon, and he cleared the operation with the Irish Minister of Defence, James Gibbons. Kelly thereafter kept Gibbons informed about how the operation was proceeding.[89] The consignment, which was due to contain pistols, machine guns and bullet proof vests, was seized by the Irish Special Branch in April 1970 at Dublin Airport. Captain Kelly met Hefferon, Neil Blaney and Gibbons on 23 April.

The two ministers did most of the talking; both seemed to be puzzled as to why the Special Branch should have mounted the weekend operation to seize the expected arms.[90]

The Special Branch had not been kept informed and the situation was complicated by the fact that Hefferon had retired on 9 April and his successor, Colonel Delaney, had also not been briefed. Jack Lynch feigned outrage that this had been going on, fearing the bad publicity, although Chief Superintendent Fleming (head of Special Branch) told Captain Kelly he believed Lynch knew about the operation all the time.[91]

Lynch asked for the resignation of Neil Blaney and Charles Haughey in May 1970. James and John Kelly were arrested. Gibbons denied everything and was given a promotion. Gibbons was the key man. In Irish law the importation of the weapons did not need a signed certificate under the relevant act if it was under the authority of the Minister of Defence for the use of the Irish defence forces. If he said yes it was an official operation. A whole host of witnesses, including government ministers and the Director of Army Intelligence, testified that Gibbons had approved the operation in spite of his denials. The accused agreed that they had tried to bring in the weapons, but the jury took less than an hour to conclude that this was not an illegal operation as it had official approval.

Charles Haughey's role was slightly different. As Minister of Finance he had been asked by Captain Kelly to authorise the importation of a consignment without the usual customs clearance. Haughey had agreed without asking what it was, and hence also found himself in the dock. Haughey did not, however, try to distance himself from the operation. He testified that James Kelly "had a very special role by authority of the Government".[92] Anything Army intelligence wanted was alright by him.

It was present in my mind that these were items, whatever they were, which were needed by the army to fulfill the contingency plans directive.[93]

Haughey confirmed that Gibbons had been instructed by the Irish government in August 1969 to get the Irish Army to make contingency plans in relation to the North.[94] The following exchange then took place between Charles Haughey and Mr. McCarthy, a barrister at the trial:

McCarthy:　*If you had known, first, that the consignment contained arms, ammunition and bullet-proof vests, would that have made any difference?*

Haughey:　*Not the slightest, no. The contingency plans naturally envisaged items of that nature and I could also envisage the provision for the army here of special types of arms and ammunition, which would not normally be issued to them and in so far, if I had known that the consignment did consist of any particular type of arms and ammunition, I would have given the sanction just the same.*

McCarthy:　*If you had known that they were intended for possible ultimate distibution to civilians in the North would that have made any difference?*

Haughey:　*No, not really, provided, of course, that a Government decision intervened. I would have regarded it as a very normal part of army preparations in pursuance of the contingency plans that they would provide themselves with, and store here on this side of the border, arms which might ultimately, if the Government said so, be distributed to other persons.*[95]

In short Charles Haughey had no objections in principle to weapons being distributed in Ulster via IRA officers.

Our old friend Sam Dowling, Chairman of the Newry Civil Rights Association, who was to the fore of rioting in August 1969, was put on trial in the South shortly after Haughey & co. for possessing 3 sub-machine guns, a .303 rifle, a bomb and 3.25 lbs. of gelignite. He argued that "Those weapons were in our possession, were at that time in my possession, through the work of officers and agents of the Irish government." He was acquitted.[96]

Some other interesting things came out of the more famous of the Arms Trials. Minister of Defence, James Gibbons, admitted that he had authorised the enrollment of a number of people from Londonderry into the FCA (Irish reserve defence force) so that they could receive official arms training in Co. Donegal.[97] He agreed that this was in order that they could in a position to defend themselves, but denied that they were going to be given guns.[98]

Colonel Hefferon, Director of Irish Army Intelligence, testified that Gibbons had ordered the movement of 500 rifles to Dundalk on 2 April 1970. A message had been sent to James Kelly asking him to return from the Continent to help with their possible distribution. Hefferon stated:

> *Yes, I said that, at the time I sent the message, I was very worried about this shipment of rifles and ammunition, and that the meaning I took out of this sudden order to send rifles and ammunition and gas masks, I think, to Dundalk was that a very bad situation was about to break out in the North and that the possibility that these rifles, or some part of them, might require to be distributed in this event could not be ruled out.*[99]

Gibbons denied that these arms were for distribution in Ulster and said they might have been used by people in the South to defend themselves against incursions from the North![100]

The Minister of Justice at that time, Mr. O'Morain, revealed at the trial that the cabinet contingency plans included "limited incursions by the army into the North".[101] Gibbons confirmed that incursions had been discussed in a "Doomsday situation".[102] According to the Sunday Times Insight Team the Irish Army plan, which Haughey, Boland and Blaney had wanted implemented on 13 August 1969, involved a Londonderry doctor calling for an ambulance to come from Donegal.

> *Arrangments had been made for this to be fired on when it crossed the border. Outraged, the Irish Army would then take Craigavon Bridge and*

enter Derry. Meanwhile in the south-east corner of Ulster, the Sixth Brigade were to advance North across the border and take Lurgan and Toome Bridge, giving themselves control of the top and bottom of Lough Neagh which seperates Belfast from the rest of the province. Derry and Newry - the two Catholic border cities - would be occupied. When reinforcements arrived, the 'spearhead' Sixth Brigade would move on from Lough Neagh into Belfast.[103]

Captain James Kelly was to go on to become a member of Fianna Fail's Executive in the 1980s. Far from being disgraced, Charles Haughey replaced Jack Lynch (the man who had sacked him) as Fianna Fail leader in 1979. As I write the man who supported the invasion of Ulster and the distribution of guns to Northern Republicans is the Irish prime minister. This is the same man who is reverently consulted by the British government about the internal affairs of Northern Ireland through the workings of the Anglo-Irish Agreement. Until this agreement was signed we were assured that the South was doing everything possible to help with cross-border security. Then suddenly we were told that more could be done, but only in return for the right to meddle in Ulster's internal affairs. Innocent men and women have therefore died in IRA raids across the border because the South would not help until it made progress on its claim to jurisdiction over Ulster. Such is the quality of the Irish Republic's friendship.

B.   The SDLP and the IRA

The Social Democratic and Labour Party (SDLP) was launched in August 1970. The inclusion of the word "Labour" in the title owed much to the Belfast Socialists Paddy Devlin, who came from the NILP, and Gerry Fitt from the Republican Labour Party. Both were to depart before the decade ended and thereafter the SDLP's support in Belfast began to crumble. Sinn Fein overtook it in the 1980s. Fitt was elected as the first leader but John Hume has always been the main strategist. Hume had been preparing the way for the SDLP throughout 1969-70 by setting up branches of his Independent Organisation in Londonderry.

The former "civil rights" leaders finally nailed their colours to the mast by including in the SDLP Constitution's Principles and Objects:

> *4. To promote the cause of Irish unity based on the consent of a majority of people*
> *in Northern Ireland.*[1]

In 1971 the SDLP came out against internment, even though it had been successfully used North and South of the border in all previous IRA campaigns. The party withdrew from Stormont in protest. Again the search for ideological reasons will not be particularly fruitful. The IRA existed by popular consent of the Catholic population. It was one weapon the community wanted to keep in its arsenal. Hence the opposition to internment. It is idle to think that the SDLP had a choice about whether or not to oppose internment. By failing to do what it was told it would have faced a collapse in its support.

Stormont went in 1972 and in October of that year the British government brought out a Green Paper called *The Future of Northern Ireland*. It was at this point, politically speaking, that the wheels fell off the wagon and to this day they have never been fixed back on. The Green Paper was the culmination of English thinking arising from guilt-ridden attitudes about the "civil rights" era. That thinking, in spite of many changes in government personnel, has remained practically unaltered to the present day. The paper is the text book on which English failure in Ulster is based.

It noted a number of factors which had to be taken into account in deciding how

Ulster should be governed in the future. At Stormont the governing parties had not alternated. The Unionists had always been in power.[2] The Cameron Report had "proved" that there had been discrimination and gerrymandering.[3] There had been a political rift with the Catholic leaders and there was little hope of "political progress".

The attitude of the Government has been consistently to seek by inter-party discussions the widest possible measure of agreement as to how Northern Ireland should in future be governed and how in particular the minority as well as the majority may be assured of an active, permanent and guaranteed role in its life and public affairs.[4]

The Green Paper quoted Ted Heath as saying on 15 November 1971:

If at some future date the majority of the people in Northern Ireland want unification and express that desire in the appropriate constitutional manner, I do not believe any British government would stand in the way.[5]

The Northern Ireland government had certain powers which were "controversial and divisive", said the Green Paper, such as those over electoral law and boundaries, security and the police. There were fears that majority government in Northern Ireland might in future use its powers "oppressively and discriminatorily". The Unionist Research Department commented on these powers:

They may be controversial but they are really no more divisive than the very existence of Government itself.

We believe this is because it is not the powers themselves that are 'divisive' but the existence of the identifiable unit of Northern Ireland linked to the United Kingdom. The fact that citizenship is so protected has always been divisive. It is divisive because of a refusal by a small minority to accept that citizenship. This is why the very existence of Government has been made to seem divisive and this is why, because it does not examine the fundamental nature of the struggle, the Green Paper appears to us to miss the real issues on policing.[6]

The Green Paper then got to its main proposals:

It is also a fact that an element of the minority in Northern Ireland has hitherto seen itself as simply part of the wider Irish community. The problem of accommodating that minority within the political structures of Northern Ireland has to some considerable extent been an aspect of a wider problem within Ireland as a whole.[7]

It is therefore clearly desirable that any new arrangements for Northern Ireland should, whilst meeting the wishes of Northern Ireland and Great Britain, be so far as possible acceptable to and accepted by the Republic of Ireland....[8]

In accordance with the specific pledges given by succesive United Kingdom Governments, Northern Ireland must and will remain part of the United Kingdom for as long as that is the wish of a majority of the people; but that status does not preclude the necessary taking into account of what has been described in this paper as the 'Irish Dimension'.[9]

A Northern Ireland assembly or authority must be capable of involving all its members constructively in ways which satisfy them and those they represent that the whole community has a part to play in the government of the Province. As a minimum this would involve assuring minority groups of an effective voice and a real influence; but there are strong arguments that the objective of real participation should be achieved by giving minority interests a share in the exercise of executive power....[10]

In 1973 the Irish Dimension and the concept of power sharing were embodied in the Sunningdale Agreement between the British and Irish governments.

The SDLP's own paper, *Towards a New Ireland,* was attached to the government's Green Paper as Annex 7. Its aggressive tone on the constitutional question tended to bear out the Unionist analysis of the problem. The SDLP proposed

(1)   *An immediate declaration by Britain that she believes that it would be in the best interest of all sections of the Communities in both Islands, if Ireland were to become united on terms which would be acceptable to all the people of Ireland and that she will positively encourage the prosecution of this viewpoint.*

(2)   *The creation of an interim system of Government for Northern Ireland which will be fair to all sections of the people of Northern Ireland.*

*(3)   The creation of Democratic Machinery in Ireland to implement the
terms of the above declaration by the agreement and consent of the
people of Ireland, North and South.*[11]

It said that "Catholics in general will continue to give their loyalty to Ireland"
and " the continuation of the present constitutional relationship with Britain
means victory for Protestants and defeat for Catholics."[12] It wanted "Joint
Sovereignty of Northern Ireland" by Britain and the Irish Republic.

*Two Commissioners to act jointly as the Representatives of the Sovereign
powers who must jointly sign all legislation passed by the Northern Ireland
Assembly.*[13]

No representation in either Westminster or Dublin Parliament is envisaged.[14]

The SDLP also wanted a National Senate of Ireland.

*The basic function of the Senate should be to plan the integration of the
whole island by preparing the harmonisation of the structures, laws and
services of both parts of Ireland to agree on an acceptable constitution for
a New Ireland and its relationship with Britain.*[15]

Britain had been told the struggle was all about "civil rights", not the
constitutional question. The "civil rights" demands were conceded. Catholics
then said that what they wanted was the abolition of the B Specials and the end
of the Stormont Parliament. Those demands were conceded. Now we were
being told they wanted a united Ireland and that other institutions under
consideration would only constitute an "interim system of Government". The
goal posts were being continually shifted, but the British government was
prepared to consider any demand to appease the minority.

Brian Faulkner, the former Northern Ireland prime minister, was persuaded to
go along with the power sharing plan. The SDLP was given ministerial posts
in the new Executive. Faulkner, during elections to the new Assembly in June
1973, promised he would not share power with parties "whose primary aim is
a united Ireland".[16] Many Unionists felt this ruled out the now strongly
Republican SDLP and voted accordingly. Many pro-Assembly Unionists were
elected. Once the SDLP was brought into government, attitudes in the Unionist
community changed. To most Unionists it was absurd to include in the
Northern Ireland Executive body, ministers who were dedicated to the overthrow

of the Northern Ireland state and the ending of the link with Britain. Government ministers must agree on basic constitutional questions. Furthermore, as the SDLP saw this as only an interim arrangement, they would clearly use their positions to promote a united Ireland from within the Northern Ireland government itself. As Eamonn McCann said:

> *in order to sell the deal to the Catholic community the SDLP had to present it not just as a means of expressing its aspiration towards a united Ireland but as a means of achieving it.*[17]

In February 1974 the Westminster general election provided an opportunity for Ulster to pass its verdict on the power sharing Executive and the Council of Ireland which was designed to promote North-South co-operation and harmonisation. Opponents of the institutions banded together as the United Ulster Unionist Council (UUUC). They won 11 out of the 12 Westminster seats (Gerry Fitt retained West Belfast) and all of the Faulknerite Unionists were defeated. By then Faulkner had had to resign as Unionist Party leader. Even T.E. Utley, who was a defeated pro-power sharing Unionist in that election, said of William Whitelaw:

> *What he had achieved, in harsh reality, was an agreement with Unionist politicians who, by virtue of signing it, had rendered themselves wholly unrepresentative of any substantial section of Northern Irish opinion.*[18]

The Executive was therefore operating without popular support. It had been soundly rejected. However it clung to power in a startlingly undemocratic way. The Ulster Workers Council (UWC) wanted new elections to the Assembly so that it would reflect the electorate's wishes. This request was refused and so began the Loyalist Workers Strike of May 1974. It had massive support and the Executive collapsed. It was a historic example of how ordinary people could engage in mass action to win back democratic rights.

The actions of the SDLP were instructive. Even though he knew he had little popular support and was faced with a strike enjoying majority approval, John Hume (a minister in the power sharing Executive) said:

> *I'll sit here until there is shit flowing up Royal Avenue...* [19]

Once it had its hands on the reins of power the SDLP was not at all interested in whether it had consent or not. But then the SDLP's idea of consent has always been an odd one. It wanted Irish unification by consent, but saw nothing contradictory between this and its request that the British government declare itself to be in favour of a united Ireland, contrary to the wishes of Ulster's majority. In its October 1974 general election manifesto the SDLP went so far as to call "for a British declaration of intent to withdraw from Northern Ireland, if loyalists rejected both power-sharing and an Irish dimension."[20]

The SDLP sees the path to a united Ireland as consisting of a number of stages which will gradually undermine Ulster's position as part of the United Kingdom and increase the role of the Irish Republic in Ulster's internal affairs. By the time we are ready for the last stage of the process, which would involve a formal handover to the Irish Republic, all of Ulster's British institutional arrangements will have been destroyed. It is only the final stage in the process which the SDLP sees as requiring consent. Things like the Irish Dimension and power sharing can be imposed by the British government against the wishes of the majority if it feels it can get away with it.

It is interesting that John Hume himself had proposed in February 1970 to the Crowther Commission that there should be a periodic referendum on the constitutional question in order to remove it from party politics.[21] This seems rather odd for a supporter of a united Ireland who must have known he would lose the vote. But his intention was clear. During the "civil rights" era there were great advantages in preventing opponents from talking about the constitutional question while Republicans pursued the policies which they believed would lead to a united Ireland. Hume wanted a referendum so that he could say: 'Right, you have won that vote. We can all stop talking about the constitutional question until the next referendum and thus free party politics of this issue.' He would then be able to work on all the intermediate plans he had to undermine the British link whilst insisting that he was not raising the constitutional question. Unionists saw through this and by the time of the Border Poll in 1973 Hume had lost interest in the ploy.

John Hume is rather like the man who comes along and smashes all the windows in your home and then assures you that you will not be forced to leave. There will be no change in your address without your consent. He then takes a sledgehammer and batters your front door off its hinges and repeats his assurance. The next day he takes the tiles off your roof and knocks a hole in your wall. Still he says: 'You won't be moved without your consent. It's entirely your decision.' Eventually the house will become uninhabitable and you may decide to leave. For consent to be genuine it has to be freely given.

But does the occupier in our example really consent to move?

Hume the strategist aims at winning a whole series of incremental changes in Ulster's constitutional position, none of which constitutes the creation of a united Ireland and hence none of which, in his view, requires the consent of the majority. At the end of the process he hopes that the British connection will become so tenuous and Ulster's position so precarious that the majority will finally fall in with his plans. His protestations that the creation of these interim arrangements does not raise the constitutional question are wearing a little thin.

Hume has developed a sweet and reasonable exterior which he hopes will appeal to the British public. He continually asks for talks which will lead to a "political settlement". But a settlement has a certain amount of finality about it. Hume therefore likes to give the impression that he is prepared to conclude an agreement with the Unionists which will be in full and final settlement of the Catholic's claim for "justice". But he continually negotiates in bad faith. His and the SDLP's position is the same as it was in 1972. The power sharing Executive was to be no more than an interim government which would eventually lead to a united Ireland. In 1984 the SDLP got together with the South's Fianna Fail and Fine Gael in the Forum Report to reaffirm that its favoured option was a unitary state covering Ireland's 32 counties. Therefore what Hume is always offering to negotiate is only an interim settlement. He is happy to take half a loaf today in the form of power sharing and the Irish Dimension, and then he will come back for the other half of the loaf (a united Ireland) tomorrow.

Unionist opposition to power sharing and the Irish Dimension, which were once again the objectives of the Anglo-Irish Agreement, are based on matters of principle. An anti-British minority which wants to overthow the Constitution is not a suitable partner in exotic governmental arrangements which would not be tolerated on the Mainland; and no foreign government, particularly one which claims jurisdiction over part of the UK, should be given a say in the internal affairs of our country. But Unionists are also opposed to such arrangements because they are not the end of the matter; they are only the beginning. John Hume has never and will never renounce the goal of a united Ireland, and hence every time he comes to the negotiating table he is trying to make as much progress as possible towards that goal. Whatever he gets he will not be satisfied with. Tomorrow he will still want more, and what he wants is a united Ireland. Any concessions on the Irish Dimension and power sharing simply encourage Republicans to believe they are on course to their ultimate objective. That is why Unionists are right not to enter into talks with the SDLP.

By winning the next general election the Conservative Party could be in power for nearly 20 years. At the end of that period it is likely that Labour Party supporters would be feeling pretty alientated. Compared with the constitutional rift between the Unionists and the SDLP, the differences between Labour and Conservative are small. They both agree on Great Britain's main constitutional arrangements. And yet no-one has suggested that Mrs. Thatcher should give Labour MPs places in her cabinet; a power sharing arrangement to prevent Socialist alienation. If such an idea is not acceptable on the British Mainland, how much less sense it makes in Northern Ireland between parties as different as chalk and cheese.

Why do we try to appease Ulster's anti-British minority? One reason is that the Unionists cannot be trusted to be fair to the Catholics they oppressed prior to 1969. We have already dealt with that myth in some detail. We can therefore reject the idea of "a moral claim for reparation" correctly associated with the SDLP by Richard Rose.[22] But what about the Catholics' alienation? Let's look again at the British Labour Party example. Labour has lost 3 general elections at the time of writing because it didn't have what the electorate wanted. Its choice, therefore, was either to take a stand on its principles regardless of the consequences, or to change its policies. It has chosen to do the latter.

The SDLP has the same option, because the cause of Catholic alienation, the thing which Protestants ultimately will not stomach, is their support for a united Ireland. This is a matter of political choice rather than of religious conscience. Contrary to what many British politicians believe the conflict is not about personal relationships. Inter-communal antagonism is just a symptom of the political differences. As long as Catholics support a united Ireland they will always have minority representation. If they really wanted something other than a united Ireland they would have voted for the Alliance Party, which supports power sharing within the United Kingdom as part of a final settlement. The miniscule electoral support which Catholics give to this party shows the fatal attraction which Irish unity holds for them.

Even as late as the 1970 Westminster general election Ulster was witnessing Mainland-style political contests between a Unionist Party taking the Conservative whip in the House of Commons and a Northern Ireland Labour Pary committed to Ulster remaining part of the UK. In East Belfast the Unionists won by 26,778 votes to 18,259 and in North Belfast by 28,668 votes to 18,894.[23] Opposition parties could therefore poll well in Protestant areas as long as they supported the constitutional position. By opposing the Constitution Catholics alienated themselves, and hence there is no reason to feel guilty about their inability to gain control of the Northern Ireland Parliament.

Moderates and Extremists

It is an essential part of English political thinking that we should identify the "moderates" and "extremists" in any given situation in order that we can give concessions to the "moderates" and isolate the "extremists". This is the policy which was tried in the colonies. We have seen that it met with mixed results and was only effective where the "moderates" and "extremists" had the same goal, and the intention was to concede this objective to the good guys rather than the bad guys. In effect the plan is to punish the "extremists" by giving something to their "moderate" opponents.

But as Ulster's majority wants to remain part of the UK, we are told (sometimes unconvincingly) that we are not trying to give the SDLP a united Ireland. From the "civil rights" era to the present day the English hope has been that Catholics would settle for something else. All the evidence shows that they will not. Catholics have only ever stated they wanted something else at times when the Republican movement was weak, as a short term political expedient. Each initiative, each concession which falls short of a united Ireland merely convinces them that the English will continue to make more concessions. All the tinkering with constitutional arrangements confirms the Catholic belief that a strategy of achieving their goal in a series of stages is perfectly sound. By a process of English concessions they will get nearer and nearer to a united Ireland until one day they will get what they really want. Republicanism thrives on hope and English policy constantly feeds that hope. In the last 20 years we have not once been able to convince Irish Catholics that a united Ireland is out of the question.

We say we want Catholics to support the SDLP rather than Sinn Fein. Why should they do that? Because we are prepared to promise that they can achieve by peaceful means the objectives which they might otherwise think could only be won by "armed struggle". The hope of a united Ireland has fuelled IRA violence, and yet we are pursuing a policy which can only work if we can convince the minority community that the SDLP might be able to achieve this goal. There has therefore been a cycle of violence and concessions. We concede Republican demands and people are happy for a short while. Then there is more violence, and we make more concessions to the "moderates". This is followed by more violence. IRA terrorism and street disorder are the engine which drives Republicanism on towards its destination. October 1968 led to the concession of the "civil rights" demands; August 1969 led to the abolition of the B Specials; the beginning of the IRA campaign resulted in the overthrow of the Stormont Parliament; more IRA violence brought power sharing and the Irish Dimension. More recently the 1981 hunger strike disturbances and the big vote for Sinn Fein in 1982 and 1983 resulted in the Anglo-Irish Agreement. Garrett Fitzgerald told Mrs. Thatcher that support for Sinn Fein showed that Catholics were "alienated".[24]

It did not matter that IRA violence had created the conditions that made the Agreement possible. For this they could expect no credit and nor could they logically ask for it. The benefits of the Agreement, no matter how intangible they might seem, would inevitably be attributed to John Hume and the SDLP.[25]

Mrs. Thatcher said she could not let the violence go on and so she signed the Anglo-Irish Agreement. Since then there has been an upsurge in violence.

The terrorist machine has been encouraged by successive British governments' lack of resolve to defend the Union and oppose a united Ireland. We have seen that the 1972 Green Paper said that if a majority in Ulster wanted a united Ireland the British government would not stand in the way. This pledge was repeated when the Sunningdale Agreement was signed. It is also contained in the Anglo-Irish Agreement. The Unionist Research Department described it as

the kind of alien disinterest that worries and alarms the Ulster public.[26]

John Hume has been running around telling people that the British have no particular interest in preserving the unity of the United Kingdom. Ulster is British *only* because a majority in Northern Ireland happens to want it for the moment. The British government says that there is a constitutional guarantee, because there will be no change in the constitutional status of Northern Ireland without the consent of the majority.

Clearly the guarantee does not apply to the many intermediate stages along the road to a united Ireland which John Hume sees as essential to make Ulster's position untenable before the formality of the final handover. The Anglo-Irish Agreement was after all concluded without any consultation with the people of

Ulster and in the face of total opposition from all sections of the Loyalist community. As the guarantee does not apply to changes in Ulster's constitutional status which give the Irish government more say in the running of Northern Ireland than Ulster's own elected representatives, it is clearly worthless. It has also never been quite what it seems. For instance, are Kent, Cornwall and Scotland only parts of the UK as long as a majority of their citizens want them to be? Obviously not. They are permanent parts of the UK and there is no question of their status changing. The very act of suggesting otherwise gives encouragement to those forces which want to break up the UK. This is what has happened in Ulster.

Certainly part of the problem has been English indifference to the loyal citizens of Ulster. But this also links with the idea of convincing Catholics that they can get a united Ireland via the SDLP by peaceful means. This tragic error in English policy making means that we have had to leave open the question of Ulster's constitutional status to appease the "moderates". This in turn gives encouragement to the IRA which, since 1969, has believed that a united Ireland is, after all, possible.

If the IRA/Sinn Fein and the SDLP are engaged in a leapfrogging operation, with concessions to the SDLP following violence from the IRA, we have to ask what the relationship is between the 2 organisations. Clearly the Republican movement as a whole benefits from this dual strategy.

Conor Cruise O'Brien turned his attention to this subject quite recently in the *Irish Independent.*

> *The SDLP by its refusal to advise co-operaton against terrorism, connives in practice at the deeds which it condemns rhetorically.... Its leaders - John Hume and Seamus Mallon - have often been praised for their stand against 'the men of violence'.*

> *It is less often noted that the stand in question is purely rhetorical, and causes no practical inconvenience to the targets of the rhetoric. The purpose of the rhetoric is not that of doing any damage to the IRA, but that of preserving a respectable image for the SDLP.*

> *The respectable image keeps the SDLP in line to be the prime beneficiaries of whatever concessions to Catholics the IRA's campaign of violence may elicit from the British government. As in the case of the Anglo-Irish*

Agreement.

As the Provos spokesman, Danny Morrison, put it, cynically but accurately: 'The SDLP's political influence rides on the back of the armed struggle.' 27

O'Brien noted that

Sinn Fein and the SDLP have co-operated in campaigns for the investigation of charges of police brutality and 'shoot to kill'; campaigns for the ending of internment; campaigns for the release of prisoners on 'dirty strike' and hunger strike; campaigns for the abolition of 'supergrasses'.

Also the SDLP campaigned against unpopular local security measures - such as manned security towers in South Armagh - required by the struggle against the IRA.

And yet

The alleged need 'to isolate the men of violence' through timely concessions to the SDLP has been the SDLP's principal political stock in trade for years.

This is the argument that eventually produced the Anglo-Irish Agreement.

The SDLP has certainly been guilty of collusion with the IRA from time to time, but is it guilty of entering into a conspiracy - a political version of the hard cop-soft cop routine? Characterising this relationship accurately has frustrated Unionists for years. But with some trepidation I shall advance my own explanation in the hope that it sheds some light on the subject.

Conor Cruise O'Brien came near to the answer, without developing his insight, when he wrote of the SDLP:

Its ambivalences, ambiguities and collusions have their roots deep in the charged history of the community to which both they and the IRA belong: the Catholics of Northern Ireland. 28

What are the SDLP and the IRA/Sinn Fein? At core they consist of at most a few hundred activists. Just like the organisations in the "civil rights" era, they owe their political influence to support in the wider community. Without this active or passive support they could not survive. Both parties exist because they meet the community's needs.

Ian McAllister, in his book on the SDLP, saw that

Catholics could support constitutional politics and physical force at the same time: it was, after all sensible to back peaceful political change, but not to the extent of ignoring the consequences of its failure. This seemingly ambiguous duality of allegiances has appertained in the relations between nationalists and republicans and the Catholic community for many years and is not new. [29]

The SDLP and Sinn Fein do not have separate and distinct constituencies of support. The example of the Fermanagh and South Tyrone constituency in 1955 and 1981 shows that Catholics will support either. When they are in competition their respective votes reflect the extent to which the Catholic community feels that peaceful or violent means are needed at a particular time to bring it nearer to a united Ireland. The SDLP's idea that force should never be used is just as extreme and unrepresentative of the Irish Catholic political tradition as the idea that force alone will win through. Both views are only held by minorities. Most Catholics want to keep both options open, because it is the combination of SDLP saintliness and IRA violence which has brought most benefits. They support the continuation of the IRA campaign in order that their other wing, the SDLP, can receive the concessions. It is a combination which my poor compatriots, ignorant of the realities of Irish politics, have been powerless to resist.

The SDLP and the IRA/Sinn Fein are both to a large extent prisoners of the community they serve. It is that community which, by giving support here, withholding support there, has created an effective dual strategy which neither of the parties involved could have worked out on their own. It does not matter to this community which of its representatives receives the concessions. It is quite happy for the naive English to "punish" the IRA by giving the SDLP what it wants. The community wins either way.

At the 1981 Sinn Fein ard fheis Danny Morrison said:

Who here really believes that we can win the war through the ballot box? But will anyone here object if with a ballot paper in this hand and an Armalite in this hand we take power in Ireland? [30]

It became known as the ballot box and Armalite strategy, but in reality this strategy had been worked out a decade earlier by the Catholic community as a whole. It had supported the SDLP through the ballot box and sheltered the IRA volunteers who wielded the Armalites. The legalisation of Sinn Fein in the North after the hunger strikes simply made the strategy easier to operate. While Sinn Fein was banned it was difficult to know how much support the IRA had at any particular time and hence after a while it was not easy to convince British politicians that they needed to make concessions in order to bolster the SDLP. The late 1970s were a time of few initiatives.

The rise of Sinn Fein sent Mrs. Thatcher scuttling to sign the Anglo-Irish Agreement. The Sinn Fein vote came to be seen as a barometer. If it was going down the policy was succeeding. If it was was going up, more concessions were needed. This hasn't been lost on the Catholic community. The SDLP did well to get the Anglo-Irish Agreement and Catholics turned out in the May 1989 local elections to give the party its reward in the form of a higher percentage vote. Sinn Fein's vote remained the same. If there are not more concessions the SDLP vote will fall and the Sinn Fein vote will rise. The Catholic community is, in short, playing us for a bunch of suckers who can be endlessly manipulated into making further concessions in a vain attempt to win its affections.

The Sins of the English

The English establishment usually approaches all political problems in the same way. By explaining this approach it will be possible to see how we got into the current mess in Ulster. The establishment likes to

1. Identify moderates and extremists. This strategy fails if, as in Northern Ireland, the moderate Republicans' final objectives are just as unacceptable as those of the extremists. It also fails if the community whose support both groups are trying to win uses them both to win concessions and refuses to accept the Constitution, no matter what we give them.

2. Establish the middle ground between 2 opposing points of view.

   this has taken the form of an assumption that in politics there can be no final incompatible aspirations; there is never a point at which it must be recognised that the wishes of one man are wholly irreconcilable with those of another;[31]

The Loyalist population is pro-British, wishes to remain part of the United Kingdom and under no circumstances does it want to join a united Ireland. The Republican population is mostly anti-British, is opposed to the existence of the Northern Ireland state, and wants a united Ireland. There is no middle position between these points of view. All the attempts to introduce forms of power sharing and Irish government interference in Ulster's affairs are seen by both sides of the argument as steps along the road to a united Ireland.

The only way to "solve" the dilemma as to what we should do is through an act of choice. We must choose which side we want to support. I humbly suggest that it makes sense to back the pro-British majority rather than the anti-British minority.

3. Puts its faith in a process of negotiation and compromise. Unfortunately such a process only works when there is agreement about fundamentals. The SDLP has never been prepared to renounce the goal of a united Ireland and sees the negotiating process as simply a way of receiving concessions from the British. It has kept the constitutional issue to the fore. It has continually picked at the wound and hence it will never heal. As compromise on this constitutional question is impossible, so negotiations are pointless.

The basic English establishment approach to politics has been totally unsuited to Northern Ireland conditions. Throughout this century we have feared day to day involvement in case we got lost in the bog, the quicksands or the quagmire. Most of our politicians were right to fear this involvement as they had practically no understanding of the problem. They were right to favour a devolved Parliament in Ulster in whose affairs they would interfere as little as possible.

Now that we are stuck in the bog we try to hide our incomprehension by saying that the problem is highly complex or intractable. I agree with the late T. E Utely, who believed that

> *What has been displayed before us has not been some dark, complex, passionate scene compounded of black magic, but a straightforward conflict of easily defensible political ambitions. What we have brought to the settlement of that conflict is a grossly inadequate political equipment, a tradition full of errors about the nature of power and of politics, and a dedicated commitment to illusion. In this we have revealed ourselves in a manner which is important not only for the future of Ulster but for that of the*

whole United Kingdom.[32]

Having said how complicated everything is, most books about Ulster fail to provide their readers with any sort of credible explanation. What the problem is all about is set out in highly complex theories with bits sprouting out of them in all directions.

So here for the confused is a statement of the problem with which most of us Loyalists would agree:

1. Ulster Loyalists (mainly Protestants) want to remain part of the United Kingdom and oppose the idea of a united Ireland. All of their actions this century are explicable in terms of these simple objectives.

2. Irish Republicans (mainly Catholics) want to destroy the link with Britain and support the idea of a united Ireland. All of their actions this century are explicable in terms of these simple objectives.

3. The objectives in 1 and 2 are quite incompatible and hence one or the other must prevail.

4. In general English politicians have no comprehension of points 1-3. They have made a complete mess of things by trying to complicate matters and by meddling in affairs they do not undersand. There is therefore not so much an Ulster Problem as an English Problem.

It follows from the above that when an Irish Republican tells an Englishman that he wants civil rights, justice, a fair percentage of housing, the abolition of Stormont, power sharing, an Irish Dimension, peace and reconciliation, an Anglo-Irish Agreement, a way for Irishmen to share the island together, or 10p to put in the meter, what he is really saying is that he wants a united Ireland. Once you have grasped this, you need never be confused again.

When I was an undergraduate I studied scientific method as part of a Philosophy of Science course. I seem to recall that scientific explanations tend to be more exact than those in the social and political sphere, but some of the principles remain the same. The aim is to contruct the simplest possible theory which accounts for all the facts. Sir Karl Popper liked to think that crucial experiments could be carried out to check the validity of theories. However even in "hard" sciences like physics this was not always possible. What happened was that when facts came along which contradicted a theory, its supporters would add a subsidiary theory to their model to account for the discrepancy. This might go on for some time until the theory was extremely unwieldy, and eventually it would seem so improbable, so complex and so difficult to understand that it would collapse under its own weight. It would be replaced by a new and more simple theory.

The beauty of the Unionist political analysis of the Ulster situation is that it is simple and it has explanatory power. It actually explains everything that has gone on. I therefore believe it has more to recommend it than some of the complex and unwieldy accounts put forward by observers who are not in sympathy with Ulster's pro-British majority.

More Lessons from the Colonies

It is not my intention to try and outline a detailed security policy for Northern Ireland. I shall leave that to my colleagues. But it is necessary to show that a sound security policy is possible. Many English people look at the last 20 years and conclude that we have tried everything to defeat the IRA and have failed. Therefore we are not likely to defeat the IRA.

We must, however, remember that the British Army was not deployed in Northern Ireland to defeat the IRA, but to defend Catholic interests. When the real shooting started British governments were not in principle opposed to taking on the IRA, but they would not do so at the cost of upsetting the SDLP and the Catholic population. This imposed so many restrictions that we have had some very able soldiers mounting no sort of counter-insurgency campaign at all. We must face the fact that defeating the IRA has in itself been given a low priority which comes well behind the aim of winning the affections of the Catholic population. If once we stood back and asked why we are appeasing this anti-British minority, we might find that we don't have a really good answer. Free from this political burden, we could look at the situation anew.

I mentioned that in the colonial campaigns some good ideas did emerge, in spite of the political failures. We did, for instance, establish the need for good intelligence. Frank Kitson, writing about terrorists in the colonial context, said:

those who are supporting them by the provision of money, food, recruits, intelligence, and supplies rely for their security on remaining anonymous.

The problem of destroying enemy armed groups and their supporters therefore consists very largely of finding them. Once found they can no longer strike on their own terms but are obliged to dance to the tune of the government's forces. It then becomes a comparitively simple matter to dispose of them.[33]

This lesson seems to have been forgotten in Ulster. There is now general agreement in the security forces that most IRA terrorists are known to them. As I write there has been a lot of fuss about sheets bearing the names, addresses and photos of hundreds of IRA suspects being taken home by policemen and soldiers. The real scandal here is that the security forces largely know who is responsible for the campaign of bombings and shootings and yet they let them walk free around the streets of Ulster. This is not acceptable.

Many English people have a sense of despair about defeating the IRA because they feel that we are dealing with faceless gunmen whom we cannot find. This is not true. We know who the IRA men are and yet we neither shoot them nor detain them. Our people go in fear of terrorist attacks and yet the members of the organisation mounting those attacks are able to walk around without fear. We do not lay a hand on them for fear of offending their supporters. Internment or detention was used in the colonies and in all previous campaigns against the IRA, North and South. It would take out of circulation most IRA members. That would solve part of the problem. The Catholic population would then riot in protest, and providing we were not surprised by this (and thus not tempted to back down) the situation could be contained as a purely military exercise. The obstacles in the way of such action are only political - our irrational fear of upsetting the anti-British minority. Once we have overcome this fear we could mount a political offensive to show that violent opposition was pointless, as we were no longer inclined to even consider a united Ireland or any steps towards it aimed at undermining Northern Ireland's constitutional status. Progress is therefore possible.

Deportation of terrorists was used in both Malaya and Aden. While Ireland was all under British rule the government deported 50 Sinn Feiners for sedition in 1920 under the Defence of the Realm Act.[34] Powers of deportation were also contained in the 1939 Prevention of Violence Act passed on the Mainland after an IRA campaign there.[35] It has long been a problem that those IRA men who have been locked up tend simply to reinforce the ranks of the organisation on their release. If we were willing to learn from past experience it might well be worth removing certain of these people from the UK completely by stripping them of their citizenship and depositing them in the Irish Republic. This could be done on a large or small scale depending on the situation. Under the South's Irish Nationality and Citizenship Act 1956, natives of Northern Ireland qualify for citizenship in the Irish Republic, so it could not refuse to take deportees. As an aside it is worth noting that SDLP leader John Hume and his predecessor Gerry Fitt both made use of this provision to obtain Irish passports.[36] Both showed how much they loved British standards by refusing to use a British document.

Those who actually visit the border between Ulster and the Irish Republic are often shocked to find that there is not even a simple fence to mark the boundary line. Most people know that the IRA stores weapons and explosives in the South and launches many attacks across the border, and most have heard the constant assurances about border security. In fact the border is wide open for anyone to walk across and we rely on the odd Army patrol to impede access. The B Specials could seal the border by sheer force of numbers with units based at all the main crossing points. Currently we don't have a big enough local force to achieve this, but it would be possible. Alternatively some form of physical barrier could be used to save lives. The main problems are not technical. If the East Germans could for many years stop people getting out of their country with miles of fencing, we could certainly stop terrorists getting into Ulster. The problem is political, or should we say psychological. Some politicians are under the odd impression that the Irish Republic is a friendly country, which we should not upset. This is the same country which claims jurisdiction over Northern Ireland in its written Constitution, which has shown little enthusiasm for extraditing suspected terrorists to the UK, and whose current prime minister, Charles Haughey, wanted to invade Ulster and hand out guns to Irish Republicans North of the border.

Counter-Insurgency Theory talks about the need to win hearts and minds. What we often forget is that at the time the troops were deployed in Ulster, the hearts and minds of the Loyalist majority were already won over. These were the people who had stood by Britain in the war against Hitler. Vital bases in Londonderry, Belfast and Larne allowed our anti-submarine patrols to be extended 100 miles westward to protect our convoys.[37] Without these bases we might have starved. Harland and Wolff produced nearly 200 ships for the war effort, and it was in Northern Ireland that American troops were marshalled for the invasion of Europe.[38] Protestants enlisted voluntarily or were engaged in vital war industries. The Catholics screamed blue murder when it was suggested that conscription should be extended to Northern Ireland, as they realised they would be the ones most affected. The South opted out of the War by declaring itself neutral.

> *On the afternoon of April 30 [1945], Hitler committed suicide in his Berlin bunker and the Taioseach [de Valera], accompanied by Joseph Walshe, paid a formal visit to the German Legation in Dublin to express his condolences on the death of the Fuhrer.*[39]

No-one needed to buy the Ulster Loyalists' support. Britain has always meant something special in the hearts and minds of this people. Starting with the most favourable of positions in 1969 from which to go and defeat an anti-British insurrection, we proceeded to alienate our friends and appease our enemies by going down the road to a united Ireland - the very road which so recently we had been told the Catholics did not want to go down. They only wanted "civil rights". What fools we were.

For 20 years we have trodden the path of appeasement and for 20 years we have paid with the lives of our young soldiers and policemen, and with the lives of countless innocent civilians. Their widows and families grieve while IRA men go free. Our pathetic half-hearted attempts to stop this terrorist assault can be seen when we compare them with the successful military campaigns in Malaya and Kenya. In Malaya, 6,710 terrorists were killed, 1,500 captured and 2,700 surrendered.[40] In Kenya 150,000 arrests were made and 64,000 brought to trial.[41] And yet we are worried about moving against what the security forces agree amounts to only a few hundred IRA men. We seem to have lost something as a nation, paralysed by irrational guilt. The Republicans sense this, and despising our weakness, press on in the almost certain knowledge that our political leaders have the capacity to surrender to them everything they want. Whether or not this is delivered to the IRA is of no importance to them. It is not the hope of an IRA victory which keeps the IRA in business - it is the Catholic community's hope that a united Ireland might be granted to any Catholic representatives. It doesn't matter who they are. The IRA is only useful because we respond to violence with concessions. If we stopped doing this then we should start to win the political battle which accompanies any successful anti-terrorist campaign.

We must turn away from the policies which brought political failure in the colonies and adopt the lessons gained from our few military victories, and above all from the successful campaigns against the IRA carried out by Ulster people with the minimum of English help.

There are 2 main lessons we can learn from the loyal citizens of Ulster. The first can be learned from the IRA's 1950s campaign. The RUC and the B Specials did well and internment took out most Northern IRA members, but the inescapable conclusion is that this terrorist offensive was defeated primarily by political means. The Unionist Northern Ireland government managed to convince the Catholic population that this was a hopeless enterprise which couldn't succeed. It could not succeed because Ulstermen were in control of the counter-insurgency campaign and those Ulstermen would never concede the political demands of the terrorists, not even to "moderate" politicians promoting those same demands on behalf of their community. This Unionist approach was considerably more effective than trying to win minority support by concessions.

Someone once asked how you defeat an idea. The answer is that you deny it all hope. When hope has gone, action is pointless. And so Northern Catholics, seeing no point in a hopeless enterprise, would not give the IRA the support it needed in the 1950s. Neither would they volunteer to replace the terrorists who were interned. The campaign withered away. Despair had been produced not just in the IRA but also in the anti-British community it relied on in order to operate freely.

We English must learn this lesson and learn it well. Our countrymen who were slaughtered at Hyde Park, at the Royal Marines School of Music and elsewhere lie dead in the ground because we gave Republicanism hope. By taking over in 1969 and believing the distorted stories of a cunning and manipulative minority, we convinced those people that they could get their way. The people of Ulster had the genie firmly held in its bottle. We listened to its pleadings and let it out. By doing so we sent thousands to their deaths.

We failed to make proper use of those people whose hearts and minds we had already won over - the Loyalist community. This brings us to the second great lesson we can learn from the Ulster people's campaigns against the IRA. In the 1950s, due to the political strength of the Unionist government, the action was on a fairly small scale. In the 1920s it was not. The IRA had not hundreds of terrorists in the North but thousands. They were backed up by many more South of the border who were aided and abetted by the Irish Free State government. That assault on Ulster was not defeated by a force of professional soldiers, but by the mobilisation of the whole Loyalist community.

It was estimated by an English civil servant that if the USC had reached its full establishment of 45,000 then 1 in 4 male Protestants would have been in some part of the security forces.[42] By the middle of 1922 over half of male Protestant adults in Co. Fermanagh were in the Special Constabulary.[43] These were mostly people who held down a job during the day and then carried out their policing duties through the night. Winston Churchill and the Army came to see this as a cheap way of defending the border and consequently handed over what was supposed to be a military responsibility to local people. In the words of Sir Arthur Hezlet "the British Army had, so to speak, largely contracted out of the Irish problem."[44]

The adjutant of the IRA's 3rd Northern Division reported to his headquarters in 1922:

> *the enemy were able to pour in lorries of [Specials]... The morale of the [Catholic] civilian population, as a result of this raiding and the enemy's display of such numerically superior forces, has been considerable weakened... 'B' Specials with their local knowledge of the people and places have played a very prominent part in these raids and have made it very difficult for our men to escape.*[45]

The 2nd Northern Division of the IRA reported that "the morale of the division had been broken up and all but a handful of men had withdrawn to Co.Donegal."[46] According to Michael Farrell, in June 1922:

> *The Northern authorities were able to concentrate more attention on Belfast, however, as the campaign in the countryside flagged. They began to establish a system of blockhouses or commandeered buildings, staffed by 'A' Specials, in the Catholic areas of the city. By the end of the month Belfast, too, was under control.*[47]

We might here recall the words of the military strategist, Clausewitz, who said: "Public opinion is ultimately gained by great victories."[48]

Since 1969 we have never dominated the Republican areas where the IRA gets its support. We have therefore never been able to convince potentially helpful Catholics that we can protect them. This rather inhibits co-operation. Clearly the capacity of the IRA to shoot informants in these areas is greater than that of the security forces to shoot or arrest IRA members.

We have seen that in the early 1920s the USC had an establishment of 45,000.

In Kenya there was a 20,000 strong home guard, and a similar force in Malaya grew to over 200,000.[49] By contrast the Ulster Defence Regiment, organised as a locally recruited regiment of the British Army, has had only 6,000-8,000 members during most of the Troubles.[50] At the height of the IRA campaign in 1975 the UDR had only 1,100-1,200 men operating by night.[51] We have failed to mobilise loyal elements in the population as we did in the 1920s, and we have hence been unable to swamp the terrorists.

The idea that it is the community's responsibility to carry out policing, rather than a small bunch of professionals, goes back to Saxon times. Then it was the duty of all citizens to produce criminals in court. It was known as "Frankpledge". Later people became constables on a rota basis. The law was enforced by raising a "posse commatatus", a group of citizens who would pursue felons by hue and cry.[52] Implicit in this philosophy was the idea that if the community as a whole was under threat it was everyone's responsibility to defend it. This attitude has been eroded in England where people "don't want to get involved" but it is strong in Northern Ireland.

It is interesting to note that the IRA decided to exempt Belfast from its 1950s campaign. One reason was "the possibility of inciting reprisals against the Catholics, which they would not be strong enough to protect".[53] Not to put too fine a point on it, they feared that if they tried anything the Loyalist community would come and sort them out. The decision to include Belfast in the August 1969 disorders was therefore a tactical error on the part of the Republicans. Having patiently watched the mayhem on 12/13 August, Loyalists were beginning to step in to sort out this nonsense by 14 August, and the Republicans were in trouble.

A Lieutenant with the Royal Regiment of Wales who was sent into Belfast at that time talked about

> *The subsequent feeling that the whole problem might have been removed if the Army hadn't gone in until the following Monday: expensive on lives and property, but perhaps that might have been the end of it all, because at that stage a number of Catholics were quite prepared to cross the border.*[54]

Any sensible security policy must involve the mobilisation of the Loyalist community, but in an organised and disciplined way. In the 1920s the Army was effectively withdrawn to barracks over a number of years and was replaced by Ulster men organised by Ulster politicians who, as history shows, had an ability to succeed where British soldiers have failed. It provides food for thought.

The Death of Democracy

When Stormont was abolished the democratic process in Ulster was fatally undermined. The loss of the Northern Ireland Parliament itself reduced the standard of democracy in the Province. But worse than that, the reorganisation of local government, which was then going through, was based on a Macrory Report which had recommended the transfer of certain key council functions to boards on which Stormont would nominate the majority of representatives.

A Housing Executive, Education and Library Boards, and Health and Social Services Boards were to have only a minority of their members nominated by local councils. The rest would be appointed by the Northern Ireland government. The abolition of this government meant that nomination rights passed to British ministers. Unlike the Stormont government, these ministers are in no way responsible to the Northern Ireland electorate.

Services like housing, education, social services and libraries are under local democratic control on the British Mainland. If we don't like the local council's policy we can vote it out. The English, Welsh and Scots can raise problems in these services with their local councillor and know that he has the power to remedy their grievances. Local government officers can ultimately be instructed to do what councillors want them to do.

In Northern Ireland councils have negligible powers. They empty the dustbins, run leisure centres and manage public toilets. In all the key policy areas there is no local democracy at all. The electorate cannot vote the Housing Executive's Board out of office. The British government nominates 7 out of 10 members. Nor can Ulster voters get rid of their local Education and Library Board or their Health and Social Services Board. If they complain to the local councillor who is on one of these boards he will do his best, but elected representatives are in a minority and are usually outvoted by the unelected government nominees.

These nominees are responsible to no-one, but as it is the government's power of patronage which has put them there, they are in practice remarkably subservient to the government of the day and pay little attention to the wishes of the Northern Ireland people. The Housing Executive meets in secret and hence its members are not exposed to public scrutiny. Charles Brett, former Chairman of the Housing Executive, defended this system by saying that board members are representative of all sections of the community, even though they are not elected representatives.[35] In fact they are not. Most Ulstermen are Unionists, but the boards are carefully selected to ensure there is not a Unionist majority on any board. That is why government nominees frequently vote en bloc against elected representatives, most of whom are Unionists. Belfast City Council got so fed up with this perversion of democracy that it withdrew its councillors from the Belfast Education and Library Board.

This manipulation of the composition of local boards means that the system is corrupt. It is ironic that those government ministers who have complained about alleged gerrymandering should so subvert the democratic process. The ministers who wield the power do not stand for election in Northern Ireland and hence Ulster people cannot vote against them. Until now the Labour and Conservative Parties have not even put up candidates in Northern Ireland and hence Unionists could not vote against the government. Even when they do put up candidates there is no reason to believe that they will take notice of the massive defeats which will be imposed upon them.

Local councillors and even MPs are forced to negotiate with professional officers they do not control. We have the extraordinary position that in an English local authority its councillors can instruct a senior officer to carry out its housing policy. In Northern Ireland councillors have to go cap in hand and ask the same officers if they would kindly consider carrying out the electorate's wishes.

The whole system is based on the myths of the "civil rights" era. The wicked Unionists cannot be trusted with democratic powers and so they must be kept in subjection. The minority, which was once screaming about British rights and British standards, is now silent. Those who were never deprived of any British rights sit back smugly and rejoice in the fact that Unionists no longer enjoy the basic democratic rights which are taken for granted in the rest of the United Kingdom. The lies and distortions of the "civil rights" movement have led to the subversion of local democracy in Northern Ireland.

But it is worse than that. The desire to appease the SDLP has resulted in the wishes of the majority of people in Ulster being systematically frustrated by successive British governments.

After the abolition of Stormont and the failure of the ridiculous power sharing Executive, the British government held elections to a Constitutional Convention in May 1975. This body was asked by the government: "What provision for the government of Northern Ireland is likely to command most widespread acceptance there?" The Constitutional Convention gave its answer. It wanted a local Parliament with law and order powers. It proposed that minority parties be included on departmental committees. The British government refused to accept its recommendations and dissolved the Convention in March 1976.[56]

When the Anglo-Irish Agreement was signed I can recall Tom King saying that Unionists could not go on saying no. They had to say yes to something. In fact they have been saying yes to the return of democracy for some considerable time. In the Constitutional Convention, and on numerous occasions since, they have told us what they want, but the British government constantly overrules the democratically expressed wishes of the Ulster people. The government argument is that any proposal must have the support of an SDLP dedicated to a united Ireland. This is madness. The real veto over progress is being exercised not by the Loyalists, who simply want a British-style democracy, but by the SDLP. Everything has been allowed to grind to a halt because the representatives of an anti-British minority have been told we won't proceed without their consent.

The Northern Ireland Assembly was elected in 1982 with powers to scrutinise legislation only. It was structured in such a way that more powers could be given to it in a "rolling devolution" programme if the SDLP agreed. Unable to extract a promise of power sharing and an Irish Dimension from the Unionists, the SDLP refused to take part. The Assembly was therefore forcibly dissolved by the government, who sent in the police to physically eject elected members from the Stormont Parliament Building.

Most of us are familiar with the events surrounding the Anglo-Irish Agreement. Ulster's representatives were not consulted before it was signed. Neither a massive vote against the government in a series of parliamentary by-elections in Northern Ireland, nor the sight of 200,000 Ulster men and women protesting outside the Belfast City Hall, has moved the government at all.

I must say frankly that we have now arrived at a situation where the British government administers Ulster without the support of any significant section of its electorate. The abuses of power have become so numerous, and the current arrangements are such an antithesis of democracy, that the government's moral authority to govern in Northern Ireland is in question. It has frustrated the majority's wishes for so long, in every sphere of public administration that we can only conclude that the democratic process has been effectively suspended in Ulster. It has come to such a pass that the power of the ballot box is non-existent. Whatever Ulster votes for will be ignored.

To the British people I would say this. All of these things have been done in our name. We have let it all happen. We have allowed our friends to be insulted and our enemies to be rewarded. We have listened to the lies of those who despise us and conducted a policy of appeasement towards them. Our foolishness has vetoed all progress towards a political solution which would be acceptable to a clear majority of Ulster people. And we have also paid the price. For 2 decades we have buried our dead. We have needlessly sacrificed men, women and children in a battle which could have been won long ago. Now is as good a time as any to start making things change and to start putting right the wrongs which we have inflicted on a community whose only crime has been loyalty to Britain.

257

Part IV

The Way Forward

Wrongheaded English policies towards Ulster are not the result of a mistake by a handful of politicians. They are a reflection of a basic approach to politics which sometimes works on the British Mainland, but will never work in Northern Ireland. Politicians may amend their policies but fundamental beliefs are resistant to change. Such changes often take a generation or more to come about. I therefore have no particular reason to believe that English policy on Ulster can be changed in the foreseeable future simply by force of argument. Fortunately politicians do not have to believe in the policies they carry out. Often they adopt them because they have no alternative. When their own favoured policies cannot be implemented, they turn to another course of action. British civil servants have made an art of choosing to do that which is inevitable.

The key to ending the suffering of Ulster is to give power to Ulstermen. There are 2 reasons. Firstly English politicians are much less likely than their Ulster counterparts to carry out the required policies. Few have an understanding of Northern Ireland realities. A Scotsman might do, but few of the good ones get to be government ministers. Secondly, even if we had the ideal English man or woman in office, Republicans would know that weak ministers are like London buses. There may not be one here at the moment, but there will be one along in a minute. There is a credibility problem. Republicans don't believe English politicians have the resolve to deny them their objectives. They would only take notice of a Loyalist administration.

This is the main reason why I don't believe that integration is a complete solution. Obviously devolution and integration will for a while progress along the same path. The achievement of the integrationist objective of being treated in the same way as the rest of the UK will require the devolution of powers which Ulster is currently lacking. But we must go on from there to give Ulster a local Parliament with powers over security. The twin goals are to restore democracy and security to Northern Ireland. A local Parliament would be a guarantee of democracy. Being subject to the whims of Westminster politicians puts Ulstermen in a precarious position. As Ulstermen are more likely to solve Ulster problems than my own countrymen, this will in the long term save English and Scottish lives.

All of this is so much wishful thinking if we do not have the means to achieve the end we want. The current problem, in the wake of the collapse of the Unionist campaign against the Anglo-Irish Agreement, is to know (at least in principle) how Unionists can achieve their objectives. The way ahead seems terribly unclear.

We must start by asking whether we want another 20 years such as we have just experienced. If not, do we believe that a continuation of current policies is likely to lead to another 20 years of suffering? If the answer is yes, do we want to bring the situation to a head rather than experience 2 more decades without either democracy or security? And if the answer is again yes, are we prepared to work, perhaps over a number of years, to acquire the means to end our suffering? That is a tough one because the Loyalist leadership has not been noted for its long term strategic planning. But my own experience of meeting Loyalist activists suggests they believe that planning there must be. There are no magic solutions. The 1974 Loyalist Workers Strike is one of the few good examples of forward planning in recent years. The rest has been all rather rushed and spontaneous. The anti-Anglo-Irish Agreement campaign, which unfortunately turned into a debacle due to poor leadership, was eloquent testimony to the fact that it is not good enough to muddle by. Sound politics now requires forward planning, a period during which a policy is sold to the Loyalist population, and good organisation.

The anti-Hillsborough campaign was full of good ideas which were never implemented. One of the best was that Northern Ireland could not be governed without the consent of the Ulster people. A campaign which denied consent, and employed civil disobedience, would make Ulster ungovernable and would prevent the implementation of undemocratic policies. It would, of course, do more than that because in such situations the power to run things begins to pass from the government to the ordinary people. They would have more influence on the ground. The government may pull on the levers of power, but it may find they are not connected to anything. During the Ulster Workers Strike the distribution of petrol came to a halt. In order that essential services could still get petrol, the Ulster Workers Council issued passes to key personnel. In that situation the undemocratic power sharing Executive was not simply prevented from governing the Province. Power over the distribution of petrol actually passed into the hands of the UWC backed by a majority of Ulster's people.

It is therefore possible in principle to acquire de facto power through the withdrawal of consent. The more complete is the withdrawal of consent, the more power is transferred into Ulster hands. The power to control something, and hence the achievement of what is effectively a devolution of power, is not dependant on legislation or government approval. It can take place by other means. Devolution therefore has the advantage that it can be implemented by

Ulster people alone, without reference to their semi-colonial governors. It is possible to envisage that a body of Ulster representatives might be formed in a situation where there was a withdrawal of consent. And it is also possible to envisage this body having more influence over what was allowed to happen in Northern Ireland than colonial-style ministers from Westminster or their unelected nominees. At that stage we would be very close to a collapse of undemocratic institutions in Ulster, and a policy of endorsing the inevitable would certainly be on the cards. It might then be possible to formalise, by agreement with Westminster, democratic institutions acceptable to the majority of Ulster's people.

This has, of course, never been tried before. Nor have any serious attempts been made to sell it to the citizens of Northern Ireland. A 2 week general strike would not fit the bill. In post-Thatcher Britain the government would simply sit it out. What would be required would be a more long term withdrawal of consent, a series of actions which could be carried out as a matter of routine in a relentless campaign. Not a short sharp shock but a slow strangulation. The selling point to the people of Ulster? They do not want another 20 years like the last, and it is no use just wishing an alternative. You have to acquire the means to achieve what you want. This way would at least be non-violent. It just might head off the violent confrontation which will become inevitable if Ulster is denied both democracy and security for many more years.

For those who have not worked in public administration it is difficult to realise how much officials rely on the co-operation of the public. Without, at the very least, people's passive consent, very little can be achieved. Public authorities are backed by the force of law, but the law is only effective in coercing minorities.   When majorities withdraw their consent, the law becomes unenforceable. Public bodies lack the resources to both administer services and engage in large scale coercion. Such bodies are, of course, also full of Loyalist sympathisers, and in the middle of an emotion-charged campaign for democracy the organisations would leak like a sieve. This information would enable them to be outmanoeuvred and the machinery of public administration would gradually grind to a halt.

This is a serious matter and no-one would wish to take such action except in the most extreme circumstances. But Ulster is being run like a dictatorship and its people are being daily slaughtered. Under our Constitution there is no appeal against a government which denies democracy to part of its kingdom. The only recourse is for ordinary people to protest in the best way they know how.

Something has to be done to win back democracy and security. Rather this strategy than men with guns on the streets. Rather we should look at frustrating the machinery of public administration than allow the current situation to continue for another 20 years.

This is a tactic which will not work tomorrow. It is a strategy which will take time to prepare and then it will be necessary to wait for the right moment when the public mood is most receptive. But it is better to be working on a strategy that may not be used for a few years than to have no strategy at all, and hence no means of achieving what the Ulster people want. A number of studies may be useful, based on advice from those with specialist knowledge. We shall then know how to take apart the machinery of dictatorship. Much has already been done. I would not wish to say any more. British officials can read just as well as Ulster Loyalists.

To readers outside Northern Ireland who sympathise with Ulster's cause I would say that there will come a time when Loyalists will be ready to reclaim the democracy which has been denied them for so long. At that time they will need everyone to rally to their aid and exert as much pressure as possible on politicians in Britain and elsewhere to bring about formal arrangements for devolved government. This would cause our government far less embarrassment than being shown to be so lacking in popular support that it could not administer part of the UK. Political devolution will come first and security powers will come later.

For any strategy to be successful it is useful if it is compatible with major trends in political thought amongst relevant groups. British politicians have no new thoughts. They haven't progressed beyond power sharing and the Irish Dimension in 1972. But then we tend to overestimate the importance of such politicians. As for the British public, many of them have been inclined to tell opinion pollsters that they favour a withdrawal of troops from Northern Ireland. British politicians, unpromising as they are, do at least say that withdrawal is out of the question. Ulster's representatives could therefore be forgiven for thinking that the British politicians are slightly more sympathetic. Not so. We have to look at motives. British politicians know that if they pulled out there would be terrible conflict, but after a while democracy and security would be achieved via a majority rule Parliament. Grass roots Loyalists will tell you that this is what would happen and many therefore do not fear a withdrawal of troops as much as English people might imagine. The British Army is, after all, being used to prevent a sensible solution, not to implement it. For this reason British politicians only want to stay to make sure there is no change in policy. Once they go they lose control.

On the other hand the motives of many of those who want to withdraw troops are not as you would imagine. They are not usually Republican sympathisers, and opinion polls show that only some of them say that the alternative is a united Ireland. A surprisingly large number plump for an independent Ulster if this option is put to them. Very many of these people favour very tough measures against the IRA. They would have been very happy to see IRA members shot dead in Gibraltar. The answer is that they would like to defeat the IRA and would support almost any action to achieve this, but they do not believe the IRA can be defeated. They are the victims of government propaganda. The government says that everything that can be done is being done. Clearly what is being, and has been, done is ineffective as we haven't defeated the IRA in 20 years. Therefore it is unlikely to be defeated. The problem in Ulster will thus go on and on with no end in sight. Hence we might as well pull the troops out, because we don't want 20 more years of stalemate.

The Ulster message which comes over on the Mainland is quite different from that which you receive by talking to Loyalists in Ulster. I believe this is partly because Unionist politicians sometimes trim their message when they are talking to the media in the belief that their Mainland audience would be frightened off by the full version. What comes across is : 'Please don't withdraw from Ulster. There would be the most awful trouble. Please carry on doing what you have been doing, if necessary for another 20 years.' This is a misrepresentation of Loyalist views, is based on a misunderstanding of English attitudes, and is also a tactical error. It breeds defeatism among the English.

It would be better to say: 'The deaths of your soliders over the last 20 years have been totally unnecessary. If I was you I would be jumping up and down demanding to know why we are carrying out a policy which is getting your young men killed. I would not dream of asking you to support 20 more minutes, let alone 20 more years of this policy. The killing has to end. We have the solution. Give us the power and we will beat the terrorists. We will thereby save English and Scottish lives.'

I would suggest that the motives of many of those who casually state that they would support a withdrawal of troops are very similar motives to those which gave Ulster the Stormont Parliament. In 1920 British people wanted an arms-length relationship following what, for many, had been a traumatic and confusing intervention in Ireland. The solution was to transfer day to day administration to the Northern Ireland Parliament, which would have responsibility for law and order. Devolution was an alternative to both total engagement and total disengagement.

Today there is a growing English discontent with the degree of day to day involvement in Northern Ireland. It has for the most part been an unhappy and confusing experience for them. Therefore there is scope for devolution to be represented as the kind of partial disengagement which many of the British public want. It has the advantage that it involves no surrender to the IRA, as Northern Ireland would remain part of the UK. I suspect that if the British public were offered the kind of arms-length relationship which operated up to 1969, with a minimal involvement of British troops, many would be ecstatic. It would come as a very pleasant surprise to them to learn of the exact nature of that relationship, about which they know little. If we Loyalists were able to link to political devolution a plan to gradually reduce the number of troops in Northern Ireland and replace them with local forces, the whole package might be very attractive to many of the supporters of withdrawal, as well as to Ulster's traditional supporters. There is scope here for an appeal direct to the British public over the head of the government.

In Ulster there is a growing interest in the idea of independence. It is still a minority point of view but it has been given impetus by the failure of successive governments to give Northern Ireland a fair deal within the UK. As an Englishman and a Loyalist I would see it as a tragedy if Ulster were forced to end the Union. The efforts of myself and my colleagues have, after all, been devoted to preserving the British link. Most Mainland supporters of Ulster would view independence as a policy of last resort. If, however, Northern Irleand was treated despicably for many more years or if a united Ireland was about to be forced on Ulster, it might become a real possibility.

There is what might be called the liberal argument for independence which I should like to dispose of before we proceed. Some argue that independence, by ending the link with Britain, would take the constitutional question out of politics. If Ulster was no longer part of the UK, this matter would no longer be an issue. In these circumstances Protestants and Catholics would learn to forget their differences and might even enter into a power sharing arrangement. The flaw in the argument is that the constitutional question can be defined in 2 ways. It can equally well be defined as a question of whether Ulster becomes part of a united Ireland. This quesion would not be settled by independence.

Catholics would see it at best as a stepping stone to a united Ireland, and power sharing in an independent Ulster would be viewed likewise. It would not solve that particular problem. The only virtue of independence would be that it would give Ulster the opportunity to have democracy and security.

I would regret this move, as there are many economic difficulties which would arise under independence. However, as a last resort I might have to support the idea. But the promoters of independence would also need the means to achieve what they want. If the government will not agree to devolution, it will not agree to independence. Independence would give Loyalists more power (and hence the SDLP less power) than devolution. Negotiated independence as a way of getting round a refusal to grant devolution is therefore quite out of the question. Independence could only be won by the kind of withdrawal of consent which I have outlined.

Most Loyalists who are tempted to go-it-alone see this as a solution to a particular problem - the suspension of democracy in Ulster over the last 20 years. Most of them would accept a satisfactory devolved administration as an alternative to independence. Their course of action is therefore clear. They have to acquire the means to achieve what they want, and hence for a time they have to travel the same civil disobedience road as a devolutionist like myself. If, at the end of this road, with effective power in the hands of the Ulster people, it is not possible to establish a satisfactory form of devolution, I would have to admit that independence might be worth considering. But the British government might, at that juncture, want to consider that, from its point of view, establishing a devolved government would be the lesser of 2 evils.

The Anglo-Irish Agreement Campaign

Regretfully I have to return to the Unionist campaign against the Anglo-Irish Agreement. For as many years as I can remember, John Hume has told the British government that it must face down the Loyalists. After the recent Loyalist campaign ground to a halt he was keen to point out that he had been right all along. Once you call the Loyalists' bluff they back down.

The strategy I have outlined assumes that the Unionist community is capable of mounting a civil disobedience campaign. Hume would argue that the recent failure shows that it cannot, and Loyalists can therefore, in the final analysis, be ignored. It is likely that the British government at least partly shares Hume's view about the capabilities of the Loyalist community. This is therefore a very serious issue.

There are basically 2 theories about what went wrong: a) poor leadership and b) weakness at the grass roots. The 2 Unionist party leaders floated the idea of a civil disobedience campaign but it didn't happen. The leaders said, as part of the internal Loyalist debate, that they were prepared to lead but the people would not follow. Now for this to be true a significant body of people would have had to be consulted on this question of engaging in civil disobedience, and a good portion of them would have had to say no. I have had the privilege of speaking to a large body of Loyalist activists from all 6 counties, the very people who would be called upon to run such a campaign. I have yet to come across someone who was asked, let alone someone who said no.

The reason for failure is therefore not in doubt. There is no evidence of activists' refusal to run a civil disobedience campaign. No great body of people said they would not follow the leaders down that path. The blame therefore lies at the top. We English Loyalists kept in touch with a whole range of senior Unionist figures during the campaign and there is plenty of evidence that Paisley and Molyneaux turned down just about every useful suggestion put to them, from industrial action to civil disobedience.

What this means for the purposes of our study is that the Loyalist people are still strong and capable of the kind of action I have outlined. John Hume cannot sleep easy in his bed. For the Unionist leaders to suggest otherwise was an act of gross irresponsibility which could still have serious consequences. Temporarily we Loyalists have a leadership problem. If English politicians have difficulties with credibility, so do the 2 Unionist leaders. They frustrated the good ideas and felt that threats alone might be enough. Like the Grand Old Duke of York they marched us up to the top of the hill and they marched us down again, until we were tired and disillusioned. In the end people would not follow leaders in whom they had no confidence.

There are those of us who have seen everthing and forgotten nothing. We shall never let it happen again. Loyalist activists no longer believe that these men are capable of leading a successful campaign against a British government 'initiative'. They certainly couldn't lead the kind of campaign I have outlined. But that is our problem. In due course they will stand down if they have any honour left in them, and then we can start again.

In Conclusion

The Protestants of Ulster must be among the most maligned people in the world. The loyal citizens of Londonderry have been made out to be villains, whereas they are in fact the victims. Over 300 years ago they made their historic sacrifice in the Siege of Londonderry to secure the Glorious Revolution. Without the Port of Londonderry in the Second World War, the menace of the U-boats might have crippled the convoys bringing food and supplies from the west.

Today Londonderry's Protestants are still besieged in their frontier town. The inconvenient distribution of Catholic voters in the city, which gave rise to accusations of gerrymandering, was not remedied by changes in boundaries or the franchise. Republicans had their own solution: drive the Protestants off the west bank of the Foyle. This process had started before 1973, when Unionists could still win 3 out of the 5 wards. The process of intimidation moved Protestants into the 2 east bank wards, creating a Republican majority in the other 3. Now barely all that remains of the old North Ward Protestant population is concentrated in the small Fountain estate. A couple of hundred families whose children can hardly be allowed to go to the shops alone for fear of being attacked. The homes which face outwards into the hostile areas around the estate have their windows covered with mesh screens to protect them against the stoning and petrol bomb attacks.

In the early days of the Troubles a local man, William King, was kicked to death by a Catholic mob. British soldiers stood around and did nothing. They had no orders to intervene. The incident sums up Ulster's predicament. Soldiers standing around with no orders to intervene. The wrongs which the English have inflicted on these people are unforgiveable. If I was an Ulsterman I could barely find it in by heart to forgive. But I am an Englishman and I am ashamed of what we have done. We have driven a loyal, law abiding people to resort to the use of Protestant paramilitaries on occasions to strike against an enemy we have done little to get off their backs. If we were doing our job properly and instructing the security forces to deal with the IRA, and if we were not constantly making Ulstermen suspect we were going down the road to a united Ireland, the need for Protestant paramilitaries would disappear.

I have heard of instances around the world of democratic rights being temporarily suspended in order to fight terrorism. I can find no other example of democratic rights being suspended in order to avoid fighting terrorism. For that is what we have done. Rather than getting stuck into the terrorists we decided to appease the Catholic community which shelters the IRA. That community has lied to us and conned us for over 20 years. And still we crave its affection.

Part of the appeasement process has involved depriving the majority of the rights which we English take for granted. We have set up a form of government in which the ballot box has been declared redundant. So Loyalists have received a twin legacy from the English: death and dictatorship. This situation cannot be allowed to go on.

The British government has conducted a political experiment for 20 years. Now is the time to acknowledge that it has failed. The strategy of trying to defeat the IRA by bribing Catholics into supporting measures against the terrorists has only led to their taking the bribes without delivering the support we want. Now is the time to look at an alternative strategy. It is the strategy which helped Unionists keep the IRA in check for nearly 50 years.

Catholic hopes of a united Ireland and not Catholic despair is what drives the IRA campaign forward. The denial of hope and the inducement of despair will send it into reverse. But there is a pain barrier to be crossed. At first there will be an increase in violence and a rise in the Sinn Fein vote as Catholics resort to their old tactics. They will try to replace imprisoned IRA men. It will be our duty to ignore their demands for political concessions and to ensure that we have the right kind of security forces to contain the disorder. A community which gives most of its votes to Sinn Fein will finally be seen in its true colours by the British public and will thus be easier to move against.

The SDLP will have to look to its own survival as it would be counter-productive to try and shore it up by the granting of concessions. The military side of the counter-insurgency campaign could continue unhindered by the old worries about upsetting Republicans. Public safety would be the main concern and searches, arrests and domination of hostile areas would no longer be inhibited by misguided political considerations. On the political side a new Ulster devolved government would make it clear that the rioting and terrorism is quite pointless as it will not bring political concessions. Despair will set in amongst Catholics and the IRA campaign will wind down.

Unionists have stated that they are happy to grant minority rights to the Catholic community. That community is entitled to fair treatment, and to this end Loyalists have offered to support a Bill of Rights. But what Republicans want are majority rights without winning a majority at the polls. They want to use places in government to promote a united Ireland. That is quite out of the question. They must be content to live as a minority enjoying fair treatment within the United Kingdom. If they cannot accept this then there is nothing to stop them crossing the border to live in an Irish state which seems to command more of their allegiance than our own.

A sensible policy for Ulster is a long way off. But there do exist policies which would solve the problems created by English intervention 20 years ago. August 1969 was inevitable given the mood of the times. But if we English had not meddled, the IRA campaign would have been nipped in the bud by the Loyalist community.

The important thing now is for all of us, belatedly, to throw our support behind the Loyalist population and help it to achieve both democracy and security. If we do not win this battle then the frontier of violence will move to the Mainland. We would have shown every budding terrorist that we are too weak to stand up to our enemies. I have outlined a way ahead which shows that victory is possible. Better ideas than mine may emerge, and for this I will be grateful. But no Loyalist need despair. There is a light at the end of the tunnel, and it is not just the headlights of an onrushing train. There is a way ahead if we work patiently and diligently together, extending Hands Across the Water. The meddling of English politicians in Ulster has brought shame on my country. I look forward to the day when we can look the loyal Ulsterman in the eye and deserve his forgiveness. There have been too many gravestones, too many wasted lives.

References and Notes

I have given the author and year of publication in references. For the full title and publisher see the bibliography.

Part I Londonderry: Capital City of Injustice?

A. Gerrymandering

1	Cameron Report par. 134
2	Cameron Report par. 134
3	Londonderry Sentinel 24/5/67
4	Londonderry Sentinel 24/5/67
5	R. Rose (1971) p.235
6	F. Curran (1986)
7	F. Curran (1986) p.10
8	Londonderry Sentinel 19/5/36
9	Londonderry Sentinel 8/10/36
10	Londonderry Sentinel 8/10/36
11	Londonderry Sentinel 8/10/36
12	Derry Journal 23/12/36
13	Londonderry Sentinel 19/12/36
14	S. Elliott (1971) p.406, 429
15	Derry Journal 23/12/36
16	P. Buckland (1979) p.244
17	D. Barritt and C.Carter (1972) p.122
18	Londonderry Sentinel 28/3/36
19	F. Curran (1986) p.11
20	Londonderry Sentinel 8/10/36
21	Londonderry Sentinel 24/12/36
22	Irish Times 21/4/76 "Wresting local control from the Nationalists", D. Harkness.
23	Londonderry Sentinel 8/10/36
24	Londonderry Sentinel 8/10/36
25	Derry Journal 23/12/36 and Cameron Report par. 134
26	Ulster Unionist Party - "Northern Ireland Fact and Falsehood" p.12 (undated)
27	I. Budge and C. O'Leary (1973) p.195
28	I. Budge and C. O'Leary (1973) p.195
29	Belfast Telegraph 18/5/67
30	Belfast Telegraph 18/5/67

31   I. Budge and C. O'Leary (1973) p.196
32   Calculations based on figures in Belfast Telegraph 18/5/67
33   I. Budge and C. O'Leary (1973) p.197
34   T. P. Coogan (1987 DD) p.189
35   Belfast Telegraph 5/2/69, 13/2/69
36   W. D. Flackes (1983) p.259-263 and Belfast Telegraph 5/2/69, 13/2/69
37   Daily Express 20/6/70
38   Gerry Fitt represented Belfast-Dock, the second smallest constituency at Stormont, as well as the Dock Ward on Belfast Corporation, which was the third smallest ward.
39   Times 13/6/87
40   Evening Argus 8/5/87 (author's analysis of figures)
41   Evening Argus 6/5/88 (Author's analysis of figures)
42   Londonderry Sentinel 9/7/69
43   Londonderry Sentinel 17/5/67
44   T. E. Utley (1975) p.28-29
45   B. Faulkner (1978) p.48
46   P. Arthur (1984) p.102
47   S. Nelson (1984) p.46
48   T. E. Utley (1975) p.29
49   R. Rose (1971) p.289
50   C. Hewitt (1981) p.365
51   I. Budge and C. O'Leary (1973) p.177
52   P. Arthur (1984) p.102
53   C. Hewitt (1981) p.365
54   I. Budge and C. O'Leary (1973) p.176
55   S. Elliott (1971) p.788
56   Londonderry Sentinel 4/12/68
57   P. Compton (1978) p.80
58   Londonderry Sentinel 6/6/73
59   Cameron Report par.136
60   S. Elliott (1971) p.396
61   Londonderry Sentinel 17/1/20, 20/1/20, 22/1/20
62   P. Buckland (1979) p.243
63.   Census of Population of Northern Ireland 1926 Table 3
64   S. Elliott (1971) p.70 and Ed. B. M. Walker (1978) p.186-191
65   S. Elliott (1971) p.72
66   S. Elliott (1971) p.73
67   Stormont House of Commons Hansard 114 (24 March 1919) 153
68   Stormont House of Commons Hansard 116 (27 May 1919) 1068
69   S. Elliott (1971) p.73 and Stormont House of Commons Hansard 130 (15 June 1920) 1194
70   T. P. Coogan (1987 DD) p.189
71   L.de Paor (1970) p.157

72   PRONI CAB 9B/13/2
73   PRONI CAB 9B/13/2
74   D. Barritt and C. Carter (1972) p.42
75   S. Elliott (1973) p.18-19
76   S. Elliott (1971) p.425
77   PRONI CAB 9B/13/2
78   P. Buckland (1979) p.242-3
79   PRONI CAB 9B/13/2
80   PRONI CAB 9B/13/2
81   Cameron Report par.137
82   Northern Friends Peace Board (1969) p.22
83   J Callaghan (1973) p.6

B. Housing

1.   C. C. O'Brien (1972) p.157
2.   Northern Friends Peace Board (1969) p.25
3.   M. Hastings (1970) p.28
4.   G. Adams (1986) p.29
5   NIHT Annual Report 1945-46 p.17
6   NIHT Annual Report 1945-46 p.12-13
7   Londonderry Sentinel 7/6/61, 16/10/68
8   D Barritt and C. Carter(1972) p.112
9   Northern Friends Peace Board (1969) p.25
10   Campaign For Social Justice (1965) (no page numbers)
11   NIHT Annual Report 1968-69 p.43
12   Londonderry Sentinel 23/10/68 Editorial stated that the Corporation had built
        133 houses in the 3 years prior to 16/9/68. A guestimate based on work in
        progress and building prior to September 1965 gives us the figure of 300
        houses at 1/4/69.
13   Albert Anderson thought that at least 70% of Corporation Houses and over
        80% of NIHT houses went to Catholics (Sentinel 11/12/68). A Londonderry
        Anglican writing in the Church of England News put the Catholic share of
        public sector housing in the city at 73% (Sentinel 25/6/69).
14   E. McCann (1980) p.24
15   A. Robinson (1967) p.46,52,56
16   Census of Population of Northern Ireland 1926 Table 18
17   Housing Acts (Northern Ireland) 1944 & 1945
18   NIHT Annual Report 1961-62 p.9
19   R. Stetler (1970) p.30
20   Londonderry Sentinel 7/6/61. See also NIHT Annual Report 1960-61 p.12-
        14
21   Londonderry Sentinel 1/3/61
22   M. Holland in New Statesman 2/6/72 p. 740-741

23   Londonderry Sentinel 23/10/68
24   Housing Executive Annual Report 1971-72 p.18
25   C, Brett (1986) p.62
26   C. Brett (1986) p.62-63
27   C. Brett (1986) p.70-71
28   C. Brett (1986) p.76
29   E. McCann (1980) p.24
30   R.Deutsch & V. Magowan (1973) vol.1 p.12a
31   M Hastings (1970) p.60
32   F. Curran (1986) p.94
33   F. Curran (1986) p.102
34   Londonderry Corporation Housing Sub-Committee Minutes 14/11/68
35   Londonderry Corporation Housing Sub-Committee Minutes 14/11/68
36   Londonderry Corporation File FI53, Post War Housing 1943-46
37   Londonderry Corporation File FI53, Post War Housing 1943-46
38   NIHT Annual Report 1968-69, Appendix
39   Londonderry Corporation Housing Sub-Committee Minutes 6/2/69
40   Londonderry Sentinel 12/2/69
41   Londonderry Development Commission Memorandum of Discussions on
        Housing Matters 21/4/69 (in file with minutes of Londondery Corporation
        Housing Sub-Committee)
42   L. de Paor (1970) p.158
43   Derry Journal 16/12/36
44   E. McCann (1980) p.25
45   E. McCann (1980) p.24
46   P. Arthur (1984) p.101
47   Londonderry Area Plan p.18 and 1961 Census Table 4
48   NIHT Annual Report 1965-66 p.12
49   Londonderry Area Plan p.24 & 52
50   Cameron Report par 139
51   Campaign for Social Justice (1969) p.20
52   R. Wiener (1980) p.27
53   S. Elliott (1971) p.385,387
54   Londonderry Sentinel 24/7/68
55   F. Curran (1986) p.51
56   F. Curran (1986) p.50
57   Londonderry Sentinel 27/7/66
58   Londonderry Corporation Housing Sub-Committee Minutes 6/10/66
59   Londonderry Corporation Housing Sub-Committee Minutes 10/11/66
60   Londonderry Sentinel 9/4/69
61   Housing Executive Annual Reports 1971-72 p.26 and 1972-73 p.47
62   Londonderry Sentinel 6/3/68
63   Londonderry Sentinel 24/7/68
64   Londonderry Sentinel 12/3/69

65   Londonderry Sentinel 5/2/69
66   Londonderry Sentinel 20/11/68
67   Londonderry Sentinel 6/12/68
68   F. Curran (1986) p.20
69   NIHT Annual Report 1958-59 p.8
70   F, Curran (1986) p.20 and my calculations of NIHT allocations based on figures earlier in this book re. The Bogside and Creggan plus the fact that only 21 out of 316 houses at Shantallow went to Protestants. (Sentinel Editorial 13/11/68)
71   C. Brett (1986) p.67
72   Londonderry Sentinel 23/4/69
73   C. Brett (1986) p.67
74   Londonderry Sentinel 30/10/68
75   NIHT Annual Reports 1965-66 p.12, 1968-69 p.44, official notice in Londonderry Sentinel 20/11/68
76   Londonderry Area Plan p.106
77   Londonderry Sentinel 2/10/68
78   Londonderry Sentinel 20/11/68
79   Londonderry Sentinel 30/4/69, 28/5/69
80   F. Curran (1986) p.59-60
81   Londonderry Area Plan p.79
82   Londonderry Sentinel 27/3/68
83   B. White (1984) p.50
84   Londonderry Sentinel 30/10/68
85   Londonderry Sentinel 26/2/69
86   1961 Census Table X, 1971 Census Table 13.
87   1971 Census Table 13
88   1971 Census Table 13
89   Londonderry Development Commission Annual Report 1969-70, General Manager's Report pars 32,35
90   Housing Executive Selection Scheme
91   Calculated from figures in Derry Journal 9/6/61 and Londonderry Corporation Housing Sub-Committee Minutes 7/9/67

C. Employment and Regional Development

1   Campaign for Social Justice (1965) no page numbers
2   Londonderry Sentinel 23/10/68
3   P. Shea (1981) p.113
4   B. Faulkner (1978) p.41-2
5   D. Barritt and C. Carter (1972) p.97
6   Newsletter 25/4/70 (Captain Long at Unionist Party Conference)
7   M. Smyth (1972) p.12
8   D. Barritt and C. Carter (1972) p.87-8

9   D. Barritt and C. Carter (1972) p.59
10   D. Barritt and C. Carter (1972) p.103
11   R. Rose (1971) p.296-7
12   R. Rose (1971) p.296
13   I. Adamson (1982) p.64
14   Cameron Report par 38 and calculations from CSJ figures
15   Cameron Report par 138
16   M. Hastings (1970) p.36
17   Belfast Telegraph 4/11/58
18   Newsletter 9/5/64
19   Londonderry Sentinel 17/5/67
20   Londonderry Sentinel 4/9/68
21   Londonderry Sentinel 17/5/67
22   J. Thompson (1973) p.206
23   Londonderry Sentinel 13/11/68
24   Londonderry Sentinel 29/11/34
25   F. Curran (1986) p.51
26   Londonderry Sentinel 16/5/36
27   Londonderry Sentinel 9/4/69
28   Derry Journal 6/8/65
29   R. Rose (1971) p.90
30   F. Curran (1986) p.25
31   Mathew Report par 2
32   Mathew Report par 3
33   Mathew Report par 74
34   Mathew Report par 79
35   Mathew Report par 71
36   Mathew Report par 142
37   Mathew Report par 70
38   Mathew Report par 138
39   Wilson Report Part II p.42
40   Derry Journal 6/8/65
41   Wilson Report Part I p.5
42   Wilson Report Part II p.26
43   Wilson Report Part II p.46
44   Wilson Report Part II p.135
45   Derry Journal 19/10/65
46   Londonderry Area Plan p.1
47   Londonderry Area Plan p.33
48   Benson Report p.9
49   Benson Report p.10-11
50   Benson Report p.24
51   Benson Report p.46
52   F. Curran (1986) p.32

53	F. Curran (1986) p.34
54	Independent 1//10/88
55	Lockwood Report par 219
56	Lockwood Report par 222
57	Lockwood Report pars 89 and 93
58	Lockwood Report - Government Statement and par 214
59	Lockwood Report par 213
60	Lockwood Report par 217
61	Londonderry County Borough (1963) p.18-19
62	Londonderry County Borough (1963) p.25
63	Londonderry Corporation Housing Sub-Committee Minutes 6/6/63
64	Lockwood Report par 93
65	Lockwood Report par 221
66	B. White (1984) p.18-19
67	Lockwood Report - Government Statement
68	F. Curran (1986) p.43
69	A. Robinson (1967) p.143
70	Wilson Report Part II p.39
71	A. Robinson (1967) p.161
72	Northern Ireland Economic Council (1966) p.6
73	Londonderry Sentinel 16/7/69
74	Wilson Report Part II p.37
75	Derry Journal 5/10/65
76	B. Faulkner (1978) p.45
77	R. J. Lawrence (1965) p.101
78	I. Hamilton (1955) p.27,39
79	J. S. Gibson (1962) p.25-6
80	R. Stetler (1970) p.9
81	L.M.Cullen (1987) p.174 and 182
82	Londonderry Sentinel 3/1/68 and 17/7/68
83	Londonderry Sentinel 10/1/68, 7/2/68 and 28/2/68
84	Londonderry Sentinel 10/1/68 and 31/1/68
85	A. Robinson (1976) p.163
86	Londonderry Sentinel 17/5/67 and 25/9/68
87	A. Robinson (1967) p.176 and 193
88	A. Robinson (1967) p.174,175 and 186-7
89	D. Barritt and C. Carter (1972) p.110-111
90	R. Rose (1971) p.365
91	R. Stetler (1970) p22-4
92	F. Curran (1986) p.23
93	R. Stetler (1970) p.23-4 and A. Robinson (1967) p. 143
94	Londonderry Sentinel 18/5/66 and 25/5/66
95	Londonderry Sentinel 10/4/68 and 26/6/68
96	Londonderry Sentinel 5/6/68, 26/6/68 and 9/7/68

97   Londonderry Sentinel 19/6/68
98   Londonderry Sentinel 3/7/68 and 24/7/68
99   Londonderry Sentinel 24/7/68 and 30/10/68
100   Londonderry Sentinel 4/12/68 and 5/3/69
101   B. Faulkner (1978) p.45
102   Londonderry Sentinel 12/6/68

Part II The Civil Rights Movement

1.   T. P. Coogan (1987) p.418
2.   Irish Times 5/5/64
3.   I. McAllister (1977) p.9-10
4   Derry Journal 7/4/64
5   Irish Times 18,19/4/64
6   Londonderry Sentinel 1/2/51
7   C. C. O'Brien (1972) p.120
8   Stormont Hansard, House of Commons vol. 37 col. 1320, M. Farrell (1980)
        p.204
9   B. White (1984) p.44
10   Derry Journal 21/4/64
11   Belfast Telegraph 9/2/69 (B. White "Are the politicians leading or being
        led?")
12   B. White (1984) p.54
13   Campaign for Social Justice (1964)
14   For instance the very well known CSJ booklet, "The Plain Truth" (1969
        edition) deals with Londonderry on p.19-22. (1) It repeats the myth that there
        was a separate Stormont seat for the City of Londonderry constituency prior
        to 1929, which was controlled by Republicans. (2) It states that no houses
        had been built by the Corporation since 1966 and only 136 since 1958 - both
        totally false. (3) The NIHT is supposed to have been hampered by the non-
        extension of the boundary - completely untrue. (4) What are supposed to be
        1966 local government ward figures have no basis in reality - see the Cameron
        Report. (5) The Derry Housing Association myth is resurrected. (6) Yet
        again there is a statement that the Lord Mayor alone allocated houses and it
        is said the Housing Committee did not function! Just about every statement
        in this section of the CSJ booklet is false, indicating the quality of argument
        in the "civil rights" era and the gullibility of CSJ's liberal audience.
15   M. Farrell (1980) p.197
16   J. B. Bell (1979) p.340
17   J. B. Bell (1979) p.304
18   Ed. M. Farrell (1988) p.42 and G. Adams (1986) p.4
19   P. Bishop and E. Mallie (1987) p.35
20   T. P. Coogan (1987) p.107
21   G. Adams (1986) p.8

22	M. Farrell (1980) p.244
23	G. Adams (1986) p.8-9
24	G. Adams (1986) p.6
25	Irish News 18/4/66
26	Londonderry Sentinel 13/4/66
27	Derry Journal 12/4/66
28	Londonderry Sentinel 1/1/69 and J. B. Bell (1979) p.325
29	P. Bishop and E. Mallie (1987) p.71
30	R. Deutsch and V Magowan (1973) vol.1 p.154
31	J. Thompson (1973) p.43
32	J. Thompson (1973) p.54 and R Deutsch and V. Magowan (1973) vol.1 p.154
33	G. Adams (1986) p.12
34	Ed. M. Farrell (1988) p.43
35	Stormont Hansard, Senate vol.54 No.28, 7 July 1970 col.1275
36	J. Thompson (1973) p.59-61
37	Cameron Report par.191
38	Cameron Report pars. 33 and 34
39	Cameron Report par.34
40	B. Devlin (1969) p.91 and 93
41	B. Devlin (1969) p.94
42	Dungannon Observer 15,22 and 29/6/68, Tyrone Courier 19/6/68 Sunday News 23/6/68
43	M. Hastings (1970) p.40
44	B. Devlin (1969) p.53
45	T. P. Coogan (1987) p.246
46	G. Adams (1986) p.19 and Ed. M. Farrell (1988) p.44
47	Ed. M. Farrell (1988) p.49
48	S. Nelson (1984)p.49-50
49	C. C. O'Brien (1972) p.154
50	J. Thompson (1973) p.218
51	T. P. Coogan (1987 DD) p.199
52	C. C. O'Brien (1972) p.161
53	C. C. O'Brien (1972) p.167
54	C. C. O'Brien (1972) p.193
55	D. Barritt and C. Carter (1972) p.xii
56	Cameron Report par.229
57	Londonderry Sentinel 17/9/69
58	R. Rose (1971) p.293. If NIHT housing is added to council owned property the figures are: Unionist areas - 31% of Protestants and 32% of Catholics in public sector housing; Nationalist areas - 21% of Protestants and 47% of Catholics.
59	P. Riddell (1970) p. xiv
60	P. Riddell (1970) p.31
61	A.T.O. Stewart (1986) p.179

62   T.P. Coogan (1987) p.443 and 445
63   T. O'Neill (1972) p.145
64   Londonderry Sentinel 4/9/68
65   Londonderry Sentinel 16/10/68
66   Londonderry Sentinel 30/10/68
67   Londonderry Sentinel 22/1/69
68   Newsletter 2/10/69
69   Londonderry Sentinel 17/9/69
70   M. Farrell (1980) p.265
71   M. Hastings (1970) p.171
72   T. O'Neill (1972) p.116
73   T. O'Neill (1972) p.149
74   E. McCann (1980) p.27,30 and 33
75   P. Arthur (1974) p.24 and 142
76   Irish Militant vol 2 no 3, March 1967
77   J. Thompson (1973) p.70-1
78   E. McCann (1980) p.27 and Londonderry Sentinel 9/10/68
79   E. McCann (1980) p.38
80   Sunday Times Insight Team (1972) p.51
81   Londonderry Sentinel 17/12/69
82   E. McCann (1980) p.40
83   Cameron Report par.45
84   Ed. M. Farrell (1988) p.45
85   E. McCann (1980) p.42
86   Ed. M. Farrell (1988) p.58
87   Cameron Report par.51
88   Londonderry Sentinel 9/10/68
89   F. Curran (1986) p.84
90   E. McCann (1980) p.43
91   Irish News 18/4/66
92   E. McCann (1980) p.35
93   G. Adams (1986) p. 12-13
94   Londonderry Sentinel 9/10/68
95   L. de Paor (1970) p. 178
96   F. Curran (1986) p. 100
97   Londonderry Sentinel 8/10/69 (District Inspector Francis Armstrong at the Scarman Tribunal)
98   J. Callaghan (1973) p. 17
99   D. Caute (1988) p. 81 and 185
100   Times 1/1/88
101   Ed. M. Farrell (1988) p. 55
102   C. Hewitt (1981) p. 370-1
103   T. O'Neill (1972) p. 13
104   B. Devlin (1969) p. 114

105	Belfast Telegraph 5/5/69
106	R. Rose (1971) p. 301
107	T. O'Neill (1969) p. 129
108	E. Moloney and A. Pollack (1986) p. 118-9
109	E. Moloney and A. Pollack (1986) p. 118
110	Londonderry Sentinel 16/10/68 (after Lynch had met Eddie McAteer)
111	M. Wallace (1970) p.36
112	United Irishman, December 1969, quoted in J. Thompson (1973) p. 100
113	P. Arthur (1974) p. 38
114	P. Bishop and E. Mallie (1987) p. 59
115	B. Delvin (1969) p. 137
116	P. Arthur (1974) p. 4
117	P. Arthur (1974) p. 47 quote from "Struggle in the North" p. 13 (publiched by PD)
118	J. Thompson (1973) p. 98
119	B. Devlin (1969) p. 147
120	P. Arthur (1974) p. 61
121	Irish Times 5/12/69
122	Ramparts No 4, 1969 (published by Derry Labour Party)
123	B. Devlin (1969) p. 154
124	B. Devlin (1969) p. 155
125	B. Devlin (1969) p. 26
126	New Left Review No 55, May/June 1969, "People's Democracy; a Discussion on Strategy". (Interviewed on 20/4/69) p. 6
127	E. McCann in New Left Review No 55 p.5
128	E. McCann in New Left Review No 55 p.5
129	B. Devlin (1969) p.152
130	B. Devlin (1969) p. 148 and M. Farrell in New Left Review No 55 p. 9
131	Derry Labour Party (1969) p. 2 and 5
132	Gown 3/3/70 (Queen's University, Belfast student newspaper)
133	New Left Review No55 p. 13
134	B. Devlin (1969) p. 170
135	B. Devlin (1969) p. 191
136	C.C. O'Brien (1972) p. 160
137	New Left Review No55 p. 13
138	B. Devlin (1969) p. 119
139	New Left Review No55 p.14
140	Irish Times 8/4/69
141	P. Arthur (1974) p. 54
142	P. Arthur (1974) p. 55
143	Ed. M. Farrell (1988) p. 72
144	Londonderry Sentinel 19 and 26/3/69
145	B. White (1984) p. 74
146	M. McGuire (1973) p. 124

147	R. Rose (1971) p. 444
148	Londonderry Sentinel 9/4/69
149	Londonderry Sentinel 16/4/69
150	Londonderry Sentinel 16/4/69
151	Derry Journal 22/4/69
152	F. Curran (1986) p. 124
153	F. Curran (1986) P. 124
154	C. C. O'Brien (1972) p. 163-4
155	E. McCann (1980) p. 48
156	M. Hastings (1970) p. 120
157	P. Riddell (1970) p. 127
158	Belfast Telegraph 10/2/69
159	T. P. Coogan (1987) p. 421
160	Londonderry Sentinel 2/7/69
161	P. Arthur (1974) p. 63
162	P. Arthur (1974) p. 64
163	Londonderry Sentinel 9/7/69
164	Londonderry Sentinel 11 and 18/12/68
165	Irish Times 7/7/69
166	Irish Times 7/7/69
167	Irish Times 7/7/69
168	Newsletter 7/7/69, P. Riddell (1970) p. 52, T.P. Coogan (1987) p. 167
169	Scarman Report p.32-40
170	M. Hastings (1970) p. 124
171	E. McCann (1980) p. 57
172	Londonderry Sentinel 5/11/69
173	Derry Labour Party (1969) p. 3-4
174	E. McCann (1980) p. 58
175	Scarman Report par. 10.11
176	Scarman Report par 10.12
177	Londonderry Sentinel 20/8/69
178	Scarman Report par. 10.4
179	Scarman Report par 10.13
180	Sunday Times Insight Team (1972) p. 119
181	D. Hamill (1985) p. 14
182	Derry Journal 12/8/69
183	Derry Journal 12/8/69
184	Derry Journal 12/8/69
185	Derry Journal 28/11/69
186	Derry Journal 28/11/69
187	Scarman Report par. 11.11
188	Scarman Report par. 11.14
189	Sunday Times Insight Team (1972) p. 117-8
190	Scarman Report par. 10.14

191	Londonderry Sentinel 29/10/69
192	Sunday Times Insight Team (1972) p. 120
193	Londonderry Sentinel 19/11/69 (evidence to Scarman Tribunal)
194	Scarman Report par. 11.13
195	Scarman Report par. 11.15
196	Scarman Report par. 12.3
197	Londonderry Sentinel 29/10/69
198	Londonderry Sentinel 29/10/69
199	Scarman Report par. 12.3
200	Londonderry Sentinel 8/10/69 (evidence of Deputy Inspecter-General Graham Shillington at Scarman Tribunal)
201	Londonderry Sentinel 8/10/69
202	Londonderry Sentinel 29/10/69
203	T. P. Coogan (1987DD) p. 208
204	M. Farrell (1980) p. 260
205	Scarman Report par. 13.3
206	Scarman Report par. 29.7-29.8
207	Scarman Report pars. 14. 30-14.35
208	Scarman Report pars. 14.62-14.68
209	Scarman Report pars. 15.4-15.13
210	Scarman Report pars. 16.1-16.6
211	G. Adams (1986) p. 33
212	Scarman Report pars. 18.18-18.25
213	Scarman Report par. 18.6
214	Scarman Report pars. 18.27-18.46
215	Scarman Report par. 18.34
216	Scarman Report par. 17.6
217	Scarman Report par. 17.9
218	Scarman Report par. 18.47
219	Scarman Report Volume 2 p. 44
220	Scarman Report Volume 2 p. 44
221	C. C. O'Brien (1972) p. 180
222	M. Farrell (1980) p. 261
223	Londonderry Sentinel 8/10/69
224	F. Curran (1986) p. 132
225	E. McCann (1980) p. 60
226	B. White (1984) p. 84
227	Londonderry Sentinel 23/4/69
228	B. White (1984) p. 85
229	Londonderry Sentinel 23/4/69
230	Radio 4, 17/2/88, "The Spark That Lit The Bonfire"
231	Londonderry Sentinel 12/11/69
232	R. Stetler (1970) p. 96
233	Londonderry Sentinel 22/10/69

234   Londonderry Sentinel 19/11/69 (Evidence to Scarman Tribunal)
235   Independent 14/12/87
236   Belfast Telegraph 14/8/89
237   E. McCann (1980) p. 61
238   F. Curran (1986) p. 134
239   Scarman Report par. 12.30
240   Londonderry Sentinel 24/9/69
241   Londonderry Sentinel 24/9/69
242   Londonderry Sentinel 20/8/69
243   Londonderry Sentinel 27/8/69
244   B. White (1984) p. 82
245   M. Wallace (1970) p. 4
246   M, Wallace (1970) p. 4
247   Barricade Bulletin No9, 23/8/69
248   Barricade Bulletin 25/8/69
249   Londonderry Sentinel 3/12/69 (evidence to Scarman Tribunal)
250   Londonderry Sentinel 3/12/69
251   DCDA Newsletter 28/8/69
252   Scarman Report par.21.4
253   Scarman Report pars.21.38-21.39
254   Scarman Report pars.21.26-21.31
255   Scarman Report par.21.51
256   Scarman Report pars.21.77-21.79
257   Scarman Report pars. 21.83-21.85
258   Scarman Report par.22.1
259   Scarman Report par.21.2
260   Scarman Report par.25.51
261   Newsletter 2/8/89
262   Newsletter 2/8/89
263   P. Bishop and E Mallie (1987) p.39
264   P. Bishop and E. Mallie (1987) p.86
265   P. Bishop and E. Mallie (1987) p.91
266   R. Rose (1971) p.252
267   Scarman Report pars.30.2-30.7
268   M. Farrell (1980) p.261
269   P. Bishop and E. Mallie (1987) p.75
270   G. Adams (1986) p.34
271   F. Curran (1986) p.131
272   B. White (1984) p.80 and p.89
273   B. Devlin (1969) p.205
274   Scarman Report Volume 2 p.36 (speech at Stormont 14/8/69)
275   M. Wallace (1970) p.18
276   R. Evelegh (1978) p.34
277   R. Cutterbuck (1973) p.81

278   Londonderry Sentinel 5/11/69 (evidence to Scarman Tribunal)
279   Barricade Bulletin No.1, 14/8/69
280   P. Arthur (1974) p.69
281   Londonderry Sentinel 19/11/69 (evidence to Scarman Tribunal)
282   Channel 4, 29/4/88
283   D. Caute (1988) p.189
284   A. T. Q. Stewart (1986) p.183
285   Londonderry Sentinel 13/11/68

Part III The Politics of Security Policy

A. Counter-Insurgency for Beginners

1   E. McCann (1980) p.63-4
2   Londonderry Sentinel 24/9/69
3   Londonderry Sentinel 24/9/69
4   Derry Journal 23/9/69
5   R. Evelegh (1978) p.22
6   R. Evelegh (1978) p.23
7   F. Kitson (1971) p.7
8   J. Paget (1967) p.156
9   P. Bishop and E. Mallie (1987) p.128
10   F. Kitson (1971) p.24
11   F. Kitson (1971) p.5
12   J. Paget (1967) p.22
13   R. Rose (1971) p.465
14   J. Callaghan (1973) p.2
15   J. Callaghan (1973) p.15
16   J. Callaghan (1973) p.24-5
17   J. Callaghan (1973) p.71
18   J. Callaghan (1973) p.22
19   R. Rose (1971) p.42
20   J. Callaghan (1973) p.10
21   T. O'Neill (1972) p.134
22   T. P. Coogan (1987) p.58
23   H. Wilson (1971) p.695-6
24   J. Callaghan (1973) p.57
25   Hunt Report p.21
26   Hunt Report p.12
27   M. Farrell (1983) p147-8
28   M. Farrell (1983) p.148
29   Londonderry Sentinel 29/10/69
30   E. McCann (1980) p.129-30
31   M. McGuire (1973) p.22. See also P. Bishop and E Mallie (1987) p.144-5

32   D. Hamill (1985) p.36-7
33   D. Barzilay vol.1 (1973) p.12-14
34   D. Hamill (1985) p.36-7
35   D. Hamill (1985) p.36-7
36   D. Hamill (1985) p.39
37   J. Callaghan (1973) p.148
38   P. Bishop and E. Mallie (1987) p.143
39   P. Bishop and E. Mallie (1987) p.177
40   T. P. Coogan (1987) p.494
41   G. Adams (1986) p.53
42   G. Adams (1986) p.58
43   G. Adams (1986) p.63
44   G. Adams (1986) p.64
45   D. Barritt and C. Carter (1972) p.161
46   P. Arthur (1984) p.126
47   P. Arthur (1984) p.124
48   D. Hamill (1985) p.279
49   R. Clutterbuck (1973) p.109
50   P. Bishop and E. Mallie (1987) p.290
51   P. Bishop and E. Mallie (1987) p.284-5
52   J. B. Bell (1979) p.299-300
53   P. Bishop and E. Mallie (1987) p.295
54   P. Bishop and E. Mallie (1987) p.293-4
55   J. Murray-Brown (1972) p.270
56   J. Murray-Brown (1972) p.308
57   J. Murray-Brown (1972) p.316
58   J. Paget (1969) p.122
59   J. Paget (1969) p.250-2
60   J. Reddaway (1986) p.64
61   J. Reddaway (1986) p.124, 144
62   J. Reddaway (1986) p.144
63   J. Reddaway (1986) p.151
64   M. Maguire (1973) p.74
65   D. Hamill (1985) p.22
66   J. Callaghan (1973) p.71
67   Sir. A. Hexlet (1972) p.101-2
68   P. Riddell (1970) p.36
69   P. Riddell (1970) p.35, P. Bishop and E. Mallie (1987) p.21
70   P. Bishop and E. Mallie (1987) p.22
71   R. Cielou (1983) p.93
72   J. H. Whyte (1971) p.90
73   P. Bishop and E. Mallie (1987) p.23
74   Sir. A. Hezlet (1972) p.170, 175, P. Bishop and E. Mallie (1987) p.29
75   Sir. A. Hezlet (1972) p.184

76   T. P. Coogan (1987) p.512
77   P. Bishop and E. Mallie (1987) p.347
78   M. Farrell (1980) p.216
79   Sir. A. Hezlet (1972) p.168
80   P. Bishop and E. Mallie (1987) p.348
81   T. P. Coogan (1987) p.636
82   P. Bishop and E. Mallie (1987) p.28
83   J. B. Bell (1979) p.293
84   P. Bishop and E. Mallie (1987) p.348
85   J. Kelly (1971) p.18-19
86   P. Bishop and E. Mallie (1987) p.96
87   J. B. Bell (1979) p.294
88   J. Kelly (1971) p.9
89   J. Kelly (1971) p.19-22
90   J. Kelly (1971) p.26
91   J. Kelly (1971) p.44
92   J. Kelly (1971) p.199
93   J. Kelly (1971) p.195 quoting Charles Haughey
94   J. Kelly (1971) p.193
95   J. Kelly (1971) p.195
96   R. Rose (1971) p.110
97   J. Kelly (1971) p.148
98   J. Kelly (1971) p.149-150
99   J. Kelly (1971) p.156, 186
100   J. Kelly (1971) p.159
101   J. Kelly (1971) p.134
102   J. Kelly (1971) p.141
103   Sunday Times Insight Team (1972) p.180

B. The SDLP and the IRA

1   I. McAllister (1977) p.39
2   1972 Green Paper par.14
3   1972 Green Paper par.17
4   1972 Green Paper par.36
5   1972 Green Paper par.39
6   Unionist Research Dept. (1972) p.19
7   1972 Green Paper par.76
8   1972 Green Paper par.78
9   1972 Green Paper par.79
10   1972 Green Paper par.79
11   1972 Green Paper Annex 7, p.73-4
12   1972 Green Paper Annex 7, p.74
13   1972 Green Paper Annex 7, p.74

14   1972 Green Paper Annex 7, p.75
15   1972 Green Paper Annex 7, p.76
16   B. White (1984) p.140
17   E. McCann (1980) p.141
18   T. E. Utley (1975) p.111
19   B. White (1984) p.170
20   B. White (1984) p.176
21   B. White (1984) p.110
22   R. Rose in foreward to I. McAllister (1977) p.xiii
23   W. Flackes and S Elliott (1989) p.312
24   R. Cielou (1983) p.270
25   P. Bishop and E. Mallie (1987) p.352
26   Unionist Research Department (1972) p.16
27   Irish Independent 24-25/3/89
28   Irish Independent 24-25/3/89
29   I. McAllister (1977) p.84-5
30   P. Bishop and E. Mallie (1987) p.301
31   T. E. Utley (1975) p.12
32   T. E. Utley (1975) p.12
33   F. Kitson (1971) p.95
34   Sir. A. Hezlet (1972) p.4
35   Sir. A. Hezlet (1972) p.127
36   B. White (1984) p.159
37   P. Riddell (1970) p.113
38   P. Riddell (1970) p.109,113
39   R. Fisk (1983) p.461
40   J. Paget (1967) p.74
41   J. Paget (1967) p.96
42   Sir. A. Hezlet (1972) p.81-2
43   M. Farrell (1983) p.144
44   Sir. A. Hezlet (1972) p.84
45   M. Farrell (1983) p.145
46   M. Farrell (1983) p.145
47   M. Farrell (1983) p.146
48   J. Paget (1967) p.176
49   J. Paget (1967) p.66,91
50   M. Arthur (1987) p.255-6
51   D. Barzillay vol. II (1975) p.154
52   History of Policing in Co. Fermanagh, anon. (unpublished)
53   T P. Coogan (1987) p.335
54   M. Arthur (1987) p.8
55   C. Brett (1986) p.148
56   W. Flackes and S. Elliott (1989) p.101-2

Bibliography

Reports

Benson Report *Northern Ireland Railways* (HMSO, Cmd.458,1963)

Cameron Report *Disturbances in Northern Ireland* (HMSO, Cmd. 532, 1969)

1972 Green Paper *The Future of Northern Ireland: A Paper for Discussion* (HMSO, 1972)

Hunt Report *Report of the Advisory Committee on Police in Northern Ireland* (HMSO,Cmd.535, (1969)

Lockwood Report *Higher Education in Northern Ireland* (HMSO,Cmd.475,1965)

Londonderry Area Plan (James Munce Partnership/Londonderry Area Steering Committee, 1968)

Mathew Report *Belfast Regional Survey and Plan: Recommendations and Conclusions* (HMSO, Cmd.451,1963)

Scarman Report *Violence and Civil Disturbances in Northern Ireland in 1969* (HMSO, Cmd.566,1972)

Wilson Report *Economic Development in Northern Ireland* (HMSO,Cmd.479,1965)

Books, Booklets and Articles

G.Adams (1986) *The Politics of Irish Freedom* (Brandon)

I.Adamson (1982) *The Identity of Ulster* (Pretani Press)

M.Arthur (1987) *Northern Ireland Soldiers Talking* (Sidgwick & Jackson)

P.Arthur (1974) *The People's Democracy* (Blackstaff Press)

P.Arthur (1984) *Government and Politics of Northern Ireland* (Longman)

D,Barritt & C.Carter (1972) *The Northern Ireland Problem: A Study in Group Relations* (Oxford University Press)

D.Barzilay (1973,1975,1978) *The British Army in Ulster (3 volumes)* (Century Services)

J.B.Bell (1979) *The Secret Army: the IRA, 1916-1979* (Academy Press)

P.Bew & H.Patterson (1985) *The British State and the Ulster Crisis* (Verso)

P.Bishop & E.Mallie (1987) *The Provisional IRA* (Heinemann)

C.Brett (1986) *Housing a Divided Community* (Institute of Public Administration, Dublin and Institute of Irish Studies, Queen's University, Belfast)

P.Buckland (1979) *The Factory of Grievances: Devolved Government in Northern Ireland 1921-39* (Gill & Macmillan)

I.Budge & C.O'Leary (1973) *Belfast: Approach to Crisis* (A Study of Belfast Politics 1613-1970) (Macmillan)

J.Callaghan (1973) *A House Divided - The Dilemma of Northern Ireland* (Collins)

Campaign for Social Justice (1964) *Why Justice Can Not Be Done* (CSJ)

Campaign for Social Justice (1965) *Londonderry: One Man, No Vote* (CSJ)

Campaign for Social Justice (1969) *The Plain Truth* (CSJ)

D.Caute (1988) *Sixty Eight: The Year of the Barricades* (Hamish Hamilton)

R. Cielou (1983) *Spare My Tortured People* (Whitethorn Press)

W.Clark (1967) *Guns in Ulster* (Constabulary Gazette, Belfast)

A.F.N.Clarke (1983) *Contact* (Secker & Warburg)

R.Clutterbuck (1973) *Protest and the Urban Guerrilla* (Cassell)

P.Compton (1978) *Northern Ireland: a Census Atlas* (Gill and Macmillan)

T.P.Coogan (1987 DD) *Disillusioned Decades: Ireland 1966-87* (Gill and Macmillan)

T.P.Coogan (1987) *The IRA* (Fontana paperback edition)

L.M.Cullen (1987) *An Economic History of Ireland Since 1660* (Batsford)

F.Curran (1986) *Derry: Countdown to Disaster* (Gill & Macmillan)

Derry Labour Party (1969) *Labour and Civil Rights* (Derry Labour Party)

R.Deutsch & V.Magowan (1973) *Northern Ireland 1968-73 Chronology of Events, Volume 1 1968-71* (Blackstaff Press)

B.Devlin (1969) *The Price of My Soul* (Andre Deutsch)

M.Dewar (1985) *The British Army in Northern Ireland* (Arms & Armour Press)

S.Elliott (1971) *The Electoral System in Northern Ireland Since 1920* (Unpublished PhD Thesis, Queen's University, Belfast)

S.Elliott (1973) *Northern Ireland Parliamentary Election Results 1921-1972* (Political Reference Publications, Chichester)

R.Evelegh (1978) *Peace Keeping in a Democratic Society: The Lessons of Northern Ireland* (C.Hurst & Co)

M.Farrell (1980) *Northern Ireland: The Orange State* (Pluto Press)

M.Farrell (1983) *Arming the Protestants: The formation of the Ulster Special Constabulary and Royal Ulster Constabulary, 1920-7* (Brandon)

Ed.M.Farrell (1988) *Twenty Years On* (Brandon)

B.Faulkner (1978) *Memoirs of a Statesman* (Weidenfeld & Nicolson)

R.Fisk (1983) *In Time of War - Ireland, Ulster and the Price of Neutrality 1939-45* (Andre Deutsch)

W.D.Flackes (1983) *Northern Ireland: A Political Directory 1968-83* (Ariel Books)

W.D.Flackes & S.Elliott (1989) *Northern Ireland: A Political Directory 1968-88* (Blackstaff Press)

J.S.Gibson (1962) *Port of Londonderry: a Study of the Development and Function of a Port* (Unpublished BA Thesis, Queen's University, Belfast)

D.Hamill (1985) *Pig in the Middle - The Army in Northern Ireland 1969-1984* (Methuen)

I.Hamilton (1955) *The Shirt Industry of Derry* (Unpublished BA Thesis, Queen's University, Belfast)

M.Hastings (1970) *Ulster 1969 - The Fight for Civil Rights in Northern Ireland* (Gollancz)

C. Hewitt (1981) *Catholic grievances, Catholic nationalism and violence in Northern Ireland during the Civil Rights Period: a reconsideration* (Article in the British Journal of Sociology, September 1981 p.362)

Sir A.Hezlet (1972) *The 'B' Specials - A History of the Ulster Special Constabulary* (Tom Stacey)

J.Kelly (1971) *Orders For the Captain* (James Kelly)

F.Kitson (1971) *Low Intensity Operations: Subversion, Insurgency, Peace-Keeping* (Faber & Faber)

R.J.Lawrence (1965) *The Government of Northern Ireland: Public Finance and Public Services 1921-1964* (Clarendon Press)

C.Limpkin (1972) *The Battle of Bogside* (Penguin)

Londonderry County Borough (1963) *Submission to the Government of Northern Ireland Presenting the Case for the Promotion of a University at Londonderry.*

I.McAllister (1977) *The Northern Ireland Social Democratic and Labour Party* (Macmillan)

E.McCann (1980) *War and an Irish Town* (Pluto Press)

M.McGuire (1973) *To Take Arms: A Year in the Provisional IRA* (Macmillan)

E.Moloney & A.Pollak (1986) *Paisley* (Poolbeg Press)

T.H.Mullin (1986) *Ulster's Historic City: Derry/Londonderry* (Coleraine Bookshop)

J.Murray-Brown (1972) *Kenyatta* (George Allen & Unwin)

S.Nelson (1984) *Ulster's Uncertain Defenders* (Appletree Press)

Northern Friends Peace Board (1969) *Orange and Green: A Quaker Study of Community Relations in Northern Ireland* (NFPB)

Northern Ireland Economic Council (1966) *Londonderry As a Location For New Industry*

C.C.O'Brien (1972) *States of Ireland* (Hutchinson & Co)

T.O'Neill (1969) *Ulster at the Crossroads* (Faber & Faber)

T.O'Neill (1972) *The Autobiography of Terence O'Neill* (Rupert Hart-Davis)

J.Paget (1967) *Counter-Insurgency Campaigning* (Faber & Faber)

J. Paget (1969) *Last Post: Aden 1964-67* (Faber & Faber)

L.de Paor (1970) *Divided Ulster* (Penguin)

J.Reddaway (1986) *Burdened With Cyprus: the British Connection* (Weidenfeld & Nicolson)

P.Riddell (1970) *Fire Over Ulster* (Hamish Hamilton)

A.Robinson (1967) *A Social Geography of the City of Londonderry* (Unpublished MA Thesis, Queen's University, Belfast)

R.Rose (1971) *Governing Without Consensus: An Irish Perspective* (Faber &Faber)

P.Shea (1981) *Voices and the Sound of Drums: an Irish Autobiography* (Blackstaff Press)

C.Smyth (1989) *Ireland's Physical Force Tradition Today: Reflections on the Enniskillen Massacre* (Ulster Society)

M.Smyth (1972) *The Battle for Northern Ireland* (County Grand Orange Lodge of Belfast)

R.Stetler (1970) *The Battle of Bogside* (Sheed & Ward)

A.T.Q.Stewart (1986) *The Narrow Ground* (Pretani Press)

Sunday Times Insight Team (1972) *Ulster* (Andre Deutsch)

J.Thompson (1973) *The Civil Rights Movement in Northern Ireland* (Unpublished MA Thesis, Queen's University, Belfast)

Unionist Research Dept. (1972) *The Future of Northern Ireland: A Commentary on the Government's Green Paper* (URD)

Unionist Research Dept. (1973) *Northern Ireland: The Hidden Truth* (URD)

T.E.Utley (1975) *Lessons of Ulster* (J.M.Dent & Sons)

Ed.B.M.Walker (1978) *Parliamentary Election Results in Ireland 1801-1922* (Royal Irish Academy)

M.Wallace (1970) *Drums and Guns: Revolution in Ulster* (Geoffrey Chapman)

A.J.Walmsley (1959) *Northern Ireland: Its Policies and Record* (Ulster Unionist Council)

B.White (1984) *John Hume: Statesman of the Troubles* (Blackstaff Press)

J.H.Whyte (1971) *Church and State in Modern Ireland 1923-1970* (Gill & Macmillan)

J.H.Whyte (1983) *How much discrimination was there under the unionist regime, 1921-68?* (Essay in "Contemporary Irish Studies" Ed.T.Gallagher & J.O'Connell, Manchester University Press)

R.Wiener (1980) *The Rape and Plunder of the Shankill* (Farset)

P.Wilkinson (1977) *Terrorism and the Liberal State* (Macmillan)

H.Wilson (1971) *The Labour Government 1964-1970: A Personal Record* (Weidenfeld & Nicolson and Michael Joseph)

The Author

Paul Kingsley is an Englishman who has no family connections with Northern Ireland. He was born in Yorkshire in 1952 and was educated at Hull Grammar School and the University of Brimingham, where he obtained an honours degree in Philosophy.

He later pursued a career in local government administration and developed a keen interest in trade union affairs. After serving as a Shop Steward and Branch Publicity Officer he was appointed as a full time trade union official with the National and Local Government Officers Association (NALGO) in the South of England.

Paul's support for the Ulster Loyalist cause generated some controversy and he became aware of a secret investigation into his political activities outside the workplace. He was dismissed from his post in 1987 after refusing to leave a meeting in protest against another attempt to discuss his political activities without his being present. Subsequently it was revealed that NALGO had reports from its senior officers showing that there was no evidence to support the bringing of political charges, and that Paul has at no time allowed his political views to adversely affect his work. Political and religious discrimination is unlawful in Northern Ireland, but not in England.